*Anna Letitia Barbauld and
Eighteenth-Century Visionary Poetics*

Anna Letitia Barbauld and Eighteenth-Century Visionary Poetics

DANIEL P. WATKINS

The Johns Hopkins University Press
Baltimore

© 2012 The Johns Hopkins University Press
All rights reserved. Published 2012
Printed in the United States of America on acid-free paper
2 4 6 8 9 7 5 3 1

The Johns Hopkins University Press
2715 North Charles Street
Baltimore, Maryland 21218-4363
www.press.jhu.edu

Library of Congress Cataloging-in-Publication Data
Watkins, Daniel P., 1952–
Anna Letitia Barbauld and eighteenth-century visionary poetics / Daniel P. Watkins.
p. cm.
Includes bibliographical references and index.
ISBN-13: 978-1-4214-0458-5 (acid-free paper)
ISBN-10: 1-4214-0458-3 (acid-free paper)
1. Barbauld, Mrs. (Anna Letitia), 1743–1825. Poems.   2. Barbauld, Mrs. (Anna Letitia), 1743–1825—Philosophy.   3. Poetics—History—18th century.   I. Title.
PR4057.B7Z95 2012
821'.6—dc22   2011024401

A catalog record for this book is available from the British Library.

Special discounts are available for bulk purchases of this book.
For more information, please contact Special Sales at 410-516-6936 or
specialsales@press.jhu.edu.

The Johns Hopkins University Press uses environmentally friendly book materials, including recycled text paper that is composed of at least 30 percent post-consumer waste, whenever possible.

For Joe Wittreich

CONTENTS

Preface ix
Acknowledgments xv

Introduction 1

1 Barbauld's *Poems* in Context 34

2 Politics, Vision, and Pastoral 50

3 Satire, Antipastoral, and Visionary Poetics 79

4 Personal Life and Visionary Poetics 94

5 Reflections on Writing 117

6 The Personal and Biblical Principles of Poetic Vision 144

7 God, Vision, and the Political Moment 173

Conclusion 195

Notes 205
Bibliography 223
Index 233

PREFACE

When I began writing this book, my aim was to examine three volumes of poetry, each by a separate writer: Anna Letitia Barbauld's *Poems* (1773; 1792), Ann Yearsley's *Rural Lyre* (1796), and Joanna Baillie's *Metrical Legends* (1821). Despite their many differences (including, especially, the fact that Yearsley came from a laboring-class background, while Barbauld and Baillie were from the middle class), these writers share a common Protestant Dissenting vision dedicated to free thought and the conviction that the principles of love, benevolence, and sympathy, if properly cultivated, and if informed by intellectual seriousness and historical understanding, are powerful enough to change the world.

For each writer, further, this conviction is formulated and articulated using the vocabulary of visionary poetics. Each poet defines and advances her poetic investments by positioning the troubled realities of this world in relation to an ideal vision of one sort or another. This vision, sometimes cast in terms of eternity and sometimes in terms of the expansive reach of history, seeks to jar human thought out of the conventional and constricting frameworks of identity and cultural understanding that entrap everyday life. Relying on a variety of writing strategies, from epic to pastoral to lyric to historical notes, Barbauld, Yearsley, and Baillie demonstrate that the only hope for achieving human betterment—and these writers are in fact hopeful that human experience can be remade in ways that enable peace, liberty, and stability—is by embracing and living by utopian principles that are neither rooted in nostalgia nor derived from or constrained by the rational discourses and political struggles that define the modern world. They are visionary idealists who put their idealism in the service of the material world and who understand that idealism has meaning only in relation to the particular challenges posed by lived experience.

In pursuing research on these volumes I discovered that their authors follow nearly identical methods in pursuing their visionary interests, insofar as they do not rely on individual poems to carry their ideas. Rather, they interweave their poems—and, in the case of Baillie, significant writings in prose as well—so that meaning emerges across the course of the volume, in a way that reflects Wordsworth's description of how he intended to integrate various of his poems into a major work called *The Recluse*; as he puts it in the preface to the 1814 edition of *The Excursion*,

> the preparatory poem [*The Prelude*] is biographical, and conducts the history of the Author's mind to the point when he was emboldened to hope that his faculties were sufficiently matured for entering upon the arduous labour which he had proposed to himself; and the two works [*Prelude* and *Excursion*] have the same kind of relation to each other, if he may so express himself, as the Ante-chapel has to the body of a Gothic church. Continuing this allusion, he may be permitted to add, that his minor pieces, which have been long before the public, when they shall be properly arranged, will be found by the attentive reader to have such connection with the main work as may give them claim to be likened to the little cells, oratories, and sepulchral recesses, ordinarily included in those edifices. (ix)

Neil Fraistat argues that certain other volumes of the Romantic period—poems by Wordsworth and Coleridge (*Lyrical Ballads*), Shelley (*Prometheus Unbound, with Other Poems*), and Keats (*Lamia, The Eve of St. Agnes, Isabella, and Other Poems*)—also constitute coherent and cohesive poetic statements. The volumes by Barbauld, Yearsley, and Baillie follow a similar course of composition, standing as coherent and unified statements. The poems in the volumes speak to, and correct, one another, so that meaning never ossifies and dreams never entirely collapse but rather appear as vibrant and living realities, responsive to ever-changing and ever-developing understanding. The result is that the poems are not most usefully read in isolation from one another (say, Yearsley's "Brutus" or Baillie's "Christopher Columbus") because in isolation they are often incomplete or even (as in the case of Barbauld's "Corsica") at least partly mistaken in the conclusions that they draw. Only when the volume is considered in its entirety do individual poems find their proper voice.

This poetic strategy places special and challenging demands on the critic, who must not only study individual poems but also the relations between and among all poems, which means that critical investigation can become at times tedious, and certainly more complex than study of a single short poem might be. Indeed, in time it became clear to me that I would be unable to contain all three writers in a single critical volume, as each writer's visionary method demanded more extensive and detailed consideration than could be fully examined alongside other volumes. To do justice to their work required separating the volumes of poetry from one another. This ostensibly simple decision, in turn, meant facing a surprisingly difficult question: do these little-studied volumes warrant such careful and detailed examination independent of one another? Can Barbauld's *Poems*, for instance, bear the weight of close critical investigation? It also meant embracing the task of accounting for as many poetic details as possible across a broad range of poems as a way of determining the enabling spirit of the volume, of not only examining, that is, each poem on its own terms but also in terms of its conversation with every other poem in the volume. As I became more deeply immersed in my research, it became clear that these volumes can bear the weight—and indeed demand the attention—of patient and detailed commentary. In fact, I now believe that these volumes (especially those by Barbauld and Yearsley) are among the most important poetic statements of the late eighteenth and early nineteenth centuries and should be placed alongside works by Blake and Wordsworth for their visionary sophistication and revolutionary thought.

Barbauld's *Poems* is a carefully constructed visionary statement and an especially good example of the visionary method used by poets in the eighteenth century. Ranging across political and philosophical topics, pastoral and epic poetic forms, and biblical and secular source materials in such a way that allows each poem in the volume to speak to the other, it constitutes a dynamic and compelling imaginative statement that is at once expansive and checked by self-reflection. In "Corsica," Barbauld boldly celebrates a nationalist revolution of independence, only to become convinced, by the end of the poem, that her proclamations are shortsighted; so she retreats into the environs of pastoral (in "The Invitation") to reconsider how she might most properly and usefully orient herself toward the larger, complex, and troubled world. And, later in the volume, she writes a series of hymns that applaud the divine character and human example of Christ, only to speculate later (in "A Summer Evening's Meditation") on the possibility that the biblical account of life might be insufficient for understanding the more expansive realities to which the mind has access. *Poems* follows this course of expression consistently, giving voice to the dream of what might be and checking that voice against the realities of circumstance that would stifle it. The volume is an organic, breathing work that expands and contracts in its effort to achieve a visionary position whose idealism can withstand and meaningfully shape the world that Barbauld inhabits.

More than any other scholar, Joseph Anthony Wittreich has shaped our understanding of visionary poetics. In a series of books and articles, culminating with the publication, in 1979, of *Visionary Poetics*, he draws together previous ideas on the subject by Northrop Frye, Barbara Lewalski, William Kerrigan, Angus Fletcher, and others and formulates the key features of vision, tracing what he has called the "line of vision" in British literary history and navigating often treacherous critical waters troubled by literary formalism at one moment and the claims of historical understanding at the next. In particular, he has mapped the intertextual character and interventionist and corrective strategies of visionary poetics, showing that visionary poetry is marked by engagement rather than interpretation or expression alone; it is transformative rather than fixed; it is restless rather than calm. Wittreich's argument is compelling and systematically pursued, and it is predicated on his claim that the Book of Revelation is "the purest and highest example of prophetic poetry," a claim that serves as the basis of his investigation into the poetic uses of Revelation from Milton through Blake. His work documents the debt that British poetry owes to the Bible, both as a source of formal experimentation and idealistic hope, and shows the importance of thinking systematically and historically about the British visionary imagination.

Other scholars (Terence Hoagwood, Leslie Tannenbaum, Jackie DiSalvo, and Anthony Rosso, to name a few) have taken their lead from Wittreich and expanded and (where necessary) corrected his argument. I take my direction from these scholars by retaining the critical idealism at the core of Wittreich's argument, as well as his claims about the intertextual and corrective strategies of visionary writing. But I also want to expand his argument in two main ways. First, I want to reconsider his claim that visionary poetics in Britain traces its source to the Book of Revelation, or (more generally) to the Bible, and sets as its goal leading people into the gates of heaven, by probing additional sources and goals with which visionary thinkers often worked. Second, I want to fill in some of the gaps in Wittreich's argument by showing that visionary expression does not overleap the eighteenth century by proceeding directly from Milton to Blake but rather is very much alive during the period, especially after 1750. Indeed, particularly when women writers are considered, these points become evident. Anna Letitia Barbauld, Elizabeth Hands, Ann Yearsley, Anna Seward, Ann Batten Cristall, and Ann Bannerman, among many others, wrote compellingly from a visionary stance, using the strategies of poetic engagement to contest dominant and more culturally conservative modes of literary expression. And often they did so without relying on the Bible or Milton as guides. Drawing on a rich variety of source materials and situating their visionary interests in specific relation to the historical conditions under which they were writing, they help us to understand the extent to which a mode of disruptive and idealistic thought was kept alive, even if underground, during an extended period of what might otherwise appear to be visionary dreariness, or, as Wittreich puts it, a period dominated by writers who form a "line of wit."

Without question, Barbauld is a visionary poet who engages with other texts for inspiration and in order to correct them and who is motivated by an idealistic spirit committed to the promise and possibility of a world transformed from violence and struggle to peace and stability: even if she does not write specifically about building Jerusalem in "England's green and pleasant land," she nevertheless imagines, with Blake, a similarly renovated world. And she certainly draws on biblical texts at times to shape her poetic strategies. But she also looks to other sources—classical and contemporary, religious and secular—to guide her visionary spirit. She does not work directly out of a biblical tradition or under the influence of Milton alone; her poetry reaches into the historical past, beyond any single textual representation, to draw on many texts and events (from Virgil to Tibullus and from Paoli to Barbauld's grandmother), and it looks to the future, though not necessarily to the heavenly gates promised by Revelation. The idealism at the center of her vision, indeed, never entirely escapes the bounds of historical reality but, instead, pushes that reality ever further outward so that its grip on human experience is lessened and so that it can accommodate the expansive reach of the imagination.

Following Wittreich's compelling formulation of visionary poetics, then, my objective is to trace the complex workings of Barbauld's imagination across the entirety of *Poems* in the hope that, by searching out her sources and particularizing the sort of future that Barbauld imagines, we can better understand the radical nature of her corrective intervention into the tradition of British thought and poetry. In pursuing such a task it becomes clear how deeply invested Barbauld is in visionary writing, even if she cannot be easily placed within a clear "line" of visionary thought extending from the Bible through Milton. Indeed, if anything, given the range of her sources and influences, it is more accurate to say that she does not belong to a line of vision but rather to a kaleidoscopic collection of visionary influences, drawing her interests from a broad and diverse range of literary source materials and using them to shape a vision that brings her idealism directly to bear on the modern age. Still, Wittreich's description of visionary poetics is a necessary guide to understanding Barbauld, insofar as she engages with and corrects those materials (from Boswell to Priestley, from the Bible to Wilberforce) to suit her own visionary purpose, which is to expand historical understanding so that it can comfortably accommodate and implement (in a nonsimplistic and nonsentimental way) the principles of benevolence, peace, and love. While the Bible may be only one of her sources, and while Milton figures marginally in her writing, her commitment to her visionary project is constant and unyielding. And the depth of her visionary investment and the contours of her visionary purpose can be discovered only by examining *Poems* from the assumption that it is of a piece, an organic combination of integrated parts that constitute a single poetic expression.

ACKNOWLEDGMENTS

This project would not have been possible without the interest and assistance of several students, colleagues, editors, and readers, all of whom contributed significantly to my efforts to understand Barbauld's poetry. Because my interest in Barbauld began in the classroom, and developed over a period of years when I was teaching courses on Romantic women poets, my first debt of gratitude is to my graduate students, whose patience, intelligence, dedication, and challenging conversations contributed immeasurably to my efforts to think clearly about Barbauld. Among these students, Andrea Beranek, Nicola Brooke, Michelina Cersosimo, Jade Higa, Timothy Ruppert, Moria Torrington, Matthew Vickless, and Melissa Wehler were especially helpful and supportive.

In addition, several present and former colleagues in the Department of English at Duquesne University read sections of the manuscript, assisted with tracking down source materials, answered computer questions, and provided important and patient responses to my many queries about eighteenth-century poetry: these were Bernard Beranek, Laura Engel, John Fried, Kathy Glass, Sue Howard, Joseph Keenan, Jim Purdy, Danielle St. Hilaire, and Samuel Tindall. Christopher Duncan, the dean of the McAnulty College and Graduate School of Liberal Arts, also provided important funding for a research assistant over the course of one summer. Several research assistants—Maureen Gallagher, Shreyashi Mukherjee, and Madhuchhanda Ray Choudhury—were solicitous and prompt in helping me with various aspects of the research. The chair of the Department of Classics at Duquesne, Stephen Newmeyer, provided helpful conversation on matters related to classical literature; two tutors in the classics lab, Michael Coulter and Sarah Whitlock, were helpful in translating parts of Virgil's *Georgics*. Nora McBurney and Gabrielle Kokanos provided much efficient and cheerful assistance with printing the manuscript, handling correspondence, and other important matters. Also, Bonnie Badger and John Henderson offered much patient guidance in helping me with computer and formatting matters.

Among the many scholars in the field to whom I am indebted, I am especially grateful to Stephen Behrendt, whose encouragement on an earlier project gave me the confidence to proceed with the present one. Greg Kucich has provided much wonderful support and guidance at times when I most needed them. John Thomson was my first teacher of English literature and remains a wonderful resource of knowledge. I would also be remiss if I did not express my gratitude to Stuart Curran, whose groundbreaking studies of women's poetry of the long eighteenth century not only make the current project possible but also make possible the work of an entire generation of scholars. I also want to thank the anonymous readers of the present manuscript for their support and encouragement. My deepest and most abiding scholarly debt is to Terence Hoagwood and Joseph Wittreich, who, across the entire span of my career, have been steady friends and unfailing advocates on my behalf.

Matthew McAdam, humanities acquisitions editor at the Johns Hopkins University Press, provided much excellent and indispensable advice, especially during the early stages of the project, and M. J. Devaney was superb in editing the manuscript. I also want to thank Deborah Bors for her excellent work preparing the manuscript in its final stages to ensure its professional presentation. Additionally, I thank Tom Broughton-Willett for his meticulous work on the index. Needless to say, any errors or shortcomings in the project are my own and should not in any way be attributed to those who graciously guided and assisted me along the way.

Finally, my greatest debt is to Joanna Foster, who, for more than forty years, has been my constant support.

*Anna Letitia Barbauld and
Eighteenth-Century Visionary Poetics*

Introduction

It is a critical commonplace that visionary poetry and poetics became dormant and sank into obscurity after the age of Milton and reemerged during the later eighteenth century in the figure of William Blake, whose subversive and transformative engagement with Milton and the Bible signaled the awakening of Romantic idealism and its attendant preoccupation with remaking history, politics, and society. The eloquent and detailed scholarly arguments put forward by Northrop Fry, Harold Bloom, and especially Joseph A. Wittreich map this course of development in British literary history and argue persuasively that Blake is the major visionary poet and prophetic voice of the period of visionary reawakening.[1] As Wittreich puts it in his important essay, "Opening the Seals: Blake's Epics and the Milton Tradition,"

> Blake turned from the poets of the eighteenth century, who seemed more adept at theorizing about epics than writing them, to the examples of Spenser and Milton, who, harnessing prophecy to epic, created a new kind of epic poetry. Spenser, because he fostered the experimentation that Milton continued, requires notice; but it is finally Milton who made the great advances, forging a new tradition of the old one—a tradition that Blake could embrace as his own and, once mastering, could use as the informing context for his epic endeavors (25).

In the wake of the American and French revolutions, the rigid formalisms of the early eighteenth century were broken, and the great British visionary imagination became a dominant cultural presence. And Blake was the loud voice calling out to time and eternity that change was at hand; his fiery spirit and remarkable poetic force defined the age, providing what many scholars have come to regard as the explanatory key to the literary achievements of the late eighteenth and early nineteenth centuries, especially the achievements of writers such as Wordsworth, Coleridge, and Shelley.

But Blake was not the only visionary poet of the late eighteenth century, nor the first. Nor was he the only eighteenth-century poet to think systematically about how to use vision for the purpose of changing the world. Further, while his imaginative investments in Milton and the Bible animate an astonishingly vibrant and original poetic sensibility, they do not constitute a definitive cultural and literary context for visionary poetry in the period. Indeed, Blake was only one of a large number of poets who bore witness to the events of the age by attempting to devise visionary systems that might point the way toward transforming the world so as to secure liberty and justice for all. These poets looked to many sources, including but not restricted to Milton and the Bible, for this purpose, ranging from their contemporaries and early eighteenth-century counterparts (Edward Young, James Thomson), to their classical forbears (Tibullus, Virgil); they also acknowledged but looked beyond the epic form (on which Blake relied) in shaping their visions, drawing on a variety of poetic modes, ranging from pastoral to satire to chronicles to poetic epistles, to give depth and dimension to their imaginations. Moreover, while, as visionary poets, they often looked at the world from the perspective of eternity, as the visionary impulse would seem to demand, more often they used their visionary strategies (including their understanding of eternity) to deepen and expand historical understanding.

Vision and Gender

Many, if not most, of the writers who remade visionary poetics after the age of Milton and prior to (or around the time of) Blake were women. Indeed, even the briefest survey of writers during the second half of the eighteenth century reveals that many female poets were, to varying degrees, interested in dreams and visions as a way of approaching their work as poets. In her *Poems upon Several Occasions* (1748), for instance, Mary Leapor includes a poem entitled "A Moral Vision" (65–69), which is a dream vision about how to live in the world, as well as another poem entitled "The Ten-Penny Nail" (125–31), which is also a dream vision in which a nail asks the author to write the story of its life. Other poems in the volume, too, make at least passing references to visionary experiences; for instance, in "On Discontent," Leapor remarks that "while it lasts, the pleasing Vision charms" (171).[2] In her poetry, Leapor taps into a reality beyond the borders of consciousness as a way of gaining leverage on the world around her.

Other poets were similarly drawn to the powers of visionary imagination. Anna Letitia Barbauld, the subject of the present study, wrote, in *Poems* (1773), with even greater intensity and focus than Leapor on visionary themes, using multiple poetic strategies in an effort to reshape human consciousness in such a way as to enable the remaking of the world along nonviolent and humane lines. In *The Death of Amnon* (1789), Elizabeth Hands, too, although not speaking explicitly in visionary terms, places poems with clear visionary aspirations (the titular poem, for instance) alongside pastorals, satires, epistles, and other modes of poetic expression as a means of challenging conventional structures of understanding and liberating the imagination. In *Genuine Poetical Compositions* (1791), Elizabeth Bentley also recognizes the power of the visionary imagination, remarking in her "Ode to Fancy":

> O thou keen Pow'r [fancy], whose radiant eye
> Can thousand shadowy forms descry,
> That cheat corporeal sight;
> Thou who canst soar above yon spheres,
> Past days recall, see future years,
> Or pierce the shades of night. (30)[3]

Mary Robinson's poem "To the Poet Coleridge" is perhaps the most explicit statement by a female writer of the period about visionary poetics. Written between December 1799 and December 1800, the poem directly engages Coleridge's "Kubla Khan," which Robinson had read in manuscript.[4] In the opening line of the poem, Robinson states that she is "rapt in the visionary theme!" (226) that has inspired Coleridge's imagination; she then goes on to admire Coleridge's vision but also to present a corrective to it by transforming it from a purely private dream into a dream with social dimensions and possibilities. Through the course of the poem, she shows that she understands the operation of the visionary imagination, including its corrective and revisionary purposes.

While all of these writers knew the Bible and many knew the work of Milton, and while many draw directly on both (note, for instance, Hands's use of the Bible in *Death of Amnon* and in the two "Supposition" poems immediately following it), they did not feel bound by the traditions associated with either, at least not to the degree that Blake did. Accordingly as their visions required, they integrated biblical references into pagan sensibilities or implicitly acknowledged the visionary accomplishment of Milton while engaging equally with the works (say) of Alexander Pope or Samuel Butler. Working against the grain of tradition, Anna Letitia Barbauld, Elizabeth Hands, Elizabeth Bentley, Ann Yearsley, Anne Bannerman, and Joanna Baillie, among others, wrote carefully and systematically in an effort to construct unified poetic statements intended to trouble passive understanding or acceptance of convention and thereby to create imaginative spaces for remaking reality. While Blake also sought to expose the traps set for humanity by conventional structures of belief and authority, his visionary aims were meant largely to show the way into eternity; by contrast, Barbauld and her fellow visionaries used the reach of visionary idealism as a way of showing people how to live in the world.⁵ Their visionary goal, with few exceptions, involved embracing service to others and a pacifist stance toward the conflicts of the public and political world.⁶

One important feature of the poetry by these writers is that their visionary systems, in large measure, were not set out in single poems but rather across entire volumes. In these volumes, the poets drew on a variety of literary styles and genres as well as on various source materials to create tensions and strategies that not only engage with antecedent traditions of thought but also offer self-critical commentaries on their own visions. Neil Fraistat's important study *The Poem and the Book* sets in place a helpful foundation for considering the relations among poems in the context of poetic volumes. Fraistat, for example, argues that "the major Romantic poets sought continually to create coherent volumes from seemingly disparate poems that harmonize on a sophisticated level" (40). Although he focuses only on major volumes by male Romantic poets—Wordsworth and Coleridge's *Lyrical Ballads, with a Few Other Poems* (1798); Keats's *Lamia, Isabella, The Eve of St. Agnes, and Other Poems* (1820); and Shelley's *Prometheus Unbound, with Other Poems* (1820)—his argument is generally applicable to other poets in the late eighteenth and early nineteenth centuries, many of whom paid careful attention to the ordering of individual poems within volumes as a way of putting poems in conversation with one another so as to create a large and unified poetic statement. The poetic volume, as documented by Fraistat, has particular significance for the work of the visionary poets of the long eighteenth century, not only because of its intertextual suggestiveness but also because it constitutes one means by which these poets keep their visionary investments fluid and in motion. That is, considered within the context of the poetic volume, wherein poems are in constant conversation with one another, no single poem can become a final, ossified statement of doctrine or truth; rather, it must always contend for its place and meaning within the larger volume. Meanings reside most often *across* poems rather than *within* them.⁷

Although much of the visionary poetry that emerged during the latter years of the eighteenth century was written by women, visionary expression, of course, was not the province of women writers alone. Nor, in general, did these women writers view themselves as producing poetic statements intended to work solely against the grain of patriarchal poetic traditions or as writing from a polemical feminist position intended to distinguish kinds of poetry along lines of gender. Indeed, their visionary projects were expansive, engaging smartly with the full spectrum of issues, interests, and concerns spanning their world; to view these writers and their works only through the lens of gender or to consider gender as the first principle of their poetic interest would greatly limit understanding of the reach of their imaginations.

In recent years, scholars have begun to develop new paths of inquiry into the women poets of the long eighteenth century, expanding critical interest along lines that complicate issues of gender and enrich study of the poetry. While they recognize the important ways that gender often inflects the poems written by women, these scholars also recognize that gender often was not the dominant conceptual category for many women poets and that even when it was of major importance, it was not imagined in restrictive or reductive ways. By moving beyond the singular emphasis on gender, and beyond the idea that gender is a necessary leverage point for reading women's poetry against the grain of their male counterparts, scholars have begun to place the poetry of women more richly into conversation with the broader culture in which it was produced.

Paula Backscheider provides some helpful general guidelines on how one might approach the women poets of this period, specifically by urging a revision of the tendency among some feminist critics to define women's poetry against the grain of the dominant (masculinist) tradition of poetic writing. In her monumental study, *Eighteenth-Century Women Poets and Their Poetry*, Backscheider endeavors to shift critical focus away from a narrow interest in gender and away from the notion that poetry written by women, by definition, must be polemical, directed against patriarchal authority. According to Backscheider, to begin from the critical assumption that women's poetry is, prima facie, essentially distinct from poetry written by men effectively diminishes the authority of the female imagination by situating it on the outskirts of the dominant (masculine) poetic culture. By focusing too sharply on the differences between women and their culture as a means of illustrating the characteristics of the defiant female imagination, critical endeavor risks becoming trapped in a purely negative dialectic that relegates women poets to the margins of literary history or (perhaps more accurately) leaves them isolated on the margins of literary history, exactly where they always have been. As she puts it in the early pages of her study,

> to seek and privilege anti-patriarchal themes falsifies women's—and human— literary history, and while I give the theme of defiance its due, I believe that emphasis on it has been almost as much a detriment to assessment as trivialization. (xvi)

Women poets of the eighteenth century of course were aware of their status as women and often wrote self-consciously about that status, as can be seen (to name only one famous example) in Sarah Fyge Egerton's *The Female Advocate* (1686), but just as often they were motivated by other interests: "Defiance and resistance to patriarchy," Backscheider notes, "are not primary motivations for many of these women" (xvi). To recognize this fact, Backscheider suggests, makes it possible for scholarship and criticism to begin recuperating women poets in such a way as to elucidate the breadth of their cultural interests and the depth of their cultural investment and enables a richer assessment of women's place within the larger contexts of eighteenth-century culture and society. In particular, to approach the women poets of the period from an integrative rather than separatist critical perspective will not only enable a more credible assessment of the character and worth of their poetry in relation to the period; it will also compel "major revisions in literary history" (xix), revisions that, Backscheider says, will require "a structural reorganization and reconception" of literary production (xiv).

In her important *Borderlines: The Shiftings of Gender in British Romanticism*, Susan Wolfson follows a similar line of argument. In her discussion of the influence that women writers in the 1790s have had on the history of criticism down to the present day, Wolfson observes that the writings of Catherine Macaulay and Mary Wollstonecraft portrayed the cultural dynamics defining the lives of men and women in such as way as to make "gender . . . a subject for explanation" (2), and, in so doing, Wolfson says, these writers laid the groundwork for a line of critical inquiry that eventually

> identified a "masculine" bias and a subjected "feminine," both in the literature and in a literary history that suppressed women's writing. Romanticism was then remapped to relativize received tradition: there was the "masculine" canon and the "feminine" of (excluded) women's writing; the first a nexus of values and practices summed (variously) as egotistical, colonizing, appropriative, imperialistic, anti-domestic, sublime; the other, a matrix summed (variously) as selfless, object-oriented, empathetic, sympathetic, communal, domestic. (3)

The result was a criticism that was "polemically important" in making visible writers who had disappeared from the Romantic canon. But ultimately, Wolfson says, the feminist project of recovery and assessment became too limited, leaving women writers still marginalized, though in a different way: "Its poles could feel too sheer, too schematic, slighting not only the aberrations, contradictions, or double-exposures across the divide, but also the instabilities and complexities of particular encounters" (3).

Wolfson's general line of argument helps to clarify my approach to women visionary poets, even though she does not examine the writers I have mentioned. She does not contest the important contribution of feminist scholarship; rather she seeks to open a space for a more comprehensive critical approach to women writers, one that focuses on how gender functions in works by women and men and encourages critical models that historicize the poetic concerns of women writers without reducing those concerns to a single subject matter or without reducing gender to an essentialist category. As she puts it, the most interesting thinking about gender occurs along the "often traversable borderlines that vex and complicate the symbolic order": "My work on the borders has called for flexible approaches and sympathies" (35).

By enlarging the intellectual and critical framework within which writers might be considered, Wolfson's argument provides a means of opening up the works written by the women I have mentioned—particularly Barbauld—and putting the poetic volumes of these writers in dialogue with the larger social, political, economic, and cultural conditions under which they were produced. In light of Wolfson's argument, it becomes possible to consider gender as one of many concerns of women writers and to recognize that the conditions under which they wrote were defined by matters in which gender often figured but not exclusively.[8] While Barbauld, for example, was certainly aware of the gender debates in her day, as her short poems "The Rights of Woman" and "Washing Day" show, she does not consistently organize her poetic sensibilities around questions of gender, and, indeed, she often writes against the grain of feminist intellectuals such as Wollstonecraft.[9] For Barbauld, as for others, the greatest poetic challenge was to construct a visionary poetics that reached beyond single issues to embrace the deepest and most far-reaching dimensions of human experience and consciousness.

More recently, Stephen C. Behrendt's *British Women Poets and the Romantic Writing Community* has offered a line of critique similar to Backscheider and Wolfson's. In his carefully researched and closely argued study, Behrendt examines a wide range of women poets through the lens of various cultural and aesthetic interests, concluding his study with the claim that the importance of these writers compels a wholesale reconsideration of Romantic literary history and Romantic aesthetics: "We have reached a point," he says, "at which we must collectively rise to another challenge posed to us by the recovery work that has been accomplished to date. This challenge involves reassessing the whole matter of aesthetics as it applies to romantic poetry in Britain" (299). He begins this project of reassessment by gathering a large number of women poets and placing them within various historical and literary contexts in such a way as to capture the range of influences on their imaginations, as well as the range of their poetic interests. By examining the women poets of the period in relation to "the rhetorical and ideological agendas of British radicalism," "the subject of war," "poetic form," and "national poetry," Behrendt greatly expands critical understanding of the reach of women's poetic imaginations in the long eighteenth century and indicates the direction future criticism must take (8). As he puts it in the final pages of his study,

> The more of this recovered poetry we read, and the more we do so with an openness to both its intrinsic merit and its often conspicuous intertextuality, the clearer the portrait of the literary community we will be able to paint. And this larger portrait needs to be continually redrawn, both today and long into the future, as we become still better acquainted with the lives and works of poets of both sexes who have historically been absent from the picture. (298–99)

Although gender bias on the part of a male critical establishment may account for the absence from literary history of the women writers at the center of Behrendt's study, it does not follow that contemporary examination of their poetry should be limited only to gender-specific explanations. Recovery, as Behrendt makes clear, should be accompanied, rather, by a careful consideration of the full range of writers' styles, strategies, and interests.

The virtue of the studies by Backscheider, Wolfson, and Behrendt, in addition to their redirecting the critical focus on women poets of the long eighteenth century, is their scholarly breadth. They bring into critical view numerous women poets who have been seldom studied and place them within various important cultural and critical contexts, ranging from gender to nationality. These contexts lay the necessary groundwork for more detailed studies of individual writers and works. My own work on Barbauld's *Poems* is an effort to build on the work of these scholars, not by continuing to broaden the expanse of critical investigation that they have begun to expose but rather by specifying the particulars of poetic expression. By examining one volume by one writer, I hope to show in detail how women's poetry in the eighteenth century engages deeply and smartly with the complex historical conditions under which it was produced.

Elizabeth Hands and Anne Bannerman

The nature and direction of the sort of visionary poetry written by women in the long eighteenth century can be sketched, briefly, in the writings of two poets, Elizabeth Hands and Anne Bannerman. Both writers exhibit an awareness of the biblical tradition of vision and, at least in the case of Hands, the Miltonic reliance on that tradition. At the same time, however, they situate themselves, poetically, outside that tradition and begin to construct a new sort of poetic sensibility, one that works from multiple sources and across several genres so as to produce a nuanced, textured, and multilayered vision that is both historically circumscribed and at the same time engaged in the task of transforming human consciousness, not for the purpose of creating a heavenly Jerusalem but for the purpose of reshaping the nature and direction of history. Even as Blake, Wordsworth, and Shelley were busily insinuating themselves into the Milton tradition of setting out the relations between man and God or man and an idealized, universal redemptive power, many of the women writers of the long eighteenth century were working along a parallel path in the service of a different sort of visionary poetics, whose foundations and goals were fully grounded within the realities of material circumstance and whose poetic strategies acknowledged this inexorable fact. Moreover, these writers map their visionary courses across a span of poems that they place in tension with one another in such a way as to avoid what for them might be called the pitfall of doctrinal truth. Even as the volumes by these writers construct visions for the purpose of transforming human consciousness, they check their visionary flights in such a way as to assure visionary discomfort and thus critical self-reflection.

In 1789, the domestic servant Elizabeth Hands published her only known volume of poetry, entitled *The Death of Amnon: A Poem with an Appendix, Containing Pastorals, and other Poetical Pieces.* As she indicates in her two "Supposition" poems, Hands knew that this volume would be controversial because of her gender and social class, because she chose to write about the subject of rape, and probably also because she dedicated it to the Della Cruscan poet and dramatist Bertie Greatheed.[10] Undeterred, she published the volume, drawing on a variety of poetic strategies (including satire) to establish a poetic voice sufficiently strong and confident to carry out her visionary aims. The volume not only demonstrates her poetic command of the Old Testament (the Book of Samuel) but also exhibits her familiarity with literary history and pastoral poetics in the form of a large number of pastoral poems set in the classical past. Moreover, in "Critical Fragments," the final poem in the volume, she exhibits her awareness and command of British poets who preceded her, including Milton, Shakespeare, Edward Young, and others. The volume is imaginatively bold and restless, capturing Hands's unwillingness to wed her poetic sensibility to a single tradition or style of writing. The result is a work that is astonishing in its mastery of subject matter, in its poetic range, and in its visionary power.[11]

The most immediately striking feature of the volume is its first poem, the five-canto visionary epic entitled *The Death of Amnon*. Taking its subject matter from the Book of Samuel 2:13, the poem tells the story of Amnon, the son of David, who rapes his own sister, Tamar. Hands's representation of this story in effect constitutes a rewriting of the story of the fall, except it is a man (Amnon) rather than a woman who sets in motion the course of action that destroys the peaceful order of the world. Hands's interest in rethinking the biblical and Miltonic story becomes clear in her expansion of the biblical description of David's nephew, Jonadab, as "a very subtil man" (Samuel 2:13, 3). Hands lifts this detail and develops it to the point where Jonadab becomes identical with the biblical serpent that seduces Eve and that in Genesis 3:1 is described as "more subtil than any beast of the field which the Lord God has made." Hands describes Jonadab's friendship with Amnon:

> A friend he [Amnon] had, the son of Shimlah,
> Nam'd Jonadab; a man by nature subtle,
> Proud and ambitious; yet would meanly stoop
> To the most base and most ignoble acts,
> To serve his private ends. The artless youth [Amnon]
> Oft to its plausibilities gave ear,
> Not e'en suspecting, that beneath the cloak
> Of formal flatt'ries self-interest hides
> It's [sic] serpent head. (4)

In the course of the poem, Jonadab, in fact, manipulates every detail of the plot, even to the point of persuading Achitophel to kill his brother Amnon as retribution for Amnon's crime and sin—after Jonadab had earlier persuaded Amnon to commit the crime in the first place. Over the course of the poem, Jonadab's character becomes increasingly Miltonic and Shakespearean in nature, as he is seen not only to be "subtle," like Milton's serpent (see, for example, the argument and line 307 in book 9 [385] of *Paradise Lost*), but also false and clever, like Shakespeare's Iago. As he says in a soliloquy about his plot to deceive and manipulate Achitophel:

> But I must veil my real sentiments
> With counterfeited sorrow, and observe
> Each secret movement of his [Achitophel's] varying soul,
> And sympathise with him. (20)

In pursuing her visionary theme, Hands might be viewed as providing the sort of "corrective criticism" of earlier writers and texts that Wittreich says is characteristic of visionary poetry. And, indeed, she does engage critically with her literary and biblical forbears, steering the Miltonic desire to justify the ways of God to man toward more earthly considerations, making her visionary cause a warning about how power can corrupt and destroy the human capacity for goodness. Her preoccupation in the poem, after all, is explicitly with two sorts of power, a sexual power desired by Amnon and a political power desired by Achitophel.[12] And in both cases that desire is fostered and manipulated by the blindly self-interested Jonadab. When this power is secured, the result is human unhappiness, despair, and bloodshed. Stunningly cold lines describe Amnon's murder: "Mingling with gore, the wine in currents flow'd" (43).

Further, in constructing her vision, Hands extends her reach beyond *Paradise Lost* to incorporate elements of other Miltonic texts. In particular, she draws on a segment of *Samson Agonistes* as a way of revising Satan's view of the mind in *Paradise Lost*. In *Amnon*, after Tamar is raped, she accepts her brother Absalom's offer to be her "guardian" (27) in future by remarking,

> Farewell, ye courtly scenes;
> No more shall Tamar shine in your resorts;
> But here recluse and tranquil ever 'bide;
> Regaling in that never-cloying feast,
> Th' internal calm of an untainted mind.
> This none can ravish from me; this is life. (28)

If Milton's Satan in *Paradise Lost* provides a model for Hands's Jonadab, especially in his belief that self-interest and manipulative power are the governing principles of the mind (recall, for instance, Satan's famous comment that "the mind is its own place, and in it self / Can make a Heav'n of Hell, a Hell of Heav'n" [217]), in her characterization of Tamar, Hands revises this satanic view in such a way as to make the mind a place of hope and goodness that is capable of withstanding even the worst forms of human tragedy. Tamar comes to understand that the ill that has befallen her has not destroyed the core of her spiritual identity; and, indeed, in the aftermath of her tragedy she finds within herself the resources to renew her dedication to loving God:

> That God which rais'd my father to the throne,
> And still protects him with his pow'rful arm,
> Shall be my all in all. To him I'll pray
> Incessant, and the great Jehovah's name
> Shall fire my theme, and fill my heav'nly song. (28)

Tamar's comment to Absalom provides a powerful counterpoint to the littleness of mind seen in Jonadab (and in Milton's Satan). And by constructing this counterpoint on lines from *Samson Agonistes*, Hands effectively puts Milton's last major work into critical tension with *Paradise Lost*. In the final lines of *Samson*, after Samson has killed the Philistines and himself, the chorus of Danites states:

> All is best, though we oft doubt,
> What th' unsearchable dispose
> Of highest wisdom brings about,
> And ever best found in the close.
> Oft he seems to hide his face,
> But unexpectedly returns
> And to his faithful Champion hath in place
> Bore witness gloriously; whence Gaza mourns
> And all that band them to resist
> His uncontroulable intent,
> His servants he with new acquist
> Of true experience from this great event
> With peace and consolation hath dismist,
> And calm of mind all passion spent. (593)

Tamar's "internal calm of an untainted mind" is the same "calm of mind" that comes from the view in *Samson* that "all is best," a philosophy that for Hands and the Milton of *Samson* brings the possibility of "peace and consolation."

Tamar's comments make clear that Hands does not abandon a concept of God or reject the idea that God plays a role in human experience. But she does not base her vision on the idea that God is either the foundational principle or the endpoint of human experience. Indeed, for her, God is a sort of pure mental space that allows the individual to find balance and purpose in a world full of conflict and injustice. For Hands, the vision of the world from the perspective of eternity gives way to a vision of the world from the perspective of the world itself, a vision that defines matters of spirit wholly within the framework of human experience. This poetic strategy effectively subverts and transforms the biblical and Miltonic understanding of human experience in relation to God and heaven, and Hands uses Milton himself to construct this visionary principle.

Although Hands engages directly with Milton in *Amnon*, she is not bound to Milton or to the Bible in constructing her visionary poetics, and her poetic strategy is not aimed simply at correcting these texts. Indeed, when *Amnon* is read within the larger context of the volume, it becomes clear that even as

Hands engages with the Bible and Milton for corrective purposes, she is only passing through biblical and Miltonic territory on her way to a different sort of visionary poetics. Immediately on completing *Amnon*, for instance, she turns away from her Miltonic visionary style, and away from biblical subject matter, to present two poems—"On the Supposition of an Advertisement in a Morning Paper, of the Publication of a Volume of Poems by a Servant Maid" and "On the Supposition of the Book Having Been Published and Read"—that might more properly belong to what Wittreich calls the "line of wit" (xiv). These poems imagine, for the purpose of satirizing, well-to-do readers of *Amnon*, who, in Hands's telling, lack the ability to comprehend her poetic purposes or even to take her poem seriously, because, for these readers, class and gender differences are an insurmountable obstacle.[13]

Both poems are written in anapestic tetrameter, using end-stopped rhymed couplets, a poetic strategy that looks back to Dryden and Pope's satirical method while at the same time revising their use of the heroic couplet (by shortening the rhymed lines from five to four beats) and changing their iambic meter to anapestic. The poems integrate discussions of gender and class, cooking and cleaning, with discussions of religion in such a way that the invocation of the Bible in eighteenth-century England comes to be seen as ludicrous rather than as a sign of visionary hope and redemptive possibility. For example, in discussing the story of Amnon (about which most of the people Hands is describing know little or nothing) Miss Rhymer says to her friends in the first "Supposition" poem that "if I thought I could readily find it, I'd borrow / My house-keeper's Bible, and read it to-morrow" (52). For such people as Miss Rhymer, visionary poetry is meaningless, and they are unaware that it reaches historically from Milton back to the Bible. Thus, while Hands may be aware of a visionary tradition linking the Bible and British poetry, she does not make a full poetic investment in it because, as the larger trajectory of the volume suggests, doing so would be pointless: British culture cannot be brought to understand this tradition. Instead, she situates her visionary understanding within a context of multiple poetic strategies—in this case, satire—to awaken readers to the limitations of consciousness that trap them in ignorance.

At the conclusion of the second satire, and through the use of a cryptic poetic strategy, Hands informs any reader who is capable of subtlety and understanding of her real purpose in writing. After imagining the nastiness and sardonic mockery directed toward her by the landed class, who, for instance, make fun of her poetic volume for including a poem about "a mad cow" (54), Hands describes a rector who is present at the scene and who comments to his companions on

Hands's inadequate poetic and biblical understanding. As he says to his peers about *Amnon*:

> That Amnon, you can't call it poetry neither,
> There's no flights of fancy, or imagery either;
> You may stile it prosaic, blank-verse at the best;
> Some pointed reflections, indeed, are exprest;
> The narrative lines are exceedingly poor:
> Her Jonadab is a —— the drawing-room door
> Was open'd, the gentlemen came from below,
> And gave the discourse a definitive blow. (55)

Not only does Hands here exhibit a remarkable knowledge of poetic form and style (referring to imagery, blank verse, poetic reflection, narrative, and prosaic language); she also, more importantly, brings forward one of the central characters from *Amnon*—Jonadab—and invests him with a significance that bears directly on the social reality that forms the context and points the direction of her poetics. She directly relates the diabolical associations of this figure whose absorbing self-interest corrupts the world of which he is part to people in the social gathering that she is describing. Indeed, just as Jonadab's name is mentioned, "the gentlemen came from below," like Satan's fallen angels, as if to demonstrate forcefully that the sort of evil with which Hands is concerned is of a social rather than metaphysical nature: the sins of Jonadab are identified with Satan and then transferred onto the landed class of people who deny that the poor are capable of understanding and meaningful expression. On this view, the "definitive blow" that is given to "the discourse" by "the gentlemen" does more than simply stop the conversation; it hammers home the social dimensions of Hands's visionary poetics.

The critical relation between *Amnon* and the two "Supposition" poems suggests the way that Hands shapes and interweaves her poems through the course of the volume. For example, following the "Supposition" poems, Hands presents a cluster of conventional classical pastoral poems that describe an idyllic life wherein young men and women face the mild tribulations of love at the same time that they experience its great excitement and rewards. These poems are followed immediately by two with British subject matter—"Lob's Courtship" and "The Rural Maid"—that use classical pastoral poems to comment on the British social situation, particularly the situation of the poor, and in such a way that manifestly contests the simpleminded idealism associated with the earlier pastoral poems. The first of these British pastoral poems, like the "Supposition" poems, uses satire to trouble the idealism associated with classical pastoral. Not only is the titular character, Lob, a hapless oaf who gets it "into his head to marry" (86) while feeding his cows, but his romantic pitch to Nell, the woman he has randomly selected for marriage despite the fact that she "lives a great way off" (86), is uproariously dumb, perfectly exposing the meaninglessness of the sort of idealism associated with the earlier pastoral poems. For example, in "A Pastoral," the young shepherd, Damon, asks Laura the whereabouts of Daphne in this fashion: "Where is thy friend, the lovely Daphne gone? / Ah! Has some rival led her to the grove?" (62). And again, in "A Pastoral Song," the speaker says of Delia, "She thoughtless meets me, with innocent smiles, / And trips with me into the grove" (81). Lob, however, possesses no such sophistication or verbal facility in matters of love, saying bluntly to the woman whom he wishes to marry:

What Nelly! How dost do? Says he,
Come, will you go along with me
O'er yonder stile, a little way
Along that close; Nell, what dost say? (87)

Following as it does on the cluster of poems that demonstrate a commanding grasp of pastoral voice and characterization, this poem is doubly poignant, showing just how far removed pastoral idealism really is from the lives of the poor and laboring population in England and, therefore, just how unhelpful the genre of pastoral can be as a form of poetic engagement if it is not put in relation to discernible social and historical realities.

But Hands's objective is not to reject pastoral out of hand, as becomes clear in other poems. In "Rural Maid," for instance, she approaches pastoral in an entirely different manner by describing a young woman who longs for escape from "these strange disorders" (89) of London society into the "happy grove" (88) of the rural landscape. For this young woman, the city is a place of vanity (defined by "the dear looking glass" [88]), of "tinsel joys" (89), of mindless reading of "the play-bills" (88); it is a place, that is, of banishment from the rural scene where love, song, and personal fulfillment are possible. If "Lob's Courtship" is a satirical send-up of the limitations of pastoral, "Rural Maid" reclaims the redemptive idealism that pastoral makes possible; in this poem, pastoral becomes a point of leverage against a world that views mindlessness as "pleasures" (89). On this view, for Hands, pastoral is not a fixed space or a language of pure value; it is, rather, a poetic vehicle for disrupting the corrupt values that govern the modern urban world and illustrating an alternative set of human possibilities.

"Lob's Courtship" and "Rural Maid" are not poems that comment only on the nature of pastoral, either as a limited worldview or as a preserve of visionary idealism. As they rework the ways of the pastoral imagination, they also engage with the agrarian and urban landscapes of eighteenth-century British society, creating a tension between idealism—both good and bad idealism—and realism. The fact is that pastoral idealism means nothing in the world that Lob and Nell inhabit, because they lack the leisure that is required for such idealism; their days are defined by long hours of labor that generate both the naiveté of Lob and the hard realism of Nell. At the same time, as "Rural Maid" shows, idealism is necessary as a sustaining force in life. For Hands, the important question is not whether one accepts or rejects pastoral vision outright; rather, what matters is whether one understands that idealism is always mediated by, and shaped within the circumstances of, lived experience. Pastoral is a sensibility, a vocabulary that makes it possible to talk about the world; it is not a place in which the world is located or a pure space that exists independently of the world.

Subsequent poems in the volume proceed along similar lines, speaking across cultural spaces, literary modes, and even sexual orientations, effectively creating a fluid motion of imaginative life wherein history, society, and politics are engaged, including the world of George III.[14] And the volume effects its purpose by putting individual poems into conversation with one another. For example, while she writes an ostensibly celebratory royalist poem to describe George III—"Written on Their Majesties Coming to Kew"—she precedes it and follows it with poems that make it into an ironic condemnation of royalty. She concludes "On Contemplative Ease," the poem preceding it, with the comment that

> while great ones make a splendid show,
> In equipage or dress,
> I'm happy here, nor wish below
> For greater happiness. (100)

Then, in "Contentment," which follows it, she begins her poetic commentary by stating that

> I envy not the great their joys,
> That from their riches spring.
> Let those who have in courts been bred,
> There still in splendor shine.
> . . .
> The monarch is not more secure,
> Than I beneath this shade. (103)

Sandwiched between these two poems, "Written on Their Majesties Coming to Kew" cannot plausibly be viewed as a poem celebrating monarchy. It is rather a poem in which the *idea* of monarchy, with its trappings of wealth and power, is put in tension with a poetic vision of life unconcerned with wealth and power. Under the pressure of a monarchist ideology, the pastoral imagination arises once again in "Contentment" ("Whilst I beneath this silent shade, / Contented sit and sing" [103]), though in modified form, as a vehicle for creating a space of freedom and possibility that lies not only beyond the reach of riches and courts but also beyond the naiveté of simpleminded pastoral desire. As Hands remarks at the end of "Contentment":

> These friendly trees on either side,
> From heat a shelter stand;
> The white rose on the brier hangs,
> And seems t' invite my hand.
> Ah! Rose, no longer to my eyes
> They pow'rful charms display,
> For I've a sweeter flow'r than you,
> And one that looks more gay. (103)

Taken together, these and the other poems of the volume show that Hands is not bound to the sorts of visionary understanding that are typically associated with the Bible and Milton. She destabilizes the visionary principles of the titular poem in the volume by drawing on various modes of poetic representation not because she wants to reject visionary poetry but because she wants to enliven it and make it adaptable to changing human experience. Pastoral and satire, no less than epic, are appropriate vehicles for visionary poetry, just as the realities of class and gender difference in Britain are an appropriate subject matter. To view *Amnon* as a visionary poem because of its biblical and Miltonic associations but dismiss the visionary implications of the "Supposition" poems and the pastorals because they rely on a different sort of poetic voice and on different literary sources would be a mistake. Such a critical conclusion about these poems would both miss the aims of the larger volume and distort the visionary character of *Amnon*, whose visionary impulse is shaped—and tested—by its relation to the other poems in the volume.

Hands's volume exhibits a remarkable elasticity in its approach to genres, meter and rhyme, subject matter, and literary history. In the final poem of the volume, "Critical Fragments on Some of the English Poets," Hands engages some of her major poetic forbears directly, demonstrating her knowledge of literary history and her command of the poetic styles used by the major writers of British poetry. When speaking of Milton, she writes in blank verse; when speaking about Pope, she writes in heroic couplets; when speaking of Samuel Butler, she demonstrates her facility with the hudibrastic rhyme: "From censure he's receiv'd acquittal, / And grammar, metre, rhyme submit all" (127). This range of interest and fluidity of style help to capture the nature of Hands's visionary poetics, which rejects all notions of doctrinaire understanding, moving in a direction, instead, that disrupts unreflective experiential and literary expectations. For Hands, vision requires absolute freedom of imagination and thought, as well as the courage to stand in the midst of conflict and against the oppressive power of dominant social and ideological structures so as to challenge settled opinion and release the untapped potential of the mind and possibilities of life. She refuses to be bound by heroic verse for her purposes; she uses satire, pastoral, the poetical epistle, and lyrical expression as she needs them, demonstrating that the visionary imagination is both restless and alive, pushing ever outward toward ways of seeing that might be capable of changing human consciousness.

Anne Bannerman is a very different sort of poet from Hands, but nevertheless equally invested in visionary expression. Indeed, *Tales of Superstition and Chivalry* (1802) is a radical volume that pushes further than perhaps any other volume of the period—further even than Blake's poetry—to disclose the far-reaching implications of visionary poetics.[15] Unlike Hands, Bannerman pays little attention to the pastoral imagination (except in the epigraph to the volume) and even less to biblical and Miltonic strategies of visionary expression, though in her notes to the volume she does claim the influence of Edmund Spenser. While she indicates her awareness of these poetic traditions and draws on certain familiar literary subjects such as King Arthur, she relies largely on a distinct set of literary and literary-historical interests to construct her visionary poetics, most especially gothic tales and obscure source materials that lie largely outside the line of a discernible literary tradition. That is, her vision begins from, and is situated within, the remote borders of literary and historical knowledge, using the marginalized spaces of culture as a position from which to examine and contest the governing structures of human consciousness.

Built on a series of gothic ballads that anticipate Joanna Baillie's use of gothic in *Metrical Legends* (1821), *Tales* stakes out its visionary position in the very beginning with several prefatory materials that govern everything that comes afterward. The first item in the volume is an engraving entitled *The Prophecy of Merlin*, which faces a title page that includes an epigraph (in Italian) from Giovanni Battista Guarini's *Il pastor fido* (*The Faithful Shepherd* [1590]).[16] These two prefatory materials are then followed by a brief poem that appears under the heading of "prologue." These materials form the foundation of the volume and point its direction, complicating conventional ideas of orderliness, challenging common notions of perceptual truth, and challenging the reader to reexamine assumptions that are brought to bear on an understanding of the past.

The engraving not only shocks the reader by presenting a picture of an entirely naked woman (with only a long narrow sash-like fabric draped across her back and arms and wound between the upper portion of her thighs) standing before a fully clothed man, sitting and dressed in black, gesturing toward her, as if reaching to touch her breast (though in all likelihood he is beseeching the woman to give him the chalice she is holding); its title, *The Prophecy of Merlin*, informs the reader that the picture belongs alongside the final poem in the volume. The

The Prophecy of Merlin, in Anne Bannerman's *Tales of Superstition and Chivalry*

placement of the engraving at the beginning of the volume creates a circular structure, because the linking of the picture and the final poem suggests that the volume starts where it ends. This circularity is unsettling, disrupting any expectation that a reader might have of linear progression.

Moreover, the composition of the engraving creates various sorts of tension that are, to varying degrees, unsettling. The strikingly white body of the naked woman set against the male figure dressed in black who is reaching toward her heightens the sexual suggestiveness of the picture; the portrayal of the standing and sitting figures against a backdrop that opens out onto the barren sea evokes conflicted feelings of deep loneliness, desire, and purposelessness; the (apparently) pleading gesture of the male figure creates a sense of desperation, as the female figure (with her left hand) seems to push him away or beseech him to calm down; the female figure seems both sympathetic and teasing, as she looks pityingly down on the male figure from her standing position, exposing her nakedness, while at the same time holding back the chalice for which he seems to be asking. The tensions evident in the engraving become even more pronounced when the picture is placed alongside the final poem, wherein the reader learns that the female figure is in fact the Queen of Beauty addressing the mortally wounded King Arthur, and that the chalice she is holding is in fact "a cup of sparkling pearl" (136) that she will offer to Arthur and from which he will drink. But even the beauty of the woman and the ostensible offering of sustenance do not relieve the tension present in the engraving, because, as Arthur reaches to take the cup, "he thought on what the hand of blood / Had mingled in the cave" (137), as the final poem puts it. The engraving, that is, introduces a series of tensions— nude/clothed; standing/sitting; black/white; closed space/open space—that are threaded through the volume and that are not easily resolved or explained, even in the final poem.

The epigraph to the volume is equally complicated. It is given in Italian, despite the fact that there was at least one eighteenth-century translation of Guarini's drama to which Bannerman presumably would have had access. *The Faithful Shepherd* is set in Arcadia, which has been cursed by the goddess Diana and which can be saved by only one of several sets of action; the one that is settled on in the play is the marriage of Silvio to Amarilli. By constructing his plot in this manner, Guarini makes clear his view that the pastoral landscape is never a space of pure safety and peace; it is always under threat. And the fact of that threat, for Guarini, calls into play far-reaching philosophical and spiritual considerations that must be negotiated in any effort to preserve the pastoral space. This point is made explicit in the subtitle of the play—*A Pastoral Tragi-*

comedy—which warns the reader against a naïve understanding of pastoral. For Guarini, the pastoral world—Arcadia—is not a symbol of natural plenitude, or human perfection, or the perfect harmony between humans and nature; instead, it is an example of the difficult relation between idealism and the forces of the world that threaten that idealism.

The various dramatic complications of *The Faithful Shepherd* follow from the effort of Arcadians to bring Silvio and Amarilli together in marriage. Across the course of the drama, various characters offer many statements about the troubles caused by love and in particular by women. The epigraph that Bannerman chooses for her volume is taken from a long passage spoken by Satyr, an old man who loves Corsica, and it is an excoriating criticism of women. The 1736 English version of the play translates the lines of Bannerman's epigraph thusly: "So talk or look, or think, or laugh or cry, / Seem or seem not, walk, stand, or sit, ye lye" (1.5.44).[17] The view of women expressed here may very well look forward to Bannerman's portrayal of gender in the course of her volume, particularly her interest in the way women are feared, abused, and idealized, but, read more broadly, the lines also offer a general statement about perception and knowledge that inform deep currents of thought running through the volume and that are central to her visionary concerns. That is, the lines state explicitly that everything we see or think we know is a lie. It follows from this claim, at least for Bannerman, that an adjustment of consciousness is needed to cleanse of the doors of perception, and, indeed, this is precisely the aim of her volume. And this aim, as the epigraph makes plain, entails following a path different from the one carved out by the simpleminded principles of the pastoral imagination.

The engraving and epigraph together also point to Bannerman's interest in vision, particularly visionary prophecy. The very title of the engraving, of course, informs the reader that Bannerman is well aware of the prophetic possibilities of poetry, even gothic poetry. And the epigraph, while ostensibly directing attention to Bannerman's familiarity with the pastoral tradition, also puts the idea of prophecy into play. At several points in Guarini's drama, prophecy is explicitly referenced. In the prologue to the play, for instance, Guarini combines his interest in prophecy with his recognition of the importance of pastoral:

> But whilst I prophecy [sic], and Fate prepares
> Circles of Gold and ever prosp'rous Years,
> Disdain not (Mighty Souls) this flow'ry Wreath,
> Gather'd on Pindus by those Maids that breathe
> Life in dead men. (10)

Later in the play, too, Montano remarks to Titiro that "now I see / Heav'n has suspended in thee all that Skill / In Prophecy, which it was wont t' instill" (5.6.216). The emphasis on the idea that what people see, by definition, is a lie, combined with the numerous references to prophecy by both Guarini and Bannerman, suggests Bannerman's interest in reshaping perception along a path of higher understanding.

The verse prologue to Bannerman's volume is similarly rich in its visionary suggestiveness. Beginning with a statement that rejects the nostalgic imagination—"Turn from the path; if search of gay delight / Lead thy vain footsteps back to ages past!"—the poem turns the reader's attention to "the dim regions of monastic night" that are filled with "terrors wild, and legends dear." In the "dark recesses" of these dim regions, Bannerman says, "dwells / The long-lost Spirit of forgotten times." According to these statements, the volume is rooted in history, though the past that the poem is invested in is unknown, or at least unfamiliar, rather than known. While on one level, perhaps, in the prologue Bannerman sets the scene for the gothicism of the volume with titillating images, at the same time she directly links the gothic and historical imaginations, calling attention especially to history that has been lost or marginalized. This voice from "forgotten times," she says, is important because, though now lost, it was once powerfully "prophetic," reaching "to distant climes, / And rul[ing] the nations from his witched cells." The purpose of her volume, she says, is to recall that prophetic voice, which she defines in terms of its ability to blend "with terrors wild, and legends drear, / The charmed minstrelsy of music sound," so that, ultimately, "th' unearthly habitants of faery ground" are "rous'd." For Bannerman, the worlds of "Fancy," history, mysticism, and fairyland were once all part of a single reality that, she suggests, might once more be reunited if we listen to "voice prophetic." Her prophetic vision of history is neither antiquarian nor rational in nature; it looks toward different principles of understanding altogether.

The prologue is astonishingly bold in its claims about the visionary imagination; it is also remarkably clear in its understanding of the difficult path that the visionary imagination is made to follow in the modern world. Warning the simpleminded reader that her volume is fully invested in the treacherous task of reclaiming the spirit of prophecy that is buried deep amid the dangerous regions of the past and positioning herself fully on the margins of mainstream thought in her day, Bannerman signals the direction of the volume: her serious aim is to reimagine the reach and character of the visionary imagination by turning away from the traditions (biblical and literary) that define the known line of prophecy from the Bible through Milton in her world, instead seeking the roots of vision deep in the unconscious and far away on the margins of British history. If Hands begins her heterodox visionary effort by passing through the traditions of biblical prophecy, Bannerman announces in the very beginning of her volume that she intends to proceed otherwise, and she warns that her readers will be discomfited should they choose to examine the reach and nature of her prophetic vision.

This is not to say, however, that she is unaware of literary tradition. In the ten poems that make up the heart of the volume she moves across a range of topics and imaginative landscapes, venturing into (in "The Prophetess of the Oracle of Seam") and away from (in "Basil") the visionary to varying degrees and exhibiting her awareness along the way of her literary forbears, especially Spenser. In the first and last poems in the volume, for example, Spenser is very much present in her imagination: the central character in "The Dark Ladie," Sir Guyon, is in the *Faerie Queene* the knight who destroys the Bower of Bliss; in the final poem, "The Prophecy of Merlin," Bannerman tells the story of King Arthur's death, which is also recounted in the *Faerie Queene*.[18] In the notes to the volume, too, Bannerman quotes directly from the *Faerie Queene*. But her references to Spenser, which do not constitute a direct poetic engagement with her literary forbear, seem for the most part to serve to call attention to her lesser-known sources or perhaps to indicate his marginal importance compared to these lesser-known sources, which include Michael Drayton's *Poly-Olbion* (1621); the notes to *Poly-Olbion*, written by John Selden; Gregory L. Way's translation of *Fabliaux; or, Tales* (1796, 1800), and Evan Evans's *Specimens of Welsh Poetry* (1764). This point becomes most clear, perhaps, when we consider that Spenser's aim is largely a celebration of the monarchical rule of Elizabeth I, while Bannerman's tales are built on fear that psychic and political authority are always under threat, a fear she uses to unlock her visionary imagination.

Bannerman's visionary poetic strategy, too, refuses to follow the path of literary convention. In one of the odder compositional choices she makes, for instance, she writes the whole of "The Fisherman of Lapland" in the first person and places the narrative entirely within quotation marks, even though these are unnecessary, given that no one else speaks; there is not even an omniscient narrator. The effect of this strategy is unsettling because it turns the poem into a free-floating expression that seems to desire but cannot discover a governing or stabilizing voice outside itself. Indeed, the story that Bannerman tells is, in its structural appearance, very much like the shadow that she describes in the narrative, which the fisherman finds himself unable to apprehend or comprehend: "Around it, and round, he had ventur'd to go, / But no form, that had life, threw the stamp on the snow" (95). The poem and the shadow are both like an echo without a source.

The narrative is an image that is missing that which it is an image of; it is a lie, much like the lie described in the epigraph to the volume. The sort of vision that Bannerman advances here is untethered from poetic convention and rational expectation alike, just as it is untethered from conventional understandings of time and space, and these facts push the reader to contemplate the terrifying possibilities that life—and death—lack any discernible guiding authority.

The most unsettling, and most liberating, tale in the volume is the final poem, "The Prophecy of Merlin," which tells the story of King Arthur's death at the battle of Camlann and his subsequent removal "by the Queen of the Yellow Isle" (132) to "the charmed Isle" (136). The immediate aftermath of Arthur's death is infused with supernatural elements that evoke the general gothic and superstitious tone of the volume. But these elements are not simply atmospheric add-ons meant to give the narrative excitement or to create anticipation in the reader. Bannerman also uses them to set in motion her most compelling visionary consideration of the relations between life and death. Recalling the tone of Coleridge's "Rime of the Ancient Mariner," "Prophecy" describes the ship on which Arthur is sailing as moving

> on the sleeping wave
> Like a bird upon the air;
> He knew it gained on the deep,
> But he felt no motion there! (133)

But, unlike "Rime," "Prophecy," while fraught with anxiety, does not succumb to nightmarish fear. As he sails further into the deep, and into a zone that "had no trace of time" (132), Arthur (the narrator says) "could have rested there for aye, / So sweet it seem'd to be!" (133). And after nervously drinking from the "cup of sparkling pearl" (136) proffered by the Queen of Beauty, Arthur is awakened to visionary understanding, which allows him to see beyond the dichotomous structures that govern everyday consciousness into the very heart of a unified reality, wherein the various parts of human experience are indistinguishable from one another.

The Queen of Beauty, for example, is now seen as also being "the hand of blood" (138); Arthur not only keeps a steady gaze on his immediate situation ("he call'd aloud! / And, wild, survey'd her as she stood" [138]), but he also hears a call from the past, in the form of Urien, the sixth-century King of Rheged. Most significantly, death and life meld into a single fluid reality: Arthur is told that he "must slumber in the cave" (139), even as at the same time he knows that "he would return" (139), much like Christ is destined to arise from death. But the paradoxes of Arthur's story are more complicated than those of the Christian one, as the narrator remarks that "King Arthur's body was not found, / Nor ever laid in holy grave" (139). Arthur is dead; he will arise from death; his body is lost; and his being becomes disassociated from holiness. The resolution to this disturbing and confusing set of descriptions appears in the simple lines, repeated twice with only a slight alteration near the end of the poem, that "nought has reach'd his [Arthur's] burial-place, / But the murmurs of the wave" (139). The dichotomous relations between beauty and blood, hope and fear, death and life that seem to define and give meaning to human experience are ultimately, as the epigraph to the volume says, a lie. The only certainty, the only reality that can be trusted, is stillness—"the murmurs of the waves"—and the poem and volume guide the reader toward accepting this fact, because acceptance is the only effective means of relieving the superstitions and horrors that run through the volume and that disturb mental equilibrium. The volume draws on the principles of gothic horror that suggest that the gothic is only a slightly exaggerated representation of the turmoil afflicting everyday human experience to show a way past that horror.

The notes that Bannerman appends to *Tales* call attention to her visionary aims in the volume. Rather than present a full complement of notes on each poem, Bannerman provides brief notes for only four poems: "The Prophetess of the Oracle of Seam," "Basil," "The Murcian Cavalier," and "The Prophecy of Merlin." Her emphasis here is on the explicitly prophetic poems ("Seam" and "Merlin"), and her commentary on them elucidates her understanding of marginalized spaces and the sorts of visionary power that can be associated with these spaces. In describing the inhabitants of Seam, for instance, she quotes from Drayton's *Poly-Olbion*, which states that "those nuns [of Seam] of yore / Gave answers from their caves, and took what shapes they please" (141); their power, that is, depended upon their isolation from the world. Bannerman also cites from John Selden's notes to Drayton's poem, which identify the inhabitants of Seam ("nine virgins" [141]) as "priests of a famous oracle," who were dedicated to a "religion" that not only enabled them to change shape at will but also gave them "skill in predictions" (141). What is important about these notes appended to "Seam" is not simply Bannerman's use of Drayton as a means of calling explicit attention to the sort of prophetic history and practice that can be found in *Tales*; more striking is her use of the notes as a way to exhibit her visionary strategy. That is, Bannerman's "Seam" is clarified by a note that relies on Drayton; Drayton's own poem is then given added substance by a note from John Seldon. Bannerman's effort to destabilize a reader's expectation that knowledge be firm and graspable is seen further in the note from Selden, which complicates the geography of the poem and volume by calling attention to the fact that Seam is "an isle by the coast of the French Bretagne" (141) and that its inhabitants have associations with "the witches of Lapland and Finland" (141), the latter reference gesturing toward "The Fisherman of Lapland," a later poem in the volume. Bannerman's geographical imagination is expansive, reaching across nationalistic boundaries and pushing back in time in ways that trouble conventional British expectation.

The notes appended to "The Prophecy of Merlin" are of particular interest because Bannerman's own editorial commentary in these notes exhibits her willingness to contest past authoritative accounts of King Arthur. In the very last lines of the notes, Bannerman remarks that

> it will not perhaps be very consonant to popular feeling, that legendary tradition has been violated in the fate and disposal of this great, national hero [King Arthur]. But it is all fairy-ground, and a poetical community of right to its appropriation has never been disputed. (144)

If the visionary or prophetic character, for Bannerman, resides on the outer margins of culture and speaks across cultures without regard to national identity (as other poems in the volume suggest), that character earns the right of special creative flexibility by virtue of its marginalized status. Not only does Bannerman confess that she has rewritten the story of Arthur to suit her own imaginative purpose; more tellingly, she describes the world of Arthur as "all fairy-ground" to be dealt with as the poet sees fit, thereby (for instance) effectively disrupting Spenser's positing of an actual historical British nation behind his allegorical Faeryland. Denying all claims of fixed and firm constraints on the story of Britain's "great, national hero," she in effect does with "Prophecy" what she had done with "Fisherman": she contests the underlying authority of the very story she is telling by denying that events and persons can be held to a single interpretation or grounded with a single understanding. Once again, she challenges the structuring mechanisms of rational understanding (and the traditional poetic imagination), unleashing vision in such a way that it can guide the reader beyond the empirical grounds of knowledge and beyond the binary structures that govern systems of value—beyond the lies, that is, that have been used to organize and define human experience.

Tales makes use of the literary conventions of poetic narrative, gothic horror, and textual additions (in the form of notes), all of which were prominently used by poets in Bannerman's day, and it draws on a variety of familiar poetic subjects (murder, death, fear, love) in ways that demonstrate Bannerman's command of literary expression. At the same time, however, she challenges the authority of these common literary strategies as vehicles of understanding, and she even challenges the purpose of traditional poetic expression. While Spenser, King Arthur, and Albion figure prominently in her verse, her visionary purpose is not to celebrate or tweak or correct them but to reimagine them from the remote margins of cultural experience in such a way as to break down the modes of understanding with which they have come to be identified. For Bannerman, the visionary imagination does not simply engage with the forms and ideas that preceded it for the purpose of recovering and changing them but also seeks to create its own reality that surpasses the cultural artifacts that have cut vision off from the recognition of higher truths—from the recognition that, for example, it is an illusion (or a "lie," to use the word from the epigraph to the volume) to believe that King Arthur will return, to believe that the details of past history and literature have a special and inexorable claim on the modern imagination, to believe that human experience is necessarily bound by what she calls superstitious principles or by acts of chivalry that represent a fixed code of human conduct. For her, all that we know and believe is a lie, and breaking out of the structures of value and thought that form the cultural core of that lie is the purpose of her visionary imagination.

While Hands's *Amnon* and Bannerman's *Tales* proceed differently in constructing their visionary ideals, they share a common desire to unleash the poetic imagination from the great visionary authorities that preceded them. And in this desire both poets demonstrate considerable critical self-reflexivity and boldness of spirit. Both poets make clear that they understand their marginalized status, and yet they do not step away from their visionary investments. Indeed, Hands satirically exposes the limited mindset of the world about which she is writing, disclosing that her readers, in all likelihood, are not prepared to understand the meaning of her volume, despite the fact (as she shows in "Critical Fragments") that she is every bit as capable a poet as her literary forbears. Bannerman, too, exhibits her awareness of the likely obstacles that she will face in putting forward her prophetic vision and displays her stubbornness in pursuing her visionary purpose nevertheless, going so far as to tell her readers that their views of life are a lie and that her own poetic endeavor will be to examine the deep recesses of experience (what Coleridge in "Kubla Khan" called "that deep romantic chasm") that expose that lie and that hold out the possibility of a different sort of understanding of the world. And both writers carry out their visionary aims across the entire range of their poetic volumes, Hands relying on multiple poetic styles and Bannerman relying entirely on the poetic tale while complicating it with a series of notes that reference a variety of sources. Moreover, their visions are neither one-dimensionally hopeful nor pessimistic, nor are they prescriptive;

rather they are disruptive in such a way as to compel self-reflection and a reexamination of the structural principles of history and the human psyche.

Anna Letitia Barbauld

Visionary poetry written by women in the late eighteenth and early nineteenth centuries reflects an awareness of the traditions and conventions of visionary writing through the course of British literary history, and yet this poetry possesses a voice, and deploys strategies of writing, that are distinctly its own, at least partly because its authors were women who did not enjoy the educational opportunities available to their male counterparts and did not have access (to the same degree as most men) to the sphere of public discourse of the day.[19] Reading this poetry (as far as possible) on its own terms and excavating its literary and cultural archaeological spaces demonstrates that it is not unique, untouched by masculine history and culture or positioned steadfastly against specifically masculine forms of authority; rather it shows how the cultural and historical realities bearing on the experiences of women writers give them singular access to dimensions of writing and experience that have been sealed over by traditions that are both patriarchal and (relatedly) defined largely by limited notions of what constitutes literary knowledge and poetic accomplishment. The poetry of Hands and Bannerman demonstrates this point very well.

Anna Letitia Barbauld, the author at the center of the present study, exhibits more compellingly than any poet of the eighteenth-century the sort of visionary sensibility that I am describing. She (like Hands) not only deploys a variety of poetic strategies, making use of prophecy, pastoral, lyric, satire, poetic epistle, hymns, and songs in carrying out her visionary poetic aims but also develops her visionary interests across the entirety of her volume, using her various poetic strategies to construct a unified and transformative poetic vision while at the same time self-consciously reflecting critically on the nature of visionary poetics. Perhaps the most impressive feature of her poetic endeavor in *Poems* is her fearless belief that visionary poetry is necessarily founded on and leads inexorably toward principles of love, sympathy, and virtue; for her, vision must not be constructed on, or organized around, a spirit of conflict or opposition but on a spirit of commonality, that is, a spirit of shared burdens and hopes. Across the course of her volume, she examines this spirit within the context of multiple literary traditions, from classical Latin poetry to the poetry of eighteenth-century Britain and tests it within the crucible of literary tradition and historical experience. The result is a volume of poetry that is distinct from the Miltonic line of vision but that nevertheless belongs alongside the work of Milton and those visionary poets whom Wittreich and others have helped to identify.

As a visionary poet, Barbauld keeps eternity in view in *Poems*. But, for her, eternity is not a metaphysically distinct sphere to which individuals who have been properly transformed by spiritual awakening may have access. Rather, it is a set of (for her) perdurable principles that are to be used to guide human thought and conduct. These principles are characterized by justice, truth, virtue, and love, and they undergird every dimension of experience, from friendship to religion to hope to politics to death. They are principles that encourage free thought (as in "A Summer Evening's Meditation") as well as spiritual understanding (as in the "Hymns") and worldly engagement (as in "Corsica"). The visionary proclamation of Barbauld's *Poems*, that is, interweaves life and death, body and soul, thought and feeling, personal life and public life. For Barbauld, there is but one life, and it is large, complex, and potentially beautiful; it is, indeed, identical with eternity itself.

As a result of the tireless labors by feminist scholars over the past thirty years or so to recover eighteenth-century works by women writers, Barbauld's poetry has begun to receive considerable critical attention. Much of the critical commentary on her poems has focused on her portrayals of gender, at least partly no doubt because of the critical and scholarly effort to demonstrate the self-consciousness of women poets of the period as they wrote within the cultural context of a dominant patriarchal authority.[20] In examining Barbauld's various engagements with gender, feminist criticism has done much to reveal the thematic gravity, subtlety of thought, stylistic range, and cultural awareness of her poetic output. But, almost from the beginnings of the Barbauld reassessment, other helpful lines of critical inquiry have been pursued as well. For example, William Keach, John Guillory, and Stephen Behrendt, among others, have sought to place Barbauld's thought and writing within the social, economic, and political contexts of her age, persuasively demonstrating the seriousness of her intellectual interest and the reach of her historical imagination.[21] These various threads of Barbauld criticism reflect the richness of her mind and the range and substance of her poetic interest.

In recent years, more sustained critical and scholarly efforts have confirmed Barbauld's importance. Daniel E. White's excellent *Early Romanticism and Religious Dissent* includes a detailed consideration of Barbauld's place among the British Dissenting community in the late eighteenth century. Considering, among other things, Barbauld's literary collaborations with her brother and with fellow Dissenters at Warrington Academy, White argues convincingly that Barbauld should be viewed and studied within the context of a Dissenting public sphere. His book is a carefully researched and closely argued account of Barbauld's writing and public life, and it includes critical examination of several of her poems within the context of her Dissenting principles. Beyond White, William McCarthy has performed a service of spectacular importance for Barbauld studies. His magisterial biography, *Anna Letitia Barbauld: Voice of the Enlightenment*, not only recounts the particulars of the poet's life; it is also an astonishingly detailed intellectual and critical history of Barbauld's literary output. Providing a carefully documented record of Barbauld's community of friends and acquaintances (including mentors), the compositional history of her writings, and the cultural context within which she lived and wrote, McCarthy's book stands as the most important work to date on the poet.

The recent history of Barbauld criticism, culminating with McCarthy's monumental study, demands a more systematic and comprehensive consideration of her poetry than has yet appeared. While many feminist studies of individual poems show that Barbauld was a careful and compelling poet, and while Barbauld's political self-consciousness has been well established, the works of White and McCarthy demonstrate more fully than before the degree to which she was also an intellectually gifted—and careful—thinker and writer, whose accomplishments command sustained critical attention. In particular, the range of her poetic interest and the singularity of purpose that unifies that range of interest need to be examined in detail if a fuller understanding of her poetry and her place within the context of eighteenth-century poetics are to be achieved. Such a critical effort will help to dislodge her writings from the sort of identity politics that undergirds earlier studies of eighteenth-century women writers and begin to establish Barbauld as a major visionary poet dedicated to changing human consciousness for the purpose of changing the world.

In light of the currents of critical interest in Barbauld, exemplified especially by White, Backscheider's comment describing her own argument about eighteenth-century women poets is apt, as it puts an even sharper point on the claims about gender that she, Wolfson, and Behrendt make in their studies. Gender, Backscheider says, is an important category of critical analysis, "but there are other major categories and considerations needed to balance it" (17). This claim is particularly true of Barbauld's *Poems*, a volume that appeared initially in 1773, went through several editions in the years immediately following, then appeared again in revised form in 1792, with the addition of several new pieces. Barbauld stayed with this volume for almost twenty years, reworking pieces of it, adding to it, rearranging some of its textual features; it clearly held special significance for her, and she also clearly viewed it as more than a collection of discrete poems, as the various entries appear in clusters and often are tied together by overlapping lines or references. Read individually, certain poems in the volume show that Barbauld is aware of and interested in gender, politics, and friendship, but these are not her only concerns and (to judge from the additions to the 1792 edition) perhaps not the most important ones; certainly her poetic interest does not reduce to any single issue. Indeed, as various critics have shown, other poems in the volume reflect an interest in science and speculative philosophy. A study of what the poems mean collectively—a consideration of their overarching poetic vision—has not yet been attempted, perhaps because, until now, the critical and scholarly groundwork had not yet been adequately prepared. Guided by the specific contributions of White and McCarthy, and by the more general contributions of Wolfson, Behrendt, and Backscheider, it now becomes possible to consider the extent to which, in *Poems*, Barbauld thought systematically about poetry and about the relations between poems, about the coherence of her poetic endeavor, and about the nature and trajectory of her poetic vision.

In the pages that follow, I want to examine *Poems* in a sustained and comprehensive fashion, tracking in detail Barbauld's poetic strategies, literary sources and contexts, and thematic interests in an effort to define the character and map the trajectory of her poetic vision. This effort means examining each element of the volume as closely as possible—including the many epigraphs, the textual allusions, and the arrangement of the poems—in relation to the overarching organization of the volume and in relation to the many sources and literary contexts that shape Barbauld's poetic vision. It also means examining the poems in order of their appearance to better account for their place among, and their relation to, other poems in the volume. By proceeding in this manner, it becomes possible to make a credible determination about the cohesiveness of Barbauld's poetic thought and the degree to which she aspires to construct a unified visionary statement.

With respect to the epigraphs, for instance, it is necessary not only to consider the relation of each epigraph to the poem that it introduces but also look to the larger work from which the epigraph itself is taken in order to determine whether Barbauld is working poetically with that larger text and not just with the epigraphic line or lines. Take, for example, the epigraph from "Corsica," the first poem in the volume: it matters that Barbauld drops from James Thomson's lines that poet's reference to William Wallace, the great Scottish nationalist leader, because "Corsica" is also concerned with questions of nationalism and nationalist struggle under the leadership of Pasquale Paoli. Why would she choose for her epigraph a passage from Thomson's *The Seasons* that includes explicit reference to a great nationalist leader and then eliminate that reference, while keeping the lines surrounding it? And why would she give no indication that she has done so? Does the elision of Wallace's name matter to the way one might choose to read "Corsica"? Does the abridgment of the passage from the *Seasons* suggest that Barbauld will work in a particular and knowing way with epigraphs throughout the volume?

Beyond the epigraphs, it is also necessary to consider whether, and how, Barbauld arranges the poems in the volume, particularly the way that she clusters poems together (for instance, hymns, songs, poems about women). Do these clusters speak to one another? Are they building blocks used to support a unified poetic vision? If so, how do these building blocks fit together? Do the cross references between poems and clusters of poems constitute devices meant to interweave the poems into one another? If so, to what purpose? These clusters cross a range of subjects, from religion to hedonistic desire to gender, and they do so in evocative ways that suggest that Barbauld is following a purposeful orderly principle; examining that orderliness may unlock important dimensions of Barbauld's poetic—and especially her visionary—purpose.

Finally, I want to examine the various poetic modes on which Barbauld relies in constructing her vision—epic, pastoral, songs, hymns, and so on—in an effort to map the formal dynamics of her visionary understanding. Such an effort not only will call attention to Barbauld's remarkable poetic range; it will also capture her understanding of the vital relations between the formal dynamics of poetry and visionary expression. Through the course of the volume, Barbauld's uses of various poetic forms hold a particular visionary interest. In *Poems*, pastoral, for instance, is often (though not always) used to describe the desire, and even need, for a place of retreat from the entanglements of the world, even as it exhibits the insufficiency of pure idealism as a grounding principle in life. Indeed, pastoral idealism, however attractive, is never for Barbauld a suitable final answer to worldly conflict, as can be seen, for example, in the fact that even as "Verses Written in an Alcove" concludes with a reference to "this rustic temple" (36), the very next poem, "The Mouse's Petition," transforms that "rustic temple" into "the trap where" the mouse "had been confined all night by Dr. Priestley" (37). For Barbauld, while retreat is desirable and at times rejuvenating, the world is never very far removed from her imagination.

These particular sets of related and overlapping concerns elucidate the various thematic interests of individual poems in new and interesting ways as well as capture their larger poetic purpose within the volume. That larger purpose, I hope to show, is Barbauld's effort to construct a unified and coherent visionary statement that is both humane and doggedly stubborn in its efforts to explain human experience as it is and to transform human consciousness in such a way that will encourage the remaking of the world. This visionary purpose cannot be found in a single poem but must be discovered, in its rich and nuanced fullness, across the span of the entire volume.

CHAPTER ONE

Barbauld's Poems *in Context*

When the radical bookseller Joseph Johnson published the first edition of Anna Letitia Barbauld's *Poems* in 1773, at which time Barbauld was thirty years old and writing under her maiden name of Aikin, as she was not yet married, England was still a relatively peaceful and secure nation. The American and French revolutions had not yet commenced, the industrial revolution was in its infancy, and the nation was militarily strong, having defeated France in the Seven Years' War.[1] Civil liberties, too, were largely tolerated, if not celebrated. For example, according to Ana M. Acosta, Dissenters (to which tradition Barbauld and her family belonged), while still the object of political discrimination as a result of the Corporation Act and the Test Acts (1661, 1672, 1678), nevertheless enjoyed certain freedoms of worship and assembly, thanks in part to the Act of Toleration of 1689, passed after the advent of William and Mary to the British throne; many English Dissenters, too, became wealthy merchants in the new age of industry and finance (3–5).[2] If England was not exactly the "green and pleasant land" that Blake later dreamed of recreating, it was nevertheless politically and socially stable and economically vibrant. As Barbauld would put it some years later in *Sins of Government, Sins of the Nation* (1793), "The course of events in this country has now, for a number of generations, for a long reach, as it were, or the stream of time, run smooth, and our political duties have been proportionally easy" (411).

In 1792, at age forty-nine, Barbauld issued "A NEW EDITION, CORRECTED" (see title page) of *Poems*. By this time, the situation in Britain had changed considerably. The Dissenting Warrington Academy (where her father had served as a tutor) had been closed in 1786 owing to financial difficulties; the American colonies had fought a successful war of independence against Britain; the French Revolution was in full flourish, not yet having succumbed to the tribulations of the Reign of Terror; England and France were poised to begin a war that would last twenty-two years; and a full-blown conservative backlash against progressive thought had begun in England in which the government and its supporters, fearful that the revolutionary spirit emanating from France might spark uprisings in Britain, set about crushing dissent. The most famous example of reaction

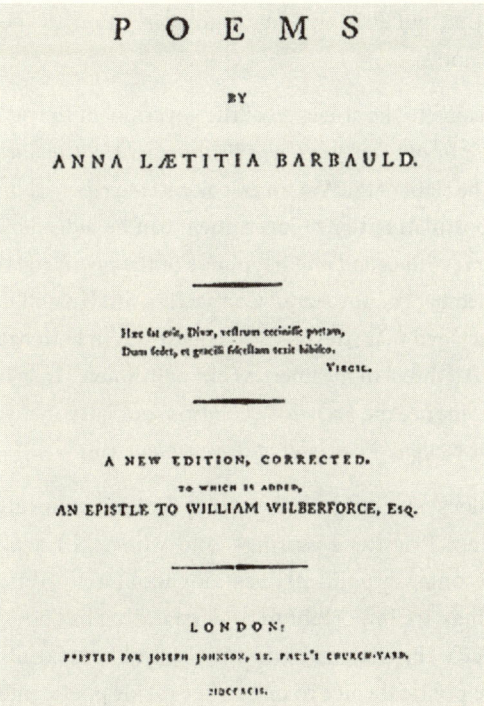

Anna Laetitia Barbauld, *Poems* (London: Joseph Johnson, 1792)

and suppression during the period immediately surrounding the publication of the new edition of *Poems* was the "Church and King" riots in 1791 during which, as Acosta observes, Joseph Priestley's "house, library, manuscripts, and laboratory equipment" in Birmingham were burned because Priestley vocally supported the principles guiding the French Revolution (16).³ In the short span of nineteen years, Britain had been transformed from a nation of relative peace, prosperity, and tolerance into a crucible for the struggle between liberty and tyranny, and the two editions of Barbauld's *Poems* seem to stand in talismanic relation to these very different historical moments, marking the trajectory and commenting on the meaning of Britain's headlong rush from social calm into political turbulence.⁴

If the 1773 and 1792 editions of *Poems* may be seen as having special significance in relation to these different historical moments, some of the political details and energies providing intellectual support to that significance are given clarifying urgency in the writings of Barbauld's friend and mentor Joseph Priestley, who wrote two important works within a few short years of Barbauld's two editions, works that put Priestley in troubled relation to the British government. As Acosta notes,

> Priestley first came to the attention of the government in 1769 when he published *Present State of Liberty in Great Britain and Her Colonies*. In this work, he supported the right of the American colonists to rebel against a tyrannical government, postulating that a government can be judged by the degree to which it preserves "the good and happiness of the members, that is, the majority of the members of any state." Connecting foreign and national policy, he further concluded that "the political conditions in both halves of the empire constituted a threat to the liberties of Englishmen." In 1791, he published a pamphlet defending the French Revolution and later that year *A Political Dialogue on the General Principles of Government*. (16)

While Barbauld does not engage in the sort of detailed political discussion about Britain that defines Priestley's writings, and while, as I argue, she disagrees with Priestley on some key political questions about how to effect social change, her friend's writings are important to understanding her poetic vision because they help to specify the personal and intellectual context of her writing and because they give political voice to one of her major poetic interests: the liberty of individual conscience, which, according to her, must not be infringed by any social or political structure of authority.[5]

A quick glance at *The Present State of Liberty in Great Britain and Her Colonies*, published four years prior to the first edition of *Poems*, reveals a direct relation between the works of Priestley and Barbauld. Like *Poems*, *Present State of Liberty* begins with an epigraph taken from Virgil. But while Barbauld takes hers from the *Eclogues*, Priestley lifts his from the epic *Aeneid*. If Priestley and Barbauld are connected literarily in their choices of a literary guidepost, at the same time their choices point to significant differences between them. Indeed, if Priestley's line from Virgil's great epic suggests his confidence and certainty in writing political commentary, Barbauld's choice of lines from Virgil's earlier pastoral poetry suggests her more measured and temperate sensibility. Even the content of the epigraphs suggests the different temperaments of the writers. The line from the *Aeneid* (in translation) reads "Whither now, whither are ye bound, ah! My wretched countrywomen? 'Tis not the foe, not the hostile Argive campe ye burn, but youre hopes" (*Present State of Liberty* 129), while the lines from *Eclogues* translate as follows: "These verses will suffice for your poet to have sung, / Goddess Pierians, while he sits and weaves a basket / Of slim hibiscus" (29). The epigraphs are linked by the fact that both address female characters. But Priestley's epigraph is defiant in tone, while Barbauld's is marked by patience and acceptance. Insofar as Barbauld might be using the epigraph to *Poems* to engage her friend and mentor on questions of large importance, she seems to be calling him back from his fiery anger to a more measured intellectual and political position.

Why Barbauld might wish to urge restraint on Priestley can be seen in the tone of his prose, which is marked by righteous and feverish indignation directed against the British government. In the preface to the essay, for instance, when he describes the oppressive measures Britain has taken against North America, measures that, he fears, will lead to a revolt among the colonies, Priestley remarks:

> Pity it is, that the iron hand of oppression should be extended to those people [in the colonies], whom nothing but a love of freedom induced to leave their native clime, in the arbitrary reigns of our former princes! How preposterous is it, that those who glory in a free constitution for themselves, should wish for a power over *their fellow-subjects*, which would make them the most abject slaves, of which there is any account in history; that a commercial nation should take measures to cut off the greatest source of their own wealth; and that a nation which, on many accounts, stands in need of *peace*, should, in asserting her unjust claims, provoke a contest, which, if the Americans be the genuine offspring of Britons, cannot but be attended with the most pernicious consequences to both! (130)

As this comment shows, the preface is written in a heated spirit of alarm that freedom is being threatened. Indeed, for Priestley, the "circumstances [are] so discouraging, all the consolation we can have, must be derived from the consideration of the *unsearchable ways of Divine Providence*" (131). In an age when Dissenters faced political discrimination simply for their religious faith, Priestley exposed himself even more fully to persecution by publicly voicing politically radical (some might say seditious) ideas.[6]

While the three sections of the essay proper are not quite so heated in tone, they are no less pointed in their criticism of the British government for violating the natural and civil rights of its citizens, including the citizens in the American colonies, or in their claim that the people of a nation have the right to form their own government as they see fit. For example, in the first section of the essay, entitled "Of Government in General," Priestley describes in unadulterated language the recourse that a society has when faced with oppressive governors, remarking that the first course of action should be to "make strong remonstrances to those governors who have betrayed their trust, expressing their sense of the injustice that has been done them" (134). But, he continues, "if through the infatuation of governors, intoxicated with power, these means be insufficient to obtain the end, nothing hinders that people, thus grossly abused and insulted by their magistrates" from stripping "them of their power, and confer[ring] it where they have reason to hope it will be less abused" (134–35). For Priestley (as for Milton before him), liberty is entirely bound to a democratic political vision rooted in the natural and inalienable rights of citizens, and the protection of liberty thus falls directly to these citizens, not to the government.[7] Such a view effectively places the control of government in the hands of the people, and it insists on the right of the people to change their government if it acts arbitrarily or fails to serve the public good.

Following his announcement of this general political principle, Priestley sharpens his argument, in the second and third sections by considering the particular offenses of the British government against its citizens. The second section, "Of the State of Liberty in England," for instance, methodically enumerates the ways that the British government has violated the trust of the people. In particular, he says, British rulers have abused their authority in six areas: "They have evaded the operation of the great writ of *Habeas Corpus*"; "They have, by a *general warrant*, in which no person was said to have been accused upon oath, or so much as named, arrested the person of an Englishman, and a member of the House of Commons"; "They restrict the liberty of the press"; "They have ... contrived to evade the great privilege of Englishmen, that of being tried by their peers"; "The great *Bill of Rights* has been invaded by a repeated refusal, to admit the first county in England, to judge of the fitness of the person who shall represent them in parliament"; "Recourse has unnecessarily been had to that great engine of arbitrary power, *a military force*, in a manner contrary to the genius and spirit of our constitution" (138–39). These strong accusations, as Priestley doubtless knew, carried within them a political sentiment that seemed to suggest the inevitability of a revolutionary uprising against the British government. And, indeed, it is only at the end of the third section of the essay, "Of the State of Liberty in England," which specifies the British offenses against its American colonies, that he pulls back from the volatile rhetoric that defines the larger part of his argument, acknowledging in a final statement that "it is never too late for any man, or body of men, to repent of, and rectify, what they are convinced they have done amiss" (144).[8]

By the time he had published *A Political Dialogue: On the General Principles of Government* in 1791, one year before the new and corrected edition of Barbauld's *Poems* was published, Priestley had become even more convinced that an elected and democratic form of government was most likely to serve the public good, his conviction having been confirmed by the recent events in France. In this essay, he again uses the dialogue form to speak forcefully against Britain's exploitation of labor for the purposes of supporting the wealth and well-being of the nation's rulers. Comparing the present situation in Britain to that in France prior to its revolution, he remarks that in Britain "an enormous proportion, it is thought two-thirds, of the fruit of its industry is at the absolute disposal of government, and this was very much the case with France" (85). Such a distribution of wealth, he says, is "a most unnatural state of society" (85) that must be rectified for the good of the country: "So long as one set of men provide the money, and another set have the disposal of it, there will be no economy" (86). And the only proper and ameliorative course of action is the implementation of representative government: "By the method of *representation* every difficulty arising from the extent of territory and the number of people, united under any government, is easily obviated" (87). Such a view leads Priestley to his most radical and (so far as his personal safety was concerned) most dangerous proposition: the abolition of hereditary government (89ff.), that is, the abolition of British monarchy. As if to confirm his understanding that he is treading in seditious waters, he presents the following dialogue:

> **A.** I think I can perceive your opinion of the great excellence of the English Constitution is somewhat changed since our last conversation, when you dropped no hint of there being any thing amiss in its general principles.
> **B.** I am not ashamed to acknowledge that this has been the case. There is no good reason why any man should be blind to the defects of his parent state, any more than to those of his natural parents. Nothing human, we will allow, is absolutely perfect; but what is imperfect may be borne with; which I think to be the case with the constitution of England. I have not, I own, that high veneration which I once had for it: since I have seen others which appear to me to be better. But I think that all the solid advantages of society may be had in ours, with such reforms as it is very capable of. And it will certainly be wisdom in our governors to listen to proposals of reform, rather than run the risk of such convulsions as may be the consequence of an obstinate refusal to reform any thing. (106)

Priestley says here that his is "not ashamed" to confess his loss of respect for the constitution of Britain, but, at the same time, he claims to believe that reforms could be made in the government that would preserve the constitution. It is therefore hard to know whether he is rejecting the British constitution outright, or warning the British government that if reforms are not forthcoming revolutionaries will arise to overthrow the government, or whether he is trying to cover his true revolutionary convictions with reformist vocabulary.⁹ In any case, his explicitly stated arguments for the redistribution of wealth and the creation of a representative form of government provided ample evidence to many royalists and loyalists that he was a traitor to the country who was calling for a revolution that would destroy the constitution.¹⁰

In her poetic engagement with the political ideas set out in Priestley's essays, and, by extension, with the political realities of her age, Barbauld adopts a less confrontational strategy than that used by her mentor, not only because she was a woman or because she feared that such outspokenness would bring into play the forces of governmental oppression. Despite her more moderate tone, Barbauld was no less interested than Priestley in remaking society, and no less insistent in her push for change. Insofar as Barbauld, in *Poems* (at least after "Corsica"), pulls back from the sort of defiant rhetoric found in Priestley's essays, she does so because she comes to believe that politics must be preceded (and accompanied) by an examination of the foundational principles on which political vision is constructed. Priestley's goal of representative government may be noble and worthy of pursuit, Barbauld's volume suggests, but unless that goal is understood within the context of equally noble principles—such as benevolence, love, and sympathy—that can be implemented in a manner consistent with their professed social meaning, then political intervention risks posing more harm than good to the nation. That is, Barbauld differs from Priestley in her interest in what comes before politics. How does one go about imagining a new social order? How does one assure that one's thinking about that social order is principled and dedicated to the public good rather than rooted, at last, in self-interest or the brute exercise of power? How does one engage in political action without losing sight of the important work of self-reflection or without succumbing to irretrievably destructive forms of social conflict? If Priestley, in his essays, seems prepared to push forward immediately for social and political change, Barbauld, in *Poems*, shows the need to establish care, caution, and self-reflection as the shaping realities of political struggle. As *Sins of Government, Sins of the Nation* makes clear, Barbauld's aim is not to put the brakes on radical social change but rather to make certain that radical change does not simply duplicate the dominant troubled structures of authority that are being contested. Her statement in her prose essay *An Address to the Opposers of the Repeal of the Test and Corporation Acts* (1790) clarifies her view on the relations between principles and politics:

> May you never lose sight of the great principle you have held forth, the natural equality of men. May you never forget that without public spirit there can be

no liberty; that without virtue there may be a confederacy, but cannot be a community. May you, and may we, consigning to oblivion every less generous competition, only contest who shall set the brightest example to the nations, and may its healing influence be diffused, till the reign of Peace shall spread
from shore to shore
Till wars shall cease, and Slavery be no more. (376)

On this view, the 1773 and 1792 editions of *Poems* were in some measure produced under the pressure of Priestley looking over Barbauld's shoulder, influencing both the character of her idealism and her sense of caution. As Priestley's thought modulated, so did Barbauld's *Poems*. That the 1792 edition of *Poems* was meant to be seen as an adjustment to the 1773 edition for the purpose of addressing the changed political and cultural climate in England, which Priestley describes clearly in his writings, is suggested by the few yet major changes that Barbauld makes to her volume, both to its front matter and to its body.[11] For example, when the volume first appeared in 1773, the title page included the title, the epigraph in Latin from Virgil, the place of publication, the publisher, and the date of publication. Barbauld's name did not appear on this page. On a following page, Barbauld included a dedication that read "TO THE RIGHT HONOURABLE LADY MARY WEST, THESE POEMS ARE RESPECTFULLY INSCRIBED BY HER LADYSHIP'S OBLIGED AND MOST OBEDIENT SERVANT, Anna Laetitia Aikin, WARRINGTON, DEC. 1ST. 1772." The dedication is largely innocuous, although the reference to Warrington doubtless would have signaled to readers that the volume was written by a Dissenter and voiced dissenting views on its subject matter: from the very beginning, at least implicitly, Barbauld therefore situated *Poems* as a political document. For the new and revised edition in 1792, however, she changed the front. She now placed her name immediately beneath the title and dropped the dedication to Lady Mary West (including the reference to Warrington), perhaps because, as William McCarthy observes, there was no real personal connection between the two women, aside from the fact that both were women of rank (108).[12] This new arrangement of the front matter serves three purposes. First, it places Barbauld's name front and center as the voice responsible for the poetic vision represented in the volume; second, by dropping the dedication, Barbauld whittles away material that is not directly relevant to her poetic vision, thereby bringing the reader more quickly and with a greater sense of purpose to the materials that follow; third, and most importantly, in dropping the reference to Warrington, Barbauld relieves the volume of any readerly expectation that it is a sharp-edged political or religious commentary.

But Barbauld's aims in the 1792 volume extend beyond matters of establishing authorial voice, achieving compositional efficiency, and muting political disquisition. Indeed, its interests are expansive, reflecting Barbauld's effort to enrich and clarify her visionary purpose in writing poetry. Her substantial addition of poems makes this point clear. Not only does she incorporate three new hymns (125–30) into the volume; she also concludes the new edition with a long poem entitled *Epistle to William Wilberforce, Esq., on the Rejection of the Bill for Abolishing the Slave Trade* (145–52). These twelve pages of new verse help to sharpen and even reshape the visionary interests that had informed the 1773 edition of *Poems*, with the hymns drawing their subject matter (largely, though not entirely) from the biblical past, and the *Epistle to William Wilberforce* drawing its subject matter from the political present, specifically 1791, the year that Wilberforce's parliamentary bill to abolish the slave trade was defeated (and the year that Priestley's house was destroyed by the "Church and King" mob). Within the historical and political context of the early 1790s, defined by revolutionary spirit and reactionary governmental actions and widespread preoccupation among artists and intellectuals with prophetic and millennial imaginings about the future and about human nature, these poems remind the reader that issues related to spirit and mind (as described in the hymns) are integrally related to the lived reality of material and political circumstance (as described in the Wilberforce poem). For the Barbauld of the 1792 *Poems*, that is, spirituality (or religion) and politics, while distinct facets of human experience, share an ontological connection: their interrelation constitutes part of the fundamental ground on which human reality is constructed. Barbauld's visionary poetics seeks to map out and define the nature of that reality, and although she uses political and religious subjects (among many others) for her purpose, she does not allow her poetics to be reduced to them. That is to say, she is neither a religious nor a political poet alone; she is rather a visionary poet.

In this visionary interest and emphasis, Barbauld draws a clear line of distinction between her poetic purpose and Priestley's political purpose. Her visionary impulse is to change the core and course of human experience; it is not intended simply to change political systems. While Priestley organizes his thought around economics, monarchy, and democratic representation in government, Barbauld organizes her imagination around human consciousness in relation to time and eternity. For her, politics matter, but politics alone ultimately cannot liberate the human situation from the hardships that afflict it. What is required is visionary reflection on the meanings and values that underlie experience and visionary liberation of consciousness. Unless the foundations and goals of human experience are fully understood and embraced, political struggle, she demonstrates in *Poems*, will be doomed to duplicate the forms of corruption that it seeks to eliminate. For Barbauld, that necessary understanding can be best pursued by means of visionary poetics.

The modifications made to the front matter and the poems suggest that Barbauld's *Poems*, in both its 1773 and 1792 versions, is not a collection of discrete poems but rather a coherent poetic statement that addresses a variety of subjects and literary and historical moments in an effort to discover those abiding principles that, for her, stand at the core of human reality and provide the basis for human experience and meaning; she also attempts to explain and organize these principles in such a way that they may be used as a foundation for building a just and free society. While in our contemporary critical climate politics, understood generally as networks of power that mediate, absorb, and define every element of human experience, may appear to be the central interpretative interest of the volume, especially in light of the "Corsica" and *Wilberforce* poems that serve as bookends, Barbauld in fact gives politics no particular authority, placing it, instead, alongside various other elements of human experience that are no less important to her vision; she is not a political thinker in the manner of (say) Priestley or Paine.

A brief glimpse at the table of contents suggests the range of her poetic interest. While she begins and ends the volume with poems about politics, she includes numerous other poems that are concerned with pastoral subject matter; she includes poems on painting, drawing, and songwriting; she includes several metaphysical poems about deity and possible realities that lie beyond a conception of deity; she includes several elegies; she includes hymns; she addresses poems to women, putting issues into play that are related to gender. Further, some poems describe aggressive engagement with the world, while others celebrate withdrawal; some are heroic, while others are mock heroic; some focus on the beauties of nature, while others complain about the unnatural doings of nature. Such a range of interests suggests a different poetic imperative altogether, beyond politics alone, and in fact may be taken as evidence of her desire to devise a poetic vision that would subsume the idea of politics into a larger category of understanding. Under the authority of Barbauld's imagination, these multiple interests and subjects are integrated and organized into a comprehensive and unified statement about human reality and possibility that neither begins nor ends with politics—or with spirit, for that matter. Indeed, when taken together, her poems both capture and challenge the dominant political, spiritual, and intellectual currents of thought in her day and, in effect, challenge the prevailing structures of consciousness that govern her world.[13]

Barbauld's vision is built on her belief that there are certain universal principles—which she describes variously as conscience, love, friendship, benevolence, sympathy—that must serve as the foundation for building a just and free society.¹⁴ Like Ann Yearsley in *The Rural Lyre* and Joanna Baillie in *Metrical Legends*, Barbauld, in *Poems*, explores, elaborates, and complicates these principles in an effort to extricate the mind as far as possible from the negative and oppositional modes of thought that define and entrap modern history and society and to replace them with sympathetic principles organized around what is possible for a benevolent and generous community of people to create. At the center of this effort is her commitment to the Dissenting principle of the immutable right of conscience and reasoned judgment. For her, this right is not simply an abstraction; it is fundamental to a just and secure lived experience. Such a position traps her, as it were, between an idealism that recognizes the freedom of the mind and realism that recognizes the political opposition to free thought. Thus, while her vision is utopian, its sights set clearly on a transformed human consciousness that is rooted in the liberty of conscience and the rights of reasoned judgment, it is not naïve. In constructing her vision, Barbauld squarely faces the realities of political struggle, slavery, industry, death, and hardship, for example, but she does not (except on rare occasions) engage them from a purely critical-intellectual or political perspective, because she recognizes (as she shows, for instance, in "Corsica") the traps that lie in that direction; rather, she urges the reader away from a resistant, or oppositional, preoccupation with corrupt and debilitating circumstances and asks that attention be given instead solely to those values and interests that might serve as a fitting foundation for a just and free world.

Sins of Government, Sins of the Nation, published (again by Joseph Johnson) anonymously in response to George III's call for a day of public fasting to prepare the British public for the war with France that was just commencing, reveals the underlying principles of Barbauld's poetic vision.¹⁵ This document spells out clearly the relations between Barbauld's pacifist and activist views, as well as her understanding of the relation between religion and politics. It also demonstrates the complexity of her thought. In the address, she concedes that "for the sake of peace and order, we ought, in general cases, to give our passive concurrence to measure[s] which we may think wrong" (407–8). Such passive submission to governmental order, however, does not require that one approve those measures, or to accept them unthinkingly. On the contrary, she says, "every good man owes it to his country and to his own character, to lift his voice against a ruinous war, an unequal tax, or an edict of persecution; and to oppose them, temperately, but firmly, by all the means in his power: and indeed this is the only way reformations can ever be brought about, or that government can enjoy the advantage of general opinion" (408–9). Barbauld's social vision is embedded in these two statements, and their relation to one another shows precisely the dilemma that she faces in her desire to construct a transformative vision: how does one give "passive concurrence" to the dominant structures of authority and at the same time "lift his voice against" those structures of authority when they are deemed to be unjust?

The answer to this question—which is a question about how one might embrace pacifist principles without sacrificing one's political responsibilities as a citizen—lies in the practice of ongoing self-reflection. And this practice, for Barbauld, is both religious and political in nature. As she puts it near the end of the address, when history reaches a certain stage of conflict and instability,

> It becomes every man . . . to examine his principles, whether they are of that firmness and texture as suits the occasion he may have for them. . . . We want principles, not to figure in a book of ethics, or to delight us with "grand and swelling sentiments"; but principles by which we may act and by which we may suffer. Principles of benevolence, to dispose us to real sacrifices; political principles, of practical utility; principles of religion, to comfort and support us under all the trying vicissitudes we see around us, and which we have not security that we shall be long exempt from. . . . Above all, let us keep our hearts pure, and our hands clean. Whatever part we take in public affairs, much will undoubtedly happen which we could by no means foresee, and much which we shall not be able to justify; the only way, therefore, by which we can avoid deep remorse, is to act with simplicity and singleness of intention, and not to suffer ourselves to be warped, though by ever so little, from the path which honour and conscience approve. (411–12)

In this description, religion, politics, society, and history are enfolded into one another; the equal authority of the material and spiritual dimensions of human experience are acknowledged. The irreducible reality of circumstance, Barbauld asserts, is inescapable, and if it is to be bent in the direction of justice, then humanity must be able to draw on spiritual resources that are strong and (hopefully) suited to it.

For Barbauld, history and politics are as serious, real, and inescapable as life itself. This fact makes self-reflection essential to the human prospect for security and freedom and, moreover, brings into view the difficulty and complexity of self-reflection. Self-reflection, on her view, is a religious or spiritual experience that is the necessary precondition for engagement in the world. As she puts it near the beginning of Sins of Government, "Every individual... who has a sense of religion, and a desire of conforming his conduct to its precepts, will frequently retire into himself to discover his faults; and having discovered, to repent of,—and having repented of, to amend them" (381–82).[16] Without this sort of religious seriousness as a basis for action, political intervention risks harming rather than healing society. But, as she makes clear, self-reflection is not the act of a moment. It is an ongoing and self-correcting process intended to expand consciousness in such a way as to create a vision of the possibility of a just and meaningful life. To discover and strengthen the sort of principles that she advocates—principles of benevolence and justice—is "not the work of a day," nor the product of "any formal act of worship" (412); it is, rather an ongoing process of learning how to think deeply and systematically about oneself, one's world, and one's principles, of acting as though God is always observing that process. Under the severe pressure of this sort of religious seriousness, Barbauld says, self-interested and nationalistic ways of thinking about life begin to transform into a more universal consideration of and love for all humanity.[17]

Nearly two decades after writing Sins of the Government, in her poem Eighteen Hundred and Eleven, Barbauld restates some of the core beliefs set out in the earlier work, showing that Britain's failure to reflect seriously and consistently on its grounding principles—its failure, that is, to assure that benevolence and justice are sufficiently strong to support the nation—has allowed the nation to become corrupt to the point of collapse. Thus, Barbauld says, it is pointless any longer to engage the nation at all with the idea of saving it; it is fruitless to work on behalf of a nation whose days are numbered. As she puts it in the poem:

> But fairest flowers expand but to decay
> The worm is in thy core, thy glories pass away;
> Arts, arms, and wealth destroy the fruits they bring;
> Commerce, like beauty, knows no second spring.
> Crime walks thy streets, Fraud earns her unblest bread,
> O'er want and woe thy gorgeous robe is spread,
> And angel charities in vain oppose:
> With grandeur's growth the mass of misery grows. (160–61)[18]

The better course of action, she suggests, is to focus on building a new reality based on principles other than brute force and power. *Poems* is an effort in that direction.

While Barbauld creates a unified vision in *Poems*, that vision is not static but dynamic, and it is fluid and vibrant rather than dogmatic. Her effort is to imagine and present a set of governing principles that will enable the building of a world that is defined by social justice and liberty of conscience and that owes as little as possible to what she considers to be the troubling and misdirected political and religious principles of British (and Western) history that have produced the turmoil and conflict of the later eighteenth century; she refuses the proposition that immoral means can be used in the effort to secure a moral goal. Yet every effort to imagine such principles requires a poetic encounter with the political, social, and economic realities of her world, and this encounter threatens to entrap her and compromise the integrity of her vision. An engagement with the conventional structures of politics and religion, in other words, requires that she step onto the landscape of their authority, thus putting her own ideal vision at risk of being subsumed into that landscape. While she desires a pure zone from which to construct her vision of a new world, there is in fact no such Archimedean point; she is therefore forced to develop her idea of radically new and different principles, which might serve as a secure foundation for a newly remade human experience, from within the historical crosscurrents of her world. *Poems* is marked by this visionary tension between the world as she wants it to be and the world as it is, and this tension necessarily mediates her visionary idealism. It is also marked by her forward movement into the world of politics, which is recurrently offset by her retreat into a zone of quiet solitude where she is able to reexamine her principles or shore up her ideals. Both moments of existence are at once necessary to her larger vision and a temptation to forego her visionary project because her idealism points to an empty space, a sphere that is uninhabited (at present) and that may be unachievable.

The visionary tension that Barbauld seeks to resolve can be seen clearly in the volume in her frequent shifts from pastoral to prophetic modes of writing. In the pastoral poems, she expresses her desire to retreat from the world into something like a bower of bliss that will allow her poetic imagination to give full voice to its desires. In these poems (see, for instance, "Verses Written in an Alcove"), her spirit is carefree, and her subject matter exemplifies the sort of peaceful existence that she wants to believe is possible and blessed by the Muses. In other poems, however ("Corsica" and "The Mouse's Petition," for instance), she expresses her awareness of the inexorable reality of politics, nations, and the need to struggle for liberty against oppressive forces. Her challenge is to find a way to position her poetic voice in relation to these two divergent areas of visionary interest. Her struggle seems to anticipate Keats in "Sleep and Poetry," where he expresses his desire to pass the realm "of Flora, and Old Pan: sleep in the grass, / Feed upon apples red, and strawberries, / And choose each pleasure that my fancy sees" (44), only to realize that eventually he must "bid these joys farewell" in favor of "a nobler life, / Where I may find the agonies, the strife of human hearts" (45). The difference, however, is that Barbauld's poetic effort does not simply reject pastoral pleasure or embrace directly "the strife of human hearts"; rather it searches for a different vision altogether, one wherein new dimensions of experience are discovered and set in motion. For Barbauld, it is not simply a matter of choosing between pastoral pleasure and political or existential hardship but rather a matter of searching for a path beyond the dichotomous relationship between the two that leads to a new reality altogether. Her visionary poetics seeks to find this path, and her prophetic call is to enlist others in the search with her.

The tensions Barbauld probes are not only marked by prophetic and pastoral impulses. She also makes extensive use of epistolary verse, hymns, satirical verse, and lyrical effusion to map out and articulate the nuances of her visionary interests. Indeed, the sweep of her formal expression reveals a poet whose vision is at once unified and multifaceted. Just as Blake uses both verbal and visual texts to express the content of his visionary imagination, so Barbauld uses a range of forms and subject matter to construct her vision. Her subject matter is widely varied, shifting from politics, to friendship, to spirituality, to recreational joy, to literary expression, and more, and this variation in subject matter requires flexibility in the choice of poetic form. But her vision is coherent, insofar as her attention to these various subjects and her use of multiple poetic forms are energized and shaped by her consistent effort to envision human experience as joyful, caring, free, and secure. The many poetic forms and subjects, that is, are required to examine and map out the complex layerings of her vision, which cannot be captured by a single mode of expression.

Barbauld's poetic strategy is complicated further by her use of epigraphs. The volume epigraph, drawn from Virgil's tenth eclogue, may be part of a conversation with Priestley, but it is also an indicator of Barbauld's interest in the visionary. The epigraph is a passage from Virgil's first major work, thereby drawing an association with her own poetic situation, as she too is publishing her first major work. It therefore may be regarded as a defensive maneuver of sorts against the prospect of negative criticism. But it is not only defensive; it is also a gentle call to love and an expression of desire for community. Virgil's eclogue tells the story of Gallus, Virgil's friend, who suffers for lack of love and who, in his suffering, imagines that solace may be found in knowledge that others care for him:

> O then how softly would my ashes rest,
> If of my love, one day, your flutes should tell!
> And would that I, of your own fellowship,
> Or dresser of the ripening grape had been,
> Or guardian of the flock!

Gallus's comments here define him as someone who even in the midst of distress, believes that love and fellowship hold the key to peaceful existence. When placed within the context of this sentiment, the lines on which Barbauld draws for her epigraph provide an important thread to lead the reader through the volume: her wager is that to sing of love and fellowship ("these things") is to find a path to human betterment. If her decision to draw on pastoral poetry for her epigraph constitutes a prophetic shadowing of her larger vision, that vision certainly will be unlike that found in the prophetic voice of her great forebear, Milton.

In turning now to an examination of the content of *Poems* (1792), I aim to provide a close reading of individual poems in the volume, considering Barbauld's deployment of various poetic modes of expression and her interweaving of themes and ideas from poem to poem. Such a strategy is intended to offer a method for mapping the nature and trajectory, as well as the self-reflective and self-correcting character, of her visionary poetics and to illustrate the intellectual coherence of the volume. Such a methodical examination, that is, will show Barbauld's multifaceted yet consistently pursued struggle to arrive at an understanding of human experience that is steadfast and historically grounded as well as idealistic and hopeful.

CHAPTER TWO

Politics, Vision, and Pastoral

The most distinctive features of Barbauld's visionary poetics, at least in the early sections of *Poems*, are her restlessness and uncertainty as she works to construct a meaningful imaginative portrait of human experience. Especially in "Corsica," the first poem in the volume, she ranges across various poetic interests— especially pastoral and prophecy—and engages with both politically specific and philosophically speculative topics in an effort to draw together the various threads of her thought and visionary idea. Her main concern through much of the poem is to develop a prophetic voice and method that might address the world and the mind in such a way that will change both. But her effort in this direction, as she confesses near the end of the poem, fails, leaving her to reevaluate the possibilities of visionary poetry as a vehicle for changing the world and compelling her to retreat into the environs of the pastoral imagination to reassess her poetic abilities and objectives. Still, even though "Corsica" is a failure according by Barbauld's own lights, it is an important poem because it helps to point the direction of her visionary poetics—including her readiness to critique and revise her own understanding—across the larger course of the volume. And, in its relation to the subsequent poem in the volume—"The Invitation: To Miss B——"—it reflects the direction of Barbauld's thought and the character of her poetic strategy in the remainder of the volume.

In revising *Poems* for reissue in 1792, Barbauld made a small but significant change on the first page of the first poem in the volume. "Corsica" is a poem describing the Corsican struggle, under the leadership of Pasquale Paoli, for independence from Genoa in the 1760s. In the 1773 edition, at the bottom of the first page of this poem, Barbauld includes a descriptive marker that reads "WRITTEN IN THE YEAR 1769." In the 1792 version she moves this marker to the top of the page, placing it between the title of the poem and the verse epigraph taken from the Scottish Presbyterian James Thomson's *The Seasons*. From the vantage point of 1792, this change is remarkable because it signifies Barbauld's retrospective understanding of the extent to which "Corsica" is a poem about crisis as much as it is a poem about the struggle for liberty. And from the perspective of 1792, with the political situation in Europe and Britain having also reached a point of crisis, Barbauld's decision to lift the date of composition from the bottom of the page and place it just beneath the title of the poem turns the events of the 1760s into a cautionary tale whose details (Barbauld implies) must be recalled and examined by the British radicals and reactionaries of the 1790s. The crisis that she associates with Corsica is clear: on the one hand, the island of Corsica stands as an emblem of liberty, and much of the verse describes its glorious struggle to attain liberty; at the same time, that struggle ultimately failed, leaving the spirit of a nation pinched between its noble desires and the hard realities of loss and subjection. The epigraph of the poem (taken from the "Autumn" segment of *The Seasons*) describes this predicament:

> A manly race
> Of unsubmitting spirit, wise and brave;
> Who still thro' bleeding ages struggled hard
> To hold a generous undiminish'd state;
> Too much in vain! (1)

By situating the date of composition between the title and the epigraph, Barbauld effectively gives it the weight of a revelation: however noble the ideals of a people and however pure the spirit guiding their struggles, the glorious resistance to the forces of oppression can all too quickly result in defeat, leaving behind the massive loss of human blood and the loss of hope. Under the strain of this revelation, "Corsica" investigates political hope and despair in an effort to discover a workable and sustainable vision of human possibility.

The epigraph to "Corsica" is equally important but for different reasons. If the date of composition provides the reader with positive, empirical data, the epigraph is marked by silences and elisions that draw the curious reader toward a more specific and, for Barbauld, more profound set of historical and political realities. By citing only a brief passage from Thomson that lacks any mention of the specific historical, political, or social details that give the lines weight, Barbauld assures that the context of Thomson's lines is hidden from the view, though nevertheless present. More importantly, without indicating that she has done so, Barbauld drops several lines from within the passage that she cites from Thomson, thereby (presumably) intentionally erasing its specific interest and meaning. By restoring the context within which the epigraph appears, and by restoring the lines that Barbauld has deleted, the historical dimensions of Thomson's comments become clear:

> And here awhile the muse,
> High hovering over the broad cerulean scene,
> Sees Caledonia, in romantic view:
> Her airy mountains from the waving main,
> Invested with a keen diffusive sky,
> Breathing the soul acute; her forests huge
> Incult, robust, and tall, by Nature's hand
> Planted of old; her azure lakes between,
> Poured out extensive, and of watery wealth,
> Full; winding, deep and green, her fertile vales,
> With many a cool translucent brimming flood
> Washed lovely from the Tweed (pure parent-stream,
> Whose pastoral banks first heard my Doric reed,
> With, sylvan Jed, thy tributary brook)
> To where the north-inflated tempest foams
> O'er Orca's or Betubium's highest peak.
> Nurse of a people, in misfortune's school
> Trained up to hardy deeds; soon visited
> By learning, when before Gothic rage
> She took her manly flight. *A manly race,*
> *Of unsubmitting spirit, wise, and brave;*
> *Who still through bleeding ages struggled hard,*
> *(As well unhappy Wallace can attest,*
> *Great patriot-hero! ill-requited chief!)*
> *To hold a generous, undiminished state;*
> *Too much in vain!* Hence of unequal bounds
> Impatient, and by tempting glory borne,
> O'er every land, for every land their life
> Has flowed profuse, their piercing genius planned,
> And swelled the pomp of peace their faithful toil:
> As from their own clear north, their radiant streams,
> Bright over Europe bursts the boreal morn. (115, emphasis added)

These lines are among the few in *Seasons* that speak directly about matters of politics, nationalism, and the struggle for equality, and they do so through their description of Scotland and by reference to William Wallace (which is dropped without indication from Barbauld's epigraph). The larger passage not only describes the "unsubmitting spirit" of the Scots, who eventually were defeated by

England and subsumed into the British kingdom in 1707, but also the reverence due to Scotland for its "toil" on behalf of "the pomp of peace." Like Corsica, Scotland is an emblem of the noblest of nations; it is marked by its relentless spirit, its dream of peace, and its "acute" soul. As suggested by Thomson's imagery, it represents a world of natural plenitude, a pastoral ideal that serves as both a foundation and goal for Barbauld's vision. But the historical reality of Scotland is also a warning—like "Corsica"—about the material hardships that threaten idealism when that idealism is pursued through military struggle. Like William Wallace before him, Pasquale Paoli (as Barbauld recounts in "Corsica") fails in his military struggles to remake his world according to the noble principle of liberty. Given her apparent rejection of military engagement, the challenge facing Barbauld is to imagine a hopeful path around the obstacles that defeated such courageous, noble, and dedicated men.

The references to Scotland and Wallace surrounding the epigraph also suggest that Barbauld's poetic interest lies not only in Corsica but in Britain as well, and the opening line of the poem makes clear the act of poetic displacement in which she engages: "Hail generous Corsica! Unconquer'd isle!" (1). If the war between Scotland and England is the unstated subject of the epigraph, the unstated yet obvious subject of this line is the island of Britain, which, increasingly in the eighteenth century, as the empire continued to expand, had come to be identified rhetorically in terms similar to those that Barbauld uses to describe Corsica, which she calls "the fort of freedom; that amidst the waves / Stands like a rock of adamant, and dares / The wildest fury of the beating storm" (1).[1] Moreover, the Corsican constitution, written under the leadership of Paoli, was modeled on the British constitution. With the force of an epic imagination carried forward on lines of blank verse, Barbauld's tone is celebratory and confident, presenting the "unconquer'd isle" as an impenetrable defense against even the worst of military and political onslaughts, setting in motion an idea, which is stated explicitly in the second verse paragraph, that the great events occurring on the island of Corsica might also become a reality on the island of Britain.

While Barbauld's celebration of Corsica's spirit of liberty and her allusion to the British interest in liberty are emphatic, the significance of her reference to liberty, for this poem and for the volume, is unclear.[2] After all, at the time the poem was published, Corsica was not unconquered but had been defeated by overwhelming French forces after having been ceded to France by Genoa. What appears in the beginning to be a poem about the struggle for political liberty is in fact, in its larger historical context, a poem about the defeat of liberty. All that remains is what Thomson calls, in the epigraph, an "unsubmitting spirit," a description that anticipates the final line of Barbauld's poem, in which, in the face of political defeat, she celebrates "the freedom of the mind" (12). Barbauld's position here on the freedom of the mind not only echoes the general sentiments of her predecessors, Thomson and Milton; it also anticipates Byron's view, say, in "Sonnet on Chillon," which describes liberty as an "Eternal Spirit of the chainless Mind!" (3) and the physical person of Bonnivard—the sixteenth-century Genevan whom Byron imagines as one of the "sons" (3) of liberty—as being "to fetters ... consigned" (3).[3] That is, like Byron will do in 1816, Barbauld not only looks backward in her poetic construction of liberty; she effectively reenvisions the past for poetic use in the present and future. The epigraph from Thomson and the final line of the poem that, as McCarthy notes, "speaks the language of Milton" ("'We Hoped the Woman Was Going to Appear'" 123), provide a literary-political framework within which the conflicts of the present (in the form of the Corsican struggle for independence) are carried out.

Barbauld's use of Thomson and Milton as a framework for the story of liberty struggling to be born exposes "Corsica" as a statement of poetic crisis. While Thomson and Milton speak to the strength of the human spirit, or mind, Barbauld shows in the body of the poem itself that she is acutely aware of social reality—"this late sickly age" (1), as she puts it—wherein one is hard pressed to discover any true devotees of freedom. Indeed, as she begins her tale about Corsica, she describes the island as "this lone speck of earth! this spot obscure" (2), stating her astonishment that it falls to an out-of-the-way island nation to bring public attention to the possibility that the modern world might commit itself to the pursuit of liberty. The story of Corsica, she suggests, should leave Britain, with its long history of celebrating the principle of freedom, embarrassed: "What then should BRITONS feel? should they not catch / The warm contagion of heroic ardour, / And kindle at a fire so like their own?" (2). In this commentary on Britain in relation to Corsica, Barbauld seems unable to identify herself as British, referring to the citizens of her own nation as "they," because Britain stands on the sidelines, leaving the important work of history to a people living on the very margins of the modern world. Britain may proclaim its dedication to the principle of freedom, but the reality, Barbauld suggests, is far different. Thus, however much she might admire the sentiments voiced by Thomson and Milton, her poetic task is to account for the struggles and failure of liberty in her own historical moment and to discover a means to overcome that failure.

The Thomson and Milton references sharpen the sense of crisis in the volume in another way as well, specifically by showing that Barbauld is caught, poetically, between the allure of pastoral retreat and the demands of prophetic engagement and conflicted about how to negotiate the use and meaning of these modes of poetry. The difficulty, for Barbauld, is figuring out how to find her way to the pastoral ideal, a world of natural plenitude and wealth that fuels the human desire for peace and fulfillment, that the passage in Thomson's *Seasons* leading up to the lines that form Barbauld's epigraph presents, when Scottish history itself suggests the impossibility of achieving it and when the world in its present form is a "sickly age." Under the historical and political circumstances that define her historical moment, the pastoral imagination risks losing the power associated with its idealism and shrinking to little more than an escapist dream; while the pastoral ideal may indeed be the foundation of human fulfillment as well as its goal, it can also tempt one to retreat into a quietist neglect of all worldly matters, especially when the fight for liberty (as seen in the examples of Wallace and Paoli) ends in political defeat, leaving only (and at best) an "unsubmitting spirit" in its wake. The pastoral sensibility is admirable and even desirable, but it is also a potential trap, as Barbauld's excision of the Wallace reference from the epigraph suggests; the removal of the lines about Wallace amount to nothing less than the removal of the specific historical and political realities that bear oppressively on the "unsubmitting spirit" and an implicit surrender (if only temporarily) to the idea that history must be rejected if a world of natural plenitude is to be discovered.

Barbauld's desire for prophetic and visionary engagement with the world, as evidenced in the body of the poem, is problematic as well, and for the same reason. Even if prophecy can expose the injustices of the world as it is, describe the nobility of the human spirit in its struggle for freedom, and serve as a clarion call for all of humanity to join in that struggle, it offers no guarantee that a return to paradise is possible, or even that the world may be improved. In fact, Barbauld fears, prophecy may be nothing more than a naïve and pointless, or misdirected, exercise of mind that finally leaves the world just as it was, unchanged and under tyrannical authority. Her use of blank verse in "Corsica" and her reference to Milton's towering prophetic work, *Paradise Lost*, point toward her wish to take on the great burden of prophesying about liberty and reenvisioning the world. At the same time, however, her embracement of the prophetic mode is marked by a potentially debilitating anxiety. Her reference to Milton, for instance, is in fact an allusion to Satan's view that "the mind is its own place" rather than an appropriation of Milton's resounding prophetic voice that speaks forcefully to the world instead of the solitary mind. The celebration of the freedom of the mind, or the view that the mind is its own place, which Barbauld hails as a freedom "worthy of Gods" (12), does not represent a prophetic vision of social transformation but a retreat. In fact, insofar as "Corsica" may be regarded as a prophetic poem, it is a failed prophecy, a poem governed, as Barbauld herself finally realizes, by vanity and foolishness (11).

Barbauld seems to understand the problematic character of pastoral and prophecy, that each holds out considerable possibilities for reinvigorating and reenvisioning the world and at the same time, under present historical conditions, represents a potential obstacle to vision. The complex relation between pastoral and prophecy, as Barbauld formulates it in "Corsica," can be seen in the various threads of disassociation and association running between the epigraph and the final line of the poem. The unsubmitting spirit celebrated in her epigraph as a sign of human strength, she suggests, may not be exactly the same thing as the freedom of the mind described in the final line of the poem, as the epigraph (silently) describes the noble efforts of William Wallace on behalf of the Scottish people, while the final line of the poem describes a retreat into the solitary recesses of the mind; on this view the poem appears to move from political and social vision toward the rejection of politics and society. At the same time, and perhaps paradoxically, the ultimate defeat of the unsubmitting spirit described in the epigraph ("Too much in vain") may be identical to the sentiment articulated in the final line of the poem; the acknowledgment voiced in the epigraph is that William Wallace's nationalist efforts, for all their admirable courage and idealism, come to naught, leaving the individual mind to find its own, private, path to freedom. It is at least possible, Barbauld seems to suggest in both the epigraph and in the final line of the poem, that the world cannot be transformed and thus is not worth the bother.

Barbauld's complicated consideration of the relations of pastoral and prophecy in the modern world is played out in the body of the poem, with one thread of her interest captured in her portrayal of James Boswell, an early and enthusiastic supporter of the Corsican struggle for freedom. In 1765, following the advice of Rousseau, Boswell traveled to Corsica to witness revolutionary political events firsthand, after which he published his *An Account of Corsica*, an odd collection of historical and geographical information of the island, combined with a journal of his travels and a memoir. After a lengthy preface to the volume, Boswell begins his account of Corsica with a stirring celebration of liberty:

> Liberty is so natural, and so dear to mankind, whether as individuals, or as members of society, that it is indispensably necessary to our happiness. Everything worthy ariseth from it. Liberty gives health to the mind, and enables us to enjoy the full exercise of our faculties. He who is in chains cannot move

either easily or gracefully; nothing elegant or noble can be expected from those, whose spirits are subdued by tyranny, and whose powers are cramped by restraint. (1)

Barbauld commends Boswell for stepping off "the narrow beaten track" (4), trodden by conventional and nostalgic tourists who are interested only in dead artifacts, to encounter "animated forms of patriot zeal" (3) on the out-of-the-way island of Corsica. For Barbauld, Boswell's decision to visit Corsica entails a rejection of the pastoral scene (Boswell leaves "Gallia's soft delicious vales" [4]) and the antiquarian's sense of history as idle pleasure seeking (Boswell rejects "the grey reliques of imperial Rome" [4]) in favor of living history, where "fearless spirit[s]" inhabit "the living majesty of virtue" (3). Boswell's bold step into living history inspires Barbauld's imagination in the direction of prophecy. Boswell in a literal sense and Barbauld poetically willfully adopt positions on the margins of human experience for the purpose of speaking truth to the world. Understanding that Boswell is motivated by a "nobler aim" (2) than the dominant attitudes of the day might endorse and entering imaginatively into Boswell's text, Barbauld travels "in thought" (3) to Corsica in order to celebrate that island's grand vision and struggle: "I kiss/With pilgrim lips devout, the sacred soil/Stain'd with the blood of heroes" (3). As a young female poet, Barbauld stands on the margins of her culture, much as Corsica, a small, out-of-the-way island, stands on the margins of Europe, and from these margins both speak loudly and prophetically of the growing "flame of LIBERTY" (2) that is dedicated to the cause of changing the world.

Barbauld's visionary hope for a transformed world draws on other aspects of Boswell's *Account* as well, including Boswell's consideration of time and space in relation to the Corsican struggle for liberty. Boswell begins his work with a chapter entitled "Of the Situation, Extent, Air, Soil, and Productions, of Corsica," which describes, among other things, the geography of the island nation. As Samuel Johnson observes, Boswell lifted much of his information on the history and geography of Corsica from earlier historical writings ("Your history was copied from books" [qtd. in "Life of the Late James Boswell," 33]), but, for Barbauld, that fact does not make the information any less compelling. In the early pages of *Account*, for instance, Boswell cites two epigrams that Seneca wrote about Corsica while the Roman dramatist was exiled on the island (41 AD). The first describes "the raging heats" (13) and "yet fiercer plagues [that] thy shores dispense" (14). The second describes the "rocks terrific" of Corsica,

where nature spreads her wildest desarts round,
In vain revolving seasons cheer thy soil,
Nor rip'ning fruits, nor waving harvests smile:
Nor blooms the olive mid the winter drear. (14)

While Boswell objects to these descriptions as "false indeed" (12), asserting that when he wrote them Seneca's "mind was then clouded with melancholy, and every object around him, appeared in rueful colors" (15), Barbauld is struck by those rueful colors and incorporates Seneca's impression into her own vision of the Corsican dream of liberty. In describing Corsica, she refers to its "hamlets brown," situated alongside "thy swelling mountains, brown with solemn shade / Of various trees" (4); the Corsican forests are "savage," "awful, deep" (5). While she acknowledges spots of color in the Corsican landscape (the "Ilex ever green," the "living verdure" of "each humbler plant," and even the "scarlet fruit" of the arbutus tree [4]), at the same time she views vegetative life as more or less under attack, as "the spinning worm" feeds upon "the green leaf" (4). Barbauld's Corsica is very much a barren land, dreadful and wild:

Hail to thy savage forests, awful, deep:
Thy tangled thickets, and thy crowded woods,
The haunt of herds untam'd; which sullen bound
From rock to rock with fierce unsocial air,
And wilder gaze, as conscious of the power
That loves to reign amid the lonely scenes
Of unquelled nature; precipices huge,
And tumbling torrents; trackless deserts, plains
Fenc'd in with guardian rocks, whose quarries teem
With shining steel, that to the cultur'd fields
And sunny hills which wave with bearded grain
Defends their homely produce. (50)

The sentiment here anticipates the terrifying possibilities associated with the "deep romantic chasm" described in Coleridge's "Kubla Khan," in its attention not only to the tumbling torrents and savage forests on the Corsican landscape but more forcefully to "the power / That loves to reign amid the lonely scenes." But, whereas Coleridge was repulsed by the power that he found in an untamed and tumultuous nature, Barbauld views it as an example of great and disturbing energy that might be tapped for human betterment. In its attention to the sublimity of the scene, Barbauld's imagination extends beyond the easy idealisms of the pastoral imagination and reaches toward the complexity of the prophetic imagination, which recognizes that beauty and liberty are inextricably bound to conflict and hardship. Not only does the rugged landscape defend the "homely produce" of the island by providing a natural barrier against invasion; it provides a natural home for liberty, which Barbauld describes as "the mountain Goddess, [who] loves to range at large / Amid such scenes, and on the iron soil / [Print] her majestic step" (5). For Barbauld, liberty "scorns / The green enamel'd vales, the velvet lap / Of smooth savannahs, where the pillow'd head / Of luxury reposes" (5–6) in favor of a harder landscape that is more appropriate to the difficult labor that is required if people are to be free.

But it is not the landscape alone that attracts the spirit of liberty to Corsica; the human spirit shapes the landscape just as much as the landscape shapes the human spirit. The island, in fact, in Barbauld's imagination, has been worn and polished to its current condition through the course of history, as Corsicans have struggled with courage and resolve to be free, to the point where Corsica is now "a beauteous gem" (6). Corsica is the proper home of liberty because the people of Corsica, through its long history, have consistently welcomed liberty onto its shores:

> Her genuine sons,
> A broken remnant, from the generous stock
> Of ancient Greece, from Sparta's sad remains,
> True to their high descent, preserv'd unquench'd
> The sacred fire thro' many a barbarous age
> Whom, nor the iron rod of cruel Carthage,
> Nor the dread scepter of imperial Rome,
> Nor bloody goth, nor grisly Saracen,
> Nor the long galling yoke of proud Liguria,
> Could crush into subjection. Still unquell'd
> They rose superior, bursting from their chains,
> And claim'd man's dearest birthright, LIBERTY. (6)

Corsica is an emblem of the resistance and idealism that were born in Greece and that stood firm against every European political or military power that sought to subdue it. It is therefore not a pastoral retreat but rather a historically and socially constructed home for liberty.

For Barbauld, the Corsicans are a people in the wilderness struggling once more to achieve their rightful status as a free nation, and Barbauld is the prophet who draws on the Miltonic poetic example (blank verse) and Scottish historical example (William Wallace), as well as the historical example of Corsica itself (as described by Boswell) so that she might steel the spirit of the people, point their way along the road to freedom, and guide Britain and Europe onto the same path. As she knows, the labor of which she speaks is difficult—Corsicans historically have fought "thro' many a hard unequal strife" (7)—but it is not impossible. In the past, Corsica has "long withstood / With single arm, the whole collected force / Of haughty Genoa, and ambitious Gaul. / And shall withstand it" (7). The confidence expressed in this statement derives from Barbauld's conviction that "it is not in the force of mortal arm, / Scarcely in fate, to bind the struggling soul" (7). The greatest power that people possess is their spirit, their undying conviction that they can and should be free. Barbauld's prophetic responsibility, as she sees it, is to persuade Corsica (and, by extension, Britain) to "trust the faithful Muse!" (7), who celebrates the spirit of liberty and inspires people to do likewise, and she is convinced that such trust is looked on favorably by heaven: "And fav'ring heaven approves" (7).

The prophetic impulse seen in these lines is inspired by, and focuses on, the great Corsican general Pasquale Paoli, who was the leader of the Corsican struggle against Genoa and subsequently against France. Barbauld draws on and interweaves history, politics, poetry, and universal spirit in an effort to capture the greatness and world-historical importance of Paoli and to inspire Corsicans to follow his leadership. According to Barbauld, Paoli's example gives "mankind / A glimpse of higher natures" (7), because heaven has instilled in him "every purer virtue" (8) and indeed all "that lifts the hero, or adorns the man" (8). Her dream is that Paoli's example will awaken the spirit of people so that they will rise up and struggle on behalf of heaven and liberty against the forces of oppression. As she says of Paoli:

> On his brow
> Serene, and spacious front, set the broad seal
> Of dignity and rule; then smil'd benign
> On this fair pattern of a God below,
> High wrought, and breath'd into his swelling breast
> The large ambitious wish to save his country.
> Oh beauteous title to immortal fame!
> The man devoted to the public, stands
> In the bright records of superior worth
> A step below the skies. (8)

This description of Paoli marks the prophetic center of the poem, as Barbauld's imagination flies from Britain to Corsica in an effort to serve that island nation poetically just as Paoli serves it militarily. While the "British Muse" is "weak and powerless" (9)—that is, while the power of prophecy seems to have abandoned Britain—through an act of poetic displacement Barbauld reassigns her imagination, placing it in the service of a different island, lifting "her fervent voice" (9) on behalf of the Corsican struggle.

Barbauld's reference to the "British Muse" helps to clarify her dilemma as a poet who wishes to write prophecy during a historical period that is not conducive to the prophetic spirit. Although she beseeches the Corsicans to "trust the faithful muse," at the same time she confesses that the British muse is "weak and powerless," incapable of spreading "blessings as the morn sheds dews" (9), suggesting that Britain has much to learn from its small, backward neighbor about liberty. At a moment when Britain has not caught "the warm contagion of heroic ardour" (2), Barbauld says that the best that she can do is be patient at home and support liberty abroad:

> But patient hope
> Must wait th' appointed hour; secure of this,
> That never with the indolent and weak
> Will freedom deign to dwell; she must be seiz'd
> By that bold arm that wrestles for the blessing. (9)

These lines go to the heart of Barbauld's visionary poetics. The events in Corsica inspire her imagination to reach toward human liberty, and yet her historical situation leaves her imaginatively unable to penetrate the stifling and oppressive realities of Britain, as spelled out in Priestley's *Present State of Liberty in Great Britain and Her Colonies*. In the face of this predicament, wherein historical necessity narrowly constrains the shape and direction of the imagination, Barbauld's consideration of Corsica drives her to accept that the visionary poet dedicated to human betterment must remain strong and insistent that "heaven's best gift" (9) can be "seiz'd," even if it "must be bought with blood" (9). If only for a moment, Barbauld entertains the possibility that political violence might be inevitable in the struggle for liberty, and she seems willing to accept this inevitability.[4] She will eventually step back from this position, but her stance here nevertheless suggests clearly her rejection of quietist withdrawal and her materialist understanding of the complex relation between history and vision. While the force of history cannot be defeated, she insists that human agency, when inspired by courage and imagination, can intervene in history and point it in the direction of human well being.

In her surprisingly direct remark that liberty sometimes "must be bought with blood," Barbauld seems to contradict the conventional (and correct) critical notion that she was consistently pacifist in her political views.[5] Indeed, the larger course of the volume confirms her discomfort with a political vision that accepts violence, even as a necessary evil. But her position here might not be simply a momentary lapse into militaristic thinking, caused by the pressure of the historical moment. It is possible that she is trying, rather, to finesse the problematic question about the relation between violence and liberty. To understand how she could make such an explicitly nonpacifist statement, one needs only to consider the extent to which her pacifism, like her prophetic impulse, is complicated by her realistic and materialist understanding of history and human conflict.[6] She consistently maintains that human experience is constructed on the hard landscape of material circumstance—presented in literal detail in her characterization of Corsica—and that human desire must negotiate this landscape, a fact that often puts the human spirit in peril, simply because blood is inextricably related to spirit. Given this fact, the reality of blood must somehow be accommodated to the desires of spirit. And it is possible that Barbauld seeks to effect this accommodation by reimagining the ways that blood may serve to purchase liberty. That is, she may not necessarily be speaking only about armed struggle, or accepting the necessity of violence, when she says that liberty must be bought with blood. Indeed, the stance on behalf of liberty, she implies, requires self-sacrifice, the pouring of one's lifeblood into the cause of human betterment, a view that need not be understood as synonymous with a militaristic ideology. On this understanding, the "patient hope" and strength of spirit that Barbauld describes is also a form of giving one's blood in the struggle for liberty. While this reading perhaps overburdens Barbauld's lines, it nevertheless looks forward to her portrayal, in the "Hymns," of Christ's willingness to shed his own blood to serve humanity in an act that is both pacifist and selfless in nature.

Barbauld's understanding of individual character in relation to the dream of freedom can be glimpsed in her commentary on virtue under fire. In her lengthy description of Paoli, she comments that the Corsican leader has been endowed by heaven "with every purer virtue" (6). And a bit later she returns to the idea of virtue as it applies more generally to the servants of liberty when she describes the sorts of sacrifice that they are required to make on behalf of their cause. Echoing Milton's famous comment on virtue—"I cannot praise a fugitive and cloistered virtue, unexercised and unbreathed, that never sallies out and sees her adversary, but slinks out of the race, where that immortal garland is to be run for, not without dust and heat" ("Areopagitica" 728)—Barbauld imagines that "virtue triumphs" (7) "when the combat burns, / And pain and death in every horrid shape / That can appal the feeble, prowl around" (9). Like liberty, virtue finds its proper home within the hard world of human struggle and through the willing sacrifice of the individual to that struggle. As the labors on behalf of liberty intensify, virtue grows, finding "joys amidst the tempest" (10): "Her tow'ring form / Dilates with kindling majesty; her mien / Breathes a diviner spirit" (9). If Barbauld's political views tend toward pacifism, she is in no way an unengaged pacifist but finds her hope amid "heroic deeds, / And godlike action" (10).

Barbauld's energetic endorsement of the life of action, which celebrates the exploits of Paoli and poetically echoes the imaginative flights of her epic forbears, seems to confirm her embrace of prophecy and rejection of simple-minded pastoral idealism. Indeed, at this moment, at least, Barbauld rejects the allure of pastoral retreat entirely, choosing instead to cast her visionary lot with the principle of purposeful engagement which represents virtue as "a firm shield against the darts of fate" (10):

>   'Tis not meats, and drinks,
> And balmy airs, and vernal suns, and showers
> That feed and ripen minds: 'tis toil and danger;
> And wrestling with the stubborn gripe of fate;
> And war, and sharp distress, and paths obscure
> And dubious. (10)

In fact, however, within the larger frame of the poem, she keeps the pastoral imagination very much alive and envisions the pastoral landscape as a place of rest following on the hard labor of winning liberty. But, like her prophetic vision of liberty, her pastoral vision is complex, not governed by principles of withdrawal or unmediated bliss but rather by principles of integration, wherein the full weight of history is folded into the peaceful landscape. Paoli's fight on behalf of Corsica, she says, will be followed by "the shining train / Of peaceful years":

> Then shall the shepherd's pipe, the muse's lyre,
> On Cyrnus' shores be heard: her grateful sons
> With loud acclaim and hymns of cordial praise
> Shall hail their high deliverers; every name
> To virtue dear be from oblivion snatch'd
> And plac'd among the stars. (11)

In an astonishing poetic flight, Barbauld here interweaves the pastoral, prophetic, and hymnal imaginations, describing a picture of the muse's soft protection of a newly won peace, which yields hymns sung in worship of the vision and courage that enabled virtue to triumph and, among the stars, become an emblem of liberty, "heaven's greatest gift."

The final section of the poem, added after the failure of the Corsican revolution, effectively undercuts the visionary path that Barbauld hitherto had been following, as she confesses her vanity and her misunderstanding of history. In celebrating Corsica, she says, her muse was vain and foolish, ill informed about "the iron fates" (11) that doomed Paoli to defeat. In her self-criticism, she makes clear that her understanding of history and liberty had been limited, even mistaken, and that her visionary shortcomings manifested themselves as a naïve prophecy that liberty is always within reach of a disenfranchised people, if only they will keep their spirits strong and dedicated to the struggle against tyranny. Her error, moreover, not only involved her belief that Corsica could win its freedom against a militarily superior enemy; it arose as well from her misunderstanding of the means by which liberty must be secured. If earlier in the poem she was quick to say that liberty "must be bought with blood" and that "virtue triumphs" through the course of violent struggle against tyranny, now she retracts that view, suggesting that even the most generous interpretation of her idea of bloodshed was mistaken and stating explicitly that liberty and virtue must be understood differently:

> Forgive the zeal
> That, too presumptuous whisper'd better things,
> And read the book of destiny amiss.
> Not with the purple colouring of success
> Is virtue best adorn'd: th' attempt is praise. (12)

Here Barbauld's well-known pacifism emerges clearly, as she divorces her notion of freedom from militarism (even if someone as noble as Paoli is leading the struggle) and resituates it within "the mind," "beyond the proud oppressor's cruel grasp / Seated secure, uninjur'd" (12). Only when the mind is free, she says, can "virtue" truly triumph; and freedom of the mind, for Barbauld at this moment, requires relinquishing the idea of oppositional struggle. Returning here to one of the foundational principles of Dissenting philosophy, Barbauld makes explicit the importance of understanding political and social liberty in a manner that is consistent with the idea of liberty of conscience, and, for her, liberty of conscience must be distinguished categorically from all principles of political violence, even if that violence is carried out against forces of tyranny.

On this view, the retreat into "the freedom of the mind" is not so much a retreat from all notions of political engagement, nor is it necessarily an echo of the radical self-interest found in Milton's Satan in *Paradise Lost*; it is, rather, a confession of the failure of Barbauld's prophetic vision and a statement of her consequent need to rethink politics and history in new and different terms. In her eagerness to see the world remade in such a way as to make the principles of liberty triumphant, she "read the book of destiny amiss" when she came to accept the proposition that the spilling of blood ("the purple colouring of success") in the struggle against tyranny is acceptable. Retreat, in this instance, then, is a retreat from prophesying; it is a decision to reconsider more carefully than before the relations of politics, society, history, the individual, and nature in an effort to arrive at a surer understanding of the world and of the means necessary to remake it in the direction of liberty. The task that Barbauld sets for herself is large and difficult, requiring not only that she examine the social and natural details of her world but also that she consider modes of poetic writing in an effort to discover the most appropriate means of capturing and presenting her vision of liberty. While, as she will make clear later in the volume, freedom of the mind carries its own risks and liabilities, for now, she suggests, it provides a space for self-reflection and self-correction.

If "Corsica" concludes with an expression of Barbauld's desire to retreat from the world of political and military struggle, the poem that follows, "The Invitation," pays tribute to that general impulse by introducing, in the epigraph to the poem, a pastoral landscape of beauty and peace where the only hardship on human life is inflicted by time itself: "Here are cool springs, here soft meadows, Lycoris,/ Here woodland. Here with you time itself would devour me" (35).[7] Taken from Virgil's tenth eclogue, these lines effectively articulate a dream of peace. They also point explicitly toward Barbauld's interest in pastoral, here and in subsequent poems as well, as a mode of writing that may help to clarify her desire for peace, liberty, and virtue in a world that is marked by strife and hardship.[8] That she did not view pastoral as a simple idealization of life and its possibilities but rather as a means of approaching life's complexities is evident when we consider the larger context of the epigraph, which directly describes some of the interests that she had pursued in "Corsica" and indeed echoes the regret that Barbauld confesses in that poem:

Violets are dark, and hyacinths are dark . . . ,
We'd lie together in willows beneath a pliant vine;

Phyllis would gather garlands for me, Amantas sing.
Here are cool springs, here soft meadows, Lycoris,
Here woodland. Here with you time itself would devour me.
Now a demented love of hard Mars restrains me in arms,
Where spears cluster and the hostile ranks confront.
(35)

Like Barbauld in "Corsica," Virgil's speaker (Gallus) dreams of a world of peace while at the same time losing sight of that dream because of his love of "spears" and war. Thus, the eclogue from which the epigraph is taken indicates the direction Barbauld's poetic interest has gone in: "The Invitation" exhibits a pastoral sensibility that dreams of peace but at the same time brings forward the memory of the mistakes that Barbauld had made in "Corsica," where she had expressed her belief that liberty "must be bought with blood." Further, the epigraph—or the larger context within which it appears, and which gives it meaning—serves as a warning to Barbauld and to her reader against the dangers of reading "the book of destiny amiss."

"The Invitation" is addressed to "Miss B——," who is Elizabeth Belsham, Barbauld's cousin and lifelong friend, addressed, in the context of the poem, by the pastoral name Delia.[9] The poem constitutes something of a regrouping of Barbauld's spirits after the failure of her vision in "Corsica"; her proclamation at the end of that poem celebrating the "freedom of the mind" seems to recall for her certain basic principles about visionary poetics, as well as about the individual's relation to society, which she now picks up for examination. Her first step toward the reconsideration of basic poetic and social principles entails imaginatively abandoning the large social reality—Corsica—with which she had been preoccupied previously; as "Corsica" demonstrates, and as Barbauld confesses, she is not yet ready to be a global visionary poet in the way (say) that Milton was. Rather, she turns to a much smaller yet no less important sphere of social interest—friendship—that for her, as for Yearsley, provides one of the necessary building blocks for sustainable and healthy large-scale social relations.[10] If there are to be meaning, pleasure, and liberty in life, Barbauld insists, then friendship is essential: pleasure "cannot fly from friendship, and from you [Delia]" (15). Moreover, in "The Invitation" Barbauld turns her geographical imagination away from Italy, France, and Corsica back to England, repositioning her visionary poetics on her home soil, which provides a familiar and comfortable zone of experience for her visionary flights. If her dream of a world remade in the name of liberty is to succeed—if her prophetic voice is to be clear, strong, and creditable—then she must find her poetic footing on familiar soil before addressing the world at large. On this view, it is not surprising that from this moment forward in the volume Barbauld casts herself primarily as a British poet dedicated to writing about British subject matter. While her vision is universal, the foundation for her universal vision is necessarily local.

Barbauld's initial portrayal of Delia makes clear that pastoral is not only a means of portraying an idealized world but also a mode of reflecting on the world, as well as on the self. First, Barbauld associates her friend with the values, principles, and ideals that are central to her larger poetic vision. She describes Delia as a "friend" and wishes her "Health," "new joys," "sunshine," and, most importantly "hope" and "peace eternal" (13). These good wishes for her friend show that Barbauld has not abandoned a social vision in favor of the pleasures of the solitary mind (as the final line of "Corsica" seems to suggest), even if for the moment this social interest is decidedly narrow and personal, and that her vision includes the possibility of social joy, or pleasure, in life. Moreover, the characterization of Delia recalls the pastoral dream that Barbauld had described in "Corsica"; after Paoli and his supporters "in that rough school have learn'd / To smile at danger" (10–11), then will "the shepherd's pipe, the muse's lyre, / On Cyrnus' shores be heard" (11). Now, however, the pastoral dream is no longer of a blissful world that appears after liberty has been "bought with blood" but rather an immediate possibility that can be discovered by retreating from the realms of political conflict. Retreat is the necessary path to happiness and purposeful life; it provides the conditions under which those matters that, for Barbauld, require reflection can be considered: what are the possibilities of pleasure in life? To what extent is social reality the necessary condition for pleasure? And can the ideal of a joyous life be discovered without bloodshed. The poet's invitation to Delia to retreat with her into refreshing rural scenes beyond the difficulties found in the modern world is, then, an invitation to reconsider life from beyond the borders of its dominant structures of thought and belief:

> Will Delia, at the Muse's call, retire
> To the pure pleasures rural scenes inspire?
> Will she from crowds and busy cities fly,
> Where wreaths of curling smoke involve the sky,
> To taste the grateful shade of spreading trees,
> And drink the spirit of the mountain breeze? (14)

The poem's portrayal of the pure pleasures available in the rural scene (which anticipates Wordsworth's "The Tables Turned," among other poems) and of friendship exhibit Barbauld's need to reconsider her poetic principles (as previously set out in "Corsica") and perhaps, as well, her poetic capacity for writing visionary poetry.[11] For the moment, at least, Barbauld views pastoral as the necessary framework for poetic reflection, her embrace of pastoral serving a function similar to that of Yearsley's "Platonic Shade"; it is a setting within which one can take stock of oneself and the world at the same time.

When placed against her acknowledgment of prophetic failure in "Corsica" and her expressed need in "The Invitation" for a space where reflection might occur, Barbauld's call for "the freedom of the mind" at the end of "Corsica" loses its isolationist or radically individualist cast—and loses its Miltonic association as well—and becomes instead a confession of her need to begin anew. And a new beginning, for her, means examining the extent to which she is capable of poetic vision. To this end, "The Invitation" reorganizes her poetic interests and emphases entirely. Rather than end this poem with a consideration of pastoral, as she had done after describing the revolutionary resistance in "Corsica," she begins with pastoral; rather than presenting the nation and the hero as starting points for poetic vision, she begins with nature and friendship as the foundational principles of vision; rather than focus on public and military action, she focuses on description and reflection. "The Invitation" is a very different kind of poem from "Corsica," and yet it is integrally related to it because both poems show Barbauld's imagination in process of discovering its proper reach and interest. The relation between these poems shows that her imagination, far from being settled, is restless and searching.

Barbauld's care in situating herself imaginatively and in crafting pastoral as a socially relevant poetic mode is seen in her portrayal of the relations between the seasons and the relations between town and country. Accepting as a matter of principle that the purpose of life is pleasure, she likens humans to migratory birds, saying that people move with the seasons in search of pleasure, retreating from the country into the city during winter and from the city into the country during the spring and summer (14–15). While "cities and courts" (14) can offer only superficial pleasures—"gold and gems with artificial blaze" (14)—they nevertheless provide a place of retreat until "the western gale, / . . . seeks the bosom of the grassy vale" (15) and brings back the purer pleasures of spring. But even in spring, Barbauld suggests, pleasure is found not only among pristine natural landscapes but also among landscapes that have been shaped by the human imagination and human labor: "We'll follow where the smiling goddess leads, / Thro' tangled forests or enamel'd meads" (15).[12] Thus the central point for Barbauld is not that the rural landscape offers pleasure because it is pure and devoid of human presence. Rather, her point is that pleasure is a search, a process, that takes people who are bound by friendship across the various spaces of natural and human experience: pleasure "cannot fly from friendship" (15). Barbauld's imagination, that is, finds its proper home in the world and among friends.

In an additional poetic turn, Barbauld complicates the idea that pastoral is a mode of poetry celebrating retreat from a complex world by including descriptions of nature as harsh and unwelcoming and portraying the city as desirable and life sustaining. When winter "deforms" (14) nature and the sun becomes "sickly" (14), she says, people move into cities and courts because that is where pleasure is to be found. Even if the offerings of the city are artificial they are nevertheless desirable until better days are forthcoming. In this portrayal, the city takes on the characteristic of a pastoral landscape to which people may resort for the purpose of finding pleasure, while its artificial quality takes on a cast of purity that is the object of human desire, thereby becoming associated with the sort of pleasure that is often imaginatively linked with the pastoral setting. This odd twist on the idea of pastoral helps to clarify the nature of Barbauld's vision by showing that her primary interest is not in any particular landscape, pastoral or otherwise, but rather in the happiness of people, which she here establishes as the foundational principle of her imagination. That is, Barbauld engages with pastoral in order to break its form and to disrupt the expectations that are often identified with it. Her interest in pastoral is identical to "Flora's breath" (15) in the spring: she wants to discover a "transforming power" (15) that will change "an icicle into a flower" (15), that will, in other words, change the world in such a way as to make human joy possible. On this view, her revisioning of pastoral is consistent with her wish to write prophetically about the need to transform the world.

The revisionary cast of Barbauld's pastoral imagination can be seen further in her portrayal of the retreat into which the pastoral muse invites Delia. Even as Delia is invited to "haste away" and "sweetly waste the careless day" among "gentle summits" and "the green slope," where the peasant farmer "winds the laboring plow," and to enjoy the "cool vales," "fresh verdure, and eternal green" (16) of the rural landscape, Barbauld broadens the reach of her pastoral imagination to encompass the early impact of the industrial revolution on Britain. Her interest, in particular, is in the network of canals that Francis Egerton, the Duke of Bridgewater, constructed to connect Worsley (where Bridgewater owned coal pits) and Manchester and Liverpool for the transport of coal.[13] The first of these two canals (which is Barbauld's focus of attention in the poem) was opened in 1761, and the second partially opened in 1767 and fully opened in 1773, the year that the first edition of Barbauld's *Poems* was published. The canals

Bridgewater's canal crossing the River Irwell at Barton in Lancashire

were marvels in engineering. One of them (which Barbauld describes in a note to the poem) included an aqueduct that traveled over the Irwell River, while, at Worsley, another was built underground, beneath the coal pits, from where coal was loaded directly onto the underground barges.[14]

At first glimpse, the canal system, as Barbauld describes it, is no intrusion on the pastoral scene but rather, indeed, a complementary scene of beauty: The "smooth canals, across th' extended plain, / Stretch their long arms to join the distant main" (16). But as she describes the labor spent in building the canals, the difference between agrarian and industrial experiences of the landscape becomes clear. And even though she still associates the industrial transformation of the land with wonder and awe and sees the possibilities of human happiness within this new landscape, she also recognizes that, within the modern world, there is a diminishing presence of unadulterated and idyllic realms of peace and ease. The organic beauty of the farmer following his "laboring plow" is countered in the construction of the canals, for example, by "the sons of toil," who "with many a weary stroke / Scoop the hard bosom of the solid rock" (17). Rather than working with the character and flow of the land, as the farmer does, industrial laborers push against it: "Resistless, thro' the stiff opposing clay, / With steady patience [they] work their gradual way" (17). The result of this negative relation to nature is the uncovering of a nightmare reality of hardship, as the laborers "compel the genius of th' unwilling flood / Thro' the brown horrors of the aged wood" (17). While the toil and horror of industrial labor ultimately produce an "alter'd landscape" of "magic scenes" that offer their own sort of pastoral pleasure and beauty and create "social plenty [that] circles round the land" (18), at the same time the cost is great, so much so that Barbauld even imagines, in her description of the underground canal, that the radical push against the living beauties of nature creates a man-made hell, much like the one that Milton imagines in *Paradise Lost*: "Now through the hidden veins of earth" the canals "flow, / And visit sulphurous mines and caves below" (17). She seems to understand that just beneath the surface of industrial accomplishment lies a hellish power hidden from public view but that is nevertheless real. Just as, in "Corsica," she had imagined liberty being purchased with blood, here she contemplates the meaning of modern industry that is bought by imposing hardship on the lives of laboring people and destroying the natural world.

Barbauld's verse commentary on Bridgewater's canals is marked by her understanding that human experience is vexed and multilayered, subject to error even if its aims and ends are noble. But she does not simply condemn the industrial and engineering feat of Bridgewater and his engineer, James Brindley, because of the ugliness and hardship of the labor entailed in building the canals. She recognizes these and presciently describes the satanic possibilities inherent in early industrialism—foreshadowing Blake's description of England's "dark Satanic Mills"—but at the same time she offers a cautious commendation of the gifts that "the guiding hand" (18) of man has been able to give to society by remaking nature and the nation.[15] Barbauld positions herself realistically in the midst of her geographical and social situation, recognizing that that situation is defined by an abiding tension between an idealistic view of the sorts of beauty there might be in the world and a distressing disappointment in the constraints imposed by historical necessity. But she does not seek to resolve this tension. Rather, she exposes it, describing equally the hopes and fears bound within it. Barbauld's pastoral imagination is self-contradictory but not with respect to poetic ideas or moods; the contradictions that she makes evident in the Bridgewater scene arise out of the realities of history, just as earlier in the poem she had described the contradictory relations between town and country.

A further matter, one that connects the Bridgewater section of the poem to its Warrington Academy section, bears consideration because it is important to Barbauld's portrayal of hope and progress. The description of the digging of the canals as well as of the students from the academy who become poets, scientists, civic leaders, ministers, and soldiers seems to wed Barbauld's visionary idealism to a middle-class sensibility. That is, she suggests that progress toward a better world will necessarily follow the path that is carved by the bourgeoisie. But although she recognizes the social authority of the bourgeoisie, that authority, as she shows through the course of the poem, is finally problematic, because the expansion of the bourgeois vision relies on principles that, for her, undermine too sharply the possibility for human betterment that the middle class promises. Thus, in the poem to a small degree, and more pointedly in the larger volume, Barbauld finds herself negotiating the class realities of her age and having to make a decision about whether she believes that the newly dominant structure of political and economic authority in an urban industrial Britain is consistent with her principles and can be harnessed to serve the purposes of her transformative poetic vision.[16]

Barbauld retains her pastoral sensibility as she pushes further into the particulars of the modern British landscape, using that sensibility as something of a tether for her idealism and a check against political and intellectual complexity, as she addresses in further detail the social and historical circumstances of her world. After completing her commentary on Bridgewater's canals, she turns her attention to education, focusing on "yon mansion," presumably Warrington Academy, which she describes as "the nursery of men for future years": "Here callow chiefs and embryo statesmen lie, / And unfledg'd poets short excursions try" (18).[17] Her engagement with the educational system at Warrington reflects the same mixture of idealism and realism that characterizes her portrayal of Bridgewater's canals. She recognizes the grand potential of the young men who attend the academy, but at the same time she understands the difficulties that even the best educated Dissenters historically have faced in an England that has refused them equal standing before the law. "Mersey's gentle current," she says, has been "too long / By fame neglected, and unknown to song" (18); but now, with Bridgewater and Brindley's engineering feats on view for all to see, and with the progressive education in the arts and sciences offered by Warrington Academy, which at the time was bringing in brilliant new tutors, such as Priestley, the Mersey "dares to emulate a classic tide" (18). In light of these advancements, exemplified particularly in the rich intellectual environment at Warrington, Barbauld allows herself freely to imagine "th' inquiring youth" wandering along the banks of the river, contemplating "the fair majestic form of truth" (19). For Barbauld, Warrington Academy is a pastoral intellectual retreat from a world scarred by resistance to progressive thought; it provides a culture of openness and freedom within which science and poetry, once "crush'd" by "bigot rage" (19), can explore ways of improving the lot of humanity.

Even as Barbauld's pastoral imagination guides her toward an idealized view of education, her realism obligates her to acknowledge that the peace and trust that characterize the academy, and the social ideals it promotes, will not easily find their way in the world, as the tutors and young students at Warrington must ultimately make their ideas known in a nation that resists truth: "So writhes the serpent round the bird of Jove; / Hangs on her flight, restrains her tow'ring wing, Twists its dark folds, and points its venom'd sting" (19).[18] The modern pastoral imagination, envisioning young men wandering along the river bank, freely and idealistically pondering large questions about life and truth, ultimately must come face to face with historical and social reality, which, in the present historical moment, Barbauld says, is marked by bigotry, abuses of power, and the desire to kill freedom of thought. In the face of this reality, hope for the future, if hope is to be possible, must be cautious and measured against a realm of circumstance that resists hope and all too often seeks to replace it with blind acceptance of the prevailing structures of authority and belief.

It is not surprising, then, that when Barbauld expresses hope in the face of restrictive and resistant circumstance, she is more careful than she had been in "Corsica," where, she was forced to confess, she had "read the book of destiny amiss." Now she says:

> Yet still (if aught aright the Muse divine)
> Her [truth's] rising pride shall mock the vain design;
> On sounding pinions yet aloft shall soar,
> And thro' the azure deep untravel'd paths explore. (19)

Here the dreams that arise from the blessings of pastoral retreat rest on a tenuous foundation ("if aught aright the Muse divine"). Barbauld insists that hope resides in the environs of Warrington Academy—"science smiles, the Muses join the train; / And gentlest arts and purest manners reign" (19)—but there is no guarantee that hope will triumph over the darker forces of the British nation that seek to poison human intellect and conscience. Such caution as she voices here serves as a guard against naiveté and as a reminder that self-reflection is always a necessary ingredient in dreaming, if dreams are to carry meaning in the world of lived experience. With this understanding in place, she allows her pastoral imagination room to dream that the Dissenting progressives at Warrington might effectively create a better world:

> Ye generous youth who love this studious shade,
> How rich a field is to your hopes display'd!
> Knowledge to you unlocks the classic page;
> And virtue blossoms for a better age. (20)

While the dream that she associates with "this studious shade" is accompanied by a sense of unease—"Oh golden days! Oh bright unvalued hours! / What bliss (did ye but know that bliss) were yours?"—at the same time she feels sufficiently confident to envision a world defined by "affections," "virtue," national honour, "spirits light," friendship," "honour," "smiles," "confidence," "vivid fancy," "simple truth," and "mental bloom" (20–21). If only briefly, the principles of pastoral retreat and prophetic engagement are interwoven, and their visionary force is powerful, yet at the same time tempered by realistic historical and political understanding.

In her portrayal of the young men at Warrington Academy, spending their days in a bucolic setting that encourages study and self-reflection, Barbauld imagines the possibility not simply of individual accomplishment but also (and more importantly) of national redemption. Looking into the future, she imagines "this little group" (21) of Warrington students being called by their country "from academic shades and learned halls, / To fix her laws, her spirit to sustain, / And light up glory thro' her wide domain!" (21). The freedom to pursue truth, about which she speaks in the immediately preceding passage, carries within in it a transformative social power capable of remaking the nation as a "friendly union" (21) that leaves "bigot rage" behind. In her dream of a Britain redeemed by truth, all individuals possess liberty of thought, and all contribute to the nation in a manner consistent with their conscience, temperament, and ability. Some will dedicate themselves to study in "the sequester'd shade" (21), while others, "impell'd by some resistless force, / O'er seas and rocks shall urge their vent'rous course" (22). Under the authority of truth, and enjoying the liberty of conscience, the world will unfold, not along the lines of power struggles and military conflict, but as a "friendly union." Imperialism and militarism will fade away under the Dissenting principles taught at Warrington, and in Barbauld's vision of the future Britain will become known globally as a nation of peace, truth, and nobility:

> Rich fruits matur'd by glowing suns behold,
> And China's groves of vegetable gold;
> From every land the various harvest spoil,
> And bear the tribute to their native soil:
> But tell each land (while every toil they share,

Firm to sustain, and resolute to dare,)
MAN is the nobler growth our realms supply,
And SOULS are ripen'd in our northern sky. (22)

In this new world, Britain will share the burden of labor with other nations and share the human spirit of mutual regard. All nations will be recognized and applauded for what they offer to humanity, and no nation will impose its sheer power on any other nation. The result will be a global community of peace and plenty.

Barbauld's vision of greatness, which arises from her faith in the powers of the unfettered mind bound only by its desire for truth, extends beyond national and global activity to include the more isolated pursuits of science, which, ultimately, also carry social significance. She pictures those individuals of a scientific bent studying "nature's changes, and her various laws" in an attempt to unlock their "hidden cause" (22). Freed from bigotry and superstition, the rational mind is able to hunt nature "to her elemental forms" (23). Such labors, she imagines, potentially will produce great human benefit, as science might discover a means "to quench disease and cool the burning wound" (23) and perhaps even to save human lives, calling "back the flitting soul" (23). Science, no less than commerce, when pursued in the service of truth and under the authority of liberty, is a human blessing whose discoveries possess the ability to ease the burden of human experience.

But Barbauld's visionary dream of a peaceful and rich future for Britain is not based in a belief that history can in truth ever come to an end, nor does it depict the end of history. The pastoral landscape onto which she invites Miss B is in fact a shifting and often troubling landscape. The further Barbauld and Miss B "retire" into the "rural scenes," the more those scenes look like that world from which they would retire. Industry, education, commerce, science: all of these constitute real dimensions of the modern world rather than a solitary pastoral zone of bliss and ease. Although Barbauld idealizes these human endeavors under the authority of her pastoral imagination so that her reader can glimpse their capacity for easing the burdens that humanity carries, history does not dissolve just because the various dimensions of human experience contain within them transformative possibilities. Ultimately, she shows, the troubling drag of historical reality returns and draws into its difficult currents even those who have been educated amid rural scenes and by tutors motivated by principles of human betterment and dedicated to the unfettered pursuit of truth.

Some young man coming out of Warrington, Barbauld says, will feel "the patriot passion" and will become a soldier who "with lips of fire shall plead his country's cause, / And vindicate the majesty of laws" (23). The result will be the return, or continuation, of British militarism: "This, cloth'd with Britain's thunder, spread alarms / Thro' the wide earth, and shake the pole with arms" (23). Moreover, as war shakes the globe, another young man who has become a poet will "to the sounding lyre his deeds rehearse." Recording the military exploits of the soldier leading his troops into battle, he will

> enshrine his name in some immortal verse,
> To long posterity his praise consign,
> And pay a life of hardships by a line. (23)

With this descriptive turn, it becomes clear that what began as a poem of pastoral retreat, from where Barbauld could imagine the capacity of Britain to remake the world along peaceful and productive lines, is finally forced to confront the hard reality that the nation equates patriotism with militarism, and that even the poet is mesmerized by war, and feels compelled to celebrate the accomplishments of the soldier who shakes the world with arms.

After acknowledging the entanglements of war and poetry in British history and society, Barbauld makes one last brief effort to counter the deep spirit of British militarism by describing another set of individuals, people of God, who "consecrate to higher aims, / Whose hallow'd bosoms glow with purer flames" (24). These individuals, she says, live with

> Love in their heart, persuasion in their tongue, [and]
> With words of peace shall charm the list'ning throng,
> Draw the dread veil that wraps th' eternal throne,
> And launch our souls into the bright unknown. (24)

While she admires those who live with their thoughts dedicated to God and who sincerely labor to "launch our souls into the bright unknown," the fact is that they do not speak to, or intervene in, the historical reality that circumscribes human experience. That is, they cannot offer any hope of change in this world but can only imagine that there is a world outside history that promises peace. This conventional religious vision, according to Barbauld, must be regarded as nothing more than yet another idealistic dimension of the middle-class worldview that defines and enlivens the activities of the poets, scientists, and soldiers of her day; it is not capable, on its own, of transforming human suffering into a lived experience of peace and plenty. Within the limited imaginations of these religious leaders, that is, the world is ultimately left just as it is. For Barbauld, such a position amounts simply to a negation of reality rather than a transformative engagement with it.

On this view, it is not surprising that, in the final verse paragraph of the poem, Barbauld, as she had done near the end of "Corsica," confesses failure. Although her retreat into a pastoral landscape enables her to envision wonderful opportunities for human betterment, which can become available when liberty serves as the foundational principle of society, the sad reality is that modern Britain has not embraced that principle. The result is that Barbauld is left facing two contradictory and unacceptable views that seem to define thought in the modern world and that she is unable to work past, intellectually and poetically: war and human degradation are inevitable; the only way to deal with this incontrovertible fact is by turning one's back on humanity and focusing all of one's hopes on heaven. On reaching this imaginative and intellectual impasse, Barbauld is compelled to stop writing once again to regroup her thoughts and reenliven her visionary aspirations:

> Such arduous themes require
> A master's pencil and a poet's fire:
> Unequal far such bright designs to pain,
> Too weak her colours, and her lines too faint,
> My drooping Muse folds up her fluttering wing,
> And hides her head in the green lap of spring. (24)

If she had previously sought refuge from failure in "the freedom of the mind," here she continues her embrace of pastoral as a poetic mode that allows self-reflection and meditation and that thus may enable, at some future time, a more productive engagement with history: an engagement that would offer the promise extended by religion but without abandoning the historical circumstances in which human experience is forever caught. By describing her muse hiding "her head in the green lap of spring," Barbauld is confessing failure for the moment yet also expressing hope that the visionary and prophetic imagination may ultimately find a viable, persuasive, and meaningful voice.

The relation between "Corsica" and "The Invitation" is defined most importantly by the different imaginative paths that Barbauld takes in her effort to map out the proper means of constructing a free and just society. "Corsica" imagines nationalist and democratic revolution as the necessary means for bringing about social transformation, while "The Invitation" imagines a utopian world arising out of the grand efforts of the bourgeoisie in the areas of industry and education. Both paths, however, lead to failure, at least partly because both rely on brute military force to effect their ends, thereby leaving the course of human history—despite the heroic spirit and grand accomplishments of those involved in remaking the world—defiled by human blood, and no amount of idealism or heroic and celebratory poetry can justify that defilement. The particular character of Barbauld's idealism insists on the fundamental incongruity between human freedom and the exercise of brute force; for her, militarism can never be the means by which a just and free society is constructed. And yet her visionary idealism cannot yet imagine a way past the debilitating realities of war.

CHAPTER THREE

Satire, Antipastoral, and Visionary Poetics

"Corsica" and "The Invitation" are powerful examples of the difficulty that Barbauld faces in her efforts to imagine a world transformed, oriented on the principles of peace, justice, and liberty. The force of the poems' resistance to her idealism—particularly in their portrayals of militarism and industrialism—in effect disrupts the linear representation of her visionary poetics, directing her attention away from the long poetic narrative toward a variety of shorter and thematically more divergent poems intended to examine smaller moments of human experience, presumably as a means of constructing a firmer poetic footing than she was able to achieve in "Corsica" and "The Invitation." By choosing pieces of experience for close examination and forgoing the attempt to assume the wide span of human desire and endeavor in her vision, Barbauld seems to suggest, she may be able to avoid the sorts of obstacles that she encountered in the first two poems in the volume. The subjects that she chooses after "The Invitation" are poetically more manageable, enabling her to maneuver her visionary interests and themes more nimbly and efficiently.

Barbauld begins her effort in this new direction with a cluster of poems—"The Groans of the Tankard," "On the Backwardness of the Spring 1771," "Verses Written in an Alcove," and "The Mouse's Petition"—that appropriate and recast the prophetic, political, and pastoral interests of the first two poems. In this cluster, Barbauld effectively disposes of her earlier grounding poetic assumptions by relying on satirical and antipastoral strategies to clear an imaginative ground for a reconsideration of visionary poetics and the means by which meaningful vision might be constructed. From this point forward, she abandons the grand Miltonic poetic model and begins to implement a visionary poetic strategy that reaches across poetic forms and metrical strategies and embraces a wide range of poetic subjects in an attempt to assure that her foundational principles are always in view and guiding her engagement with the world.

"The Groans of the Tankard," a mock-heroic poem about drinking alcohol, gathers up some of the subjects on which Barbauld had touched in "The Invitation"—students, poets—and uses these subjects as the basis for a satire on conventional prophecy:

Of strange events I sing, and portents dire;
The wondrous themes a reverent ear require:
Tho' strange the tale, the faithful Muse believe,
And what she says with pious awe receive. (25)

Her aim here seems to be designed to force the reader to reconsider the bourgeois idealism of "The Invitation," where students and poets had figured prominently, as well as the prophetic investments of "Corsica," not for the purpose of questioning the seriousness of these poems but rather their usefulness, or accuracy, as visionary representations of human history and human endeavor. In "Groans of the Tankard," Barbauld's muse seeks a distinctly new direction, as the poem meditates on the world of "strange events," telling a strange tale that leaves behind, at least for the moment, the serious assumptions that previously had led her visionary efforts astray (again, she had "read the book of destiny amiss"). Satire, as Barbauld uses it in this instance, has a cleansing effect on her visionary imagination.

The epigraph to "Groans of the Tankard" is taken from the thirteenth poem in the third book of Horace's *Odes*, and in translation it reads "worthy of sweet wine," making an apt and cogent introduction to the subject of Barbauld's poem. But the ode from which the epigraph is taken, of course, is not satirical; rather, it is a serious poem that presents a topic of considerable complexity, and thus it serves as a counterpoint to Barbauld's satire. The ode in its entirely reads as follows:

O Bandusian fountain, brighter than crystal,
Worthy of sweet wine, not lacking in flowers,
Tomorrow we'll honour you
With a kid, whose brow is budding
With those horns that are destined for love and battle.
All in vain: since this child of the playful herd will
Darken your ice-cool waters,
With the stain of its crimson blood.
The implacable hour of the blazing dog-star
Knows no way to touch you, you offer your lovely
Coolness to bullocks, weary
Of ploughing, and to wandering flocks.
And you too will be one of the famous fountains,

Now I write of the holm oak that's rooted above
The cave in the rock where your
Clear babbling waters run down.

Horace's ode is not unlike some other poems from which Barbauld selects her epigraphs, insofar as it sets a scene of idyllic beauty against a troubling scene of unrest. The young, playful goat described in the ode will be denied the natural course of its life, Horace says, as it is destined to be sacrificed, its blood pouring into and discoloring the pure waters of the spring—a description that recalls Barbauld's statement in "Corsica" that "heaven's best gift . . . must be bought with blood" (9). While in its depiction of a talking tankard the poem is as lighthearted as the innocent goat frolicking with its "playful herd" in Horace's ode, it is ultimately only a short step away from a reality as serious as life itself. Just as Barbauld often uses pastoral as a way of securing her poetic idealism, she also uses her epigraphs on occasion to remind herself and her reader that idealism (and even, in the case of "Groans of the Tankard," simple laughter) must always find its way along the path of difficult circumstance.

The ode from which the epigraph is taken informs Barbauld's poem in another way as well. In describing the Bandusian fountain as a flow of water that is "brighter than crystal," the ode anticipates the purity of the water that fills the tankard in the poem: "The TANKARD stood, replinish'd to the brink / With the cold beverage blue-ey'd Naiads drink" (26). But even as she calls attention to the similarities between the subject of her poem and the subject of Horace's ode, Barbauld at the same time uses these similarities as a basis for poetic (and satirical) complaint. While the Bandusian fountain, lamentably, is to become spoiled with the blood of sacrifice, the tankard is not and cannot be spoiled at all, and it laments the fact of its purity, as though absolute purity is a deficiency: "How chang'd the scene! For what unpardon'd crimes / Have I surviv'd to these degenerate times?" (26). Modernity, the tankard suggests, is so obsessed with purity that life becomes compromised, its joy lost. In the course of describing a past where beer flowed freely, the tankard compares the head of a draft of beer to the snow sitting atop Mount Etna, pays tribute to Ceres, the goddess of agriculture, and celebrates the rich resources of the East and West Indies. It also describes the alcohol of which it is now bereft as a socializing and ameliorative drink, better able than the purest water to spark conversations about religion, sports, and politics and to fuel the imagination with dreams of a changed world (27). It is no surprise, then, in a world where every year is "one long Lent" (29), that the tankard longs for a past that was less pure yet more joyful.

But the voice of the tankard, of course, derives from Barbauld's satirical imagination, and as such it should not be understood to represent visionary expression. Rather, it presents a perspective that contests the "Presbyterian's" (28) view of what constitutes a pure ideal. And that perspective, Barbauld says, is blind to the troubling conditions on which the tankard's understanding of pleasure is founded. Indeed, in telling the story of its own history, the tankard reveals the long history of British imperialism. Distinguishing itself from the fine teacups that come from China and that are used as containers for the tea and coffee that come from India and South America, the tankard imagines itself as a "nobler metal" that has been, and should be once again, put to "more generous use" by holding ale. That nobler metal, the tankard says, was dug from "the dark bowels of Potosi's mine" (28) in Bolivia and "endur'd the fiery test" (28) of being molded into a drinking vessel. In having the tankard tell this story of its history, Barbauld focuses squarely on its alien character and the violence inflicted on it in the process of becoming, finally, "stamp'd . . . with Britain's lofty crest" (28):

> Was I for this with violence torn away,
> And dragg'd to regions of the upper day?
> For this the rage of torturing furnace bore,
> From foreign dross to purge the bright'ning ore? (28)

While the tankard celebrates the force of British imperialism that has brought it to life and complains that its life is now being put to poor use as a container for water, at the same time it reveals the violence that accompanies the imperialist drive to take over foreign lands for the purpose of expropriating their natural resources. Barbauld's satirical imagination thus exposes the historical conditions that shape the tankard even as the tankard laments the conditions of the modern age.

The serious aim of the poem becomes clear in its final stanza, which still evinces Barbauld's satirical spirit but also reveals her much more profound interest in prophecy. The tankard stops speaking only when "an ancient Sibyl furrow'd o'er with years" (30) walks into the room to where the tankard rests on a table and shuts its lid. While this scene has a laugh-out-loud quality about it, especially in its suggestion of a wife coming into a tavern to announce control over a too-long-yabbering spouse, it also reminds the reader that satire is limited in its usefulness as a means of articulating the principles of visionary idealism. The tankard's idealism, while admirable (as is its expressed desire for joy in life), is marked, after all, by historical ignorance and even by the mistaken notion that joy must be bought with the obliteration (in this case, by drunkenness) of thought. It is no accident, on this view, that Barbauld has "an ancient Sibyl" silence the tankard, a sibyl, of course, being a prophetess. For Barbauld, the aim of poetry should not be simply to expose the limitations of the world (be it a world of Presbyterians or imperialists) but to engage in self-reflection and self-correction as well, thereby enabling a transformative rather than simply a descriptive vision.

If "Groans of the Tankard" revisits and revises the prophetic impulses of "Corsica," so "On the Backwardness of the Spring 1771" reconsiders the pastoral sensibilities of "The Invitation." Turning away from the satirical strategies of "Groans of the Tankard," "On the Backwardness of the Spring" paints a scene of visionary dreariness that contradicts the picture of pastoral beauty and the idea of forward progress that were presented in "The Invitation," offering instead an image of ugliness and backwardness in nature, thereby showing the extent to which nature and society are out of sync with each other and with themselves. This portrait of unnatural nature compels Barbauld, in subsequent poems, toward deeper visionary understanding, leading her to reflect more closely on the pastoral and middle-class sentiments on which she had previously grounded her hopes for the future.

The epigraph to "On the Backwardness of the Spring" is taken from Virgil's *Georgics*, book 4, which is about "the management of bees" (119). Its translation reads as follows: "Taunting summer for its lateness and the west winds for their delay" (125). The importance of the epigraph resides at least partly in the fact that it puts into play Barbauld's abiding interest in the vital relations between nature and the inescapable reality of society. While the epigraph itself speaks only about the natural world, the source from which it is taken keeps a steady focus on social experience, using the subject of bees as a way of sharpening that focus. At the beginning of book 4, for instance, Virgil describes the bees about which he is writing in explicitly social terms:

> In pursuance of my plan, I will now treat the divine gift of aerial honey. Look with favor, O Maecenus, on this part also of my work. I will place before you the marvelous exhibition of a miniature republic, and will tell of high-spirited chiefs, and, in due order, of the national character and the habits of the whole race, and of their pursuits, their tribes and their wars. Upon a commonplace subject is the labor spent, but not small will be the renown, should unpropitious deities permit me, and should Apollo, when invoked, bend an ear to my prayers. (119)

Virgil's commentary on managing bees is largely descriptive, though it reminds the reader that bees are "mighty souls in tiny bosoms" (122) and that their mightiness is manifested in their dedicated efforts to build workable social relations that ensure the well-being of the entire colony. Among bees, he says, there are different types of leaders and different types of followers, and it is important for bees to distinguish one from the other if their social world —the hive—is to be happy and productive. Bees, Virgil suggests, offer a picture from the world of nature that might teach human community how to strengthen its social relations.

But, while Virgil's commentary in book 4 is about bees, and Barbauld's epigraph is lifted from that commentary, Barbauld does not actually choose for her epigraph a line that describes bees. Rather, the epigraph is taken from Virgil's description of an old and poor man from Corycus who successfully establishes a productive hive. On land not rich enough to plow, the old Corycian plants "a few pot-herbs, and white lilies round them, vervain, and small-grained poppies" (124), laboring, like Blake's just man in the argument to *Marriage of Heaven and Hell*, to create a world of plenty out of a barren landscape, and eventually his labors are successful: "He equalled in the contentment of his mind the wealth of kings" (124). The old Corycian's contentment derives from his hard effort to transform nature, much as Bridgewater had labored to transform nature in "The Invitation." But there is an important difference: Virgil's poor man cultivates nature so that it will grow in harmony with the efforts of the labor that is invested in it, thereby producing in the laborer contentment that does not depend on wealth or political power; Bridgewater, on the other hand, while seeming to create a world of "social plenty," achieves his goals at the expense of nature and as a result of capital investments that set in motion the exploitation of human labor. The productive labor of the sort that the old Corycian pursues as he works through the cold of winter, "taunting the summer for its lateness," transforms the world and self, thereby exhibiting the prophetic realization of pastoral plenty in its fullest and most human form.

While "On the Backwardness of the Spring" exhibits the same impatience for summer that Virgil describes in his old Corycian, at the same time it observes a climatological difference between Britain now and Italy in Virgil's day. In the Italy of Virgil, Barbauld says, the winters were never so relentless and threatening as they are in the northern climes of Britain:

> Not thus she [spring] breath'd on Arno's purple shore,
> And call'd the Tuscan Muses to her bowers;
> Not this the robe in Enna's vale she wore,
> When Ceres' daughter fill'd her lap with flowers. (32)

Using climatological difference as a measure of historical difference, Barbauld depicts the British landscape as harsher than the Italian landscape, a fact that particularizes the social dimensions of the pastoral dream. The British pastoral dream, Barbauld says, is more strained and more difficult to sustain than Virgil's: "In vain the spring proclaims the new-born year, / No flowers beneath her lingering footsteps spring" (31). Thus, while her impatience for summer and the promise that it brings is no less intense than that of Virgil's Corycian and while her choice of epigraph suggests her willingness to work with the same degree of commitment as the Corycian, at the same time she struggles against a "dazzling waste" (32) that Virgil could not have known. A British pastoral vision, she suggests, where "indulgent nature... / Thro' opening skies [will] let genial sun-beams play" (32), requires a qualitatively different sort of poetic orientation, because the material circumstances of Britain are qualitatively different from those of the places associated with classical antiquity.

Barbauld's implicit claim that the geographical and historical features of pastoral vision must be specified and that the idealism of pastoral expression must be measured against the conditions under which it is produced if it is to be historically and socially meaningful helps to clarify the limitation of the vision presented in "The Invitation." The fact is that it is not always summer in Britain, and well-educated young men—even if they are educated in the Dissenting tradition offered by Warrington Academy—will not be able to transform the nation simply by means of their training and good intentions. The visionary aim of transforming the world, indeed, is more challenging than Barbauld had seemed to acknowledge in "The Invitation," and "On the Backwardness of the Spring" constitutes a poetic reminder that an imaginative engagement with "arduous themes" (24) requires a more thoughtful and sophisticated reckoning with the world than she has thus far been able to produce.

Following upon the stern lesson of "On the Backwardness of the Spring," "Verses Written in an Alcove" reclaims the more hopeful possibilities of pastoral, exhibiting Barbauld's belief that recognizing hardship and circumstance does not require relinquishing idealism. The poem revises the rhyme pattern (ABAB) and five-beat lines of its predecessor, offering instead four-beat lines that rhyme ABCB. The shorter lines, combined with fewer rhymes, create a lighter and more airy poetic feeling, which emphasizes the allure of "the rustic cell" (35) into which the poet and her friend Lissy intend to withdraw.[1] Moreover, in the poem Barbauld rejects prophecy as an imaginative investment and politics as a worthwhile human interest, viewing them (for the moment, at least) as inappropriate poetic concerns, calling instead on the muse of music, who plays on "her charming shell" (35), "her careless tresses / Loosely floating on the air" (36). This muse, she says, is a "smiling sister" of the other muses, and her carefree ways cause her to be "all unknown to fame and glory" (36), though her singing creates pastoral "strains of woodland harmony" (36) that, at least for now, the poet much desires.

The retreat that Barbauld celebrates, however, does not require naiveté, or innocence, as both the epigraph and poem attest. The epigraph, taken from the fourth poem in Horace's first book of odes, translates roughly as follows: "Now Cytherea leads the dance, the bright moon overhead," a line suggesting the musical interest of Barbauld's poem, as well as its evening setting, appropriate to a clandestine meeting between two women.[2] But the larger poem from which the epigraph is taken is more than a description of the joys of spring that arise from the loosening grip of winter; the new season that brings beauty and pleasure also presents a reminder that death and hardship are never far from human experience:

> Now Faunus claims his sacrifice among the shady trees,
> Lambkin or kidling, which soe'er he please.
> Pale Death, impartial, walks his round: he knocks at cottage-gate
> And palace-portal. Sestius, child of bliss!
> How should a mortal's hopes be long, when short his being's date?

The epigraph ushers the reader onto a scene that is marked in "Verses Written in an Alcove" by "the dewy green," "a flood of soften'd light" (33), and, generally, peace and pleasure, but at the same it directs the attentive and studious reader to the same sorts of tribulation that had been presented on the descriptive surface of "On the Backwardness of the Spring."

The poem, too, suggests the complexity of Barbauld's developing pastoral vision. For example, while "On the Backwardness of the Spring" concludes with an expressed desire for the "genial sun-beams," "Verses Written in an Alcove"—as evidenced in its epigraph and in its opening lines—is set during the evening hours ("Now the moon-beam's trembling luster / silvers o'er the dewy green" [33]), a setting that at first seems to offer a soft romantic picture and promise of pleasure-filled life but that is in fact situated on the edge of "the thick and twisted foliage" that "spreads the browner gloom of night" (33). The pastoral dream, from the beginning of the poem, exists alongside a terrible darkness and is accompanied by hardship, effectively illustrating its tenuousness. To get to "this rustic temple" (36) that marks a place of peace and ease, Barbauld must make her way, poetically, past "noisy clamour, / sick disgust and anxious fear; / Pining grief and wasting anguish" (34) and clear her imagination of "tales of sheeted specters/Rising from the quiet tomb" (34)—that is, of the gothic anxieties that reflect the psychological unease of modern British culture. More significantly, she must find her way past the heavy responsibilities of the prophetic and political imagination, which, even in a moment when pastoral desire is her motivating interest, haunt her poetic sensibility:

> Not the Muse who wreath'd with laurel
> Solemn stalks with tragic gait,
> And in clear and lofty vision
> Sees the future births of fate;
> Not the maid who crown'd with cypress
> Sweeps along in scepter'd pall,
> And in sad and solemn accents
> Mourns the crested hero's fall. (35–36)

If the poem is a celebration of the beauties of the natural world and of the peace that may be found therein, it is also a confession that idealism is always surrounded by rough experience and heavy responsibilities that press in relentlessly on the visionary imagination. Even the dullness, or ordinariness, of the poem's description of itself as "verses" takes some of the shine off of pastoral idealism. Barbauld clearly takes Horace's lesson to heart: despite its dream of beauty and ease, the pastoral world is never free of the spilling of blood and the presence of "pale Death."

Like Horace, her pastoral forbear, Barbauld understands that retreat—that Arcadia—is a dream rather than a real possibility and that to embrace pastoral as a pure and impenetrable zone of beauty and ease is to leave oneself without defenses against the inexorable realities of harsh circumstance, a conclusion that she seems to arrive at in "The Invitation," where she confesses her limitation of vision.[3] The rustic temple that Barbauld describes in "Verses Written in an Alcove" is a dream of momentary respite from the world; it is not an alternative to the world, nor is it truly independent of the world. Still, the portrayal of pastoral retreat is important because it exhibits the persistent and vital role of idealism in Barbauld's visionary poetics. Though in the modern world, the dream of peace and freedom has become "all unknown to fame and glory," pushed out of the light of day and relegated to a landscape overseen only by "the star of evening" (34), its vestigial presence nevertheless makes available a restorative energy that might provide a basis for transforming the world. On this view, even if the idea of pastoral as a place where "care can never cross the threshold" (34) is a myth, its dream of human happiness nevertheless sustains hope and makes possible the prophetic vision that injustice and self-interest can be overcome and the world remade on humane and just principles.

In "The Mouse's Petition," Barbauld returns to the theme of politics and uses the satirical mode as a means of correcting the political vision first set out in "Corsica." Eschewing for the moment the question of prophetic expression—that is, setting aside the interests of "Corsica" and "Groans of the Tankard"—she uses her satire here to localize and distill politics in such a way as to illuminate their pressing immediacy and to show thereby the inadequacies of simple-minded pastoral idealism as a visionary mode. In so doing, she does not abandon pastoral altogether, as subsequent poems in the volume attest, but rather places its idealism more securely than before within the material contexts and social currents of human experience. In this manner, she begins to establish a more complex and subtle ground for political thought and action. Moreover, even though the poem does not engage with prophetic or visionary subject matter, it sets out the principles that must serve as preconditions of prophecy.

"The Mouse's Petition" is one of Barbauld's most famous poems, at least partly because of the circumstances surrounding its composition.[4] But, as Margaret Anne Doody points out, the appeal of the poem also resides in its portrayal of political injustice and the outcry of the small mouse against that injustice. Doody makes the important point that on Barbauld's view, a just political system will be grounded in natural rights, compassion, and empathy. Although the poem is about a mouse, its lesson has universal and human importance, because "there is no felt difference between 'them' and 'us'—all is subsumed as 'we,' so the possibility of 'one transient gleam of day' allotted to all, man and animal, as the only portion of their existence, is truly included" (22–23). While the poem may be a criticism of animal experimentation, and, more generally, the misuses of science, it is also most certainly an appeal on behalf of compassion for all living things, an appeal that insists compassion should not be obstructed by any political system.[5]

But the poem's political sensibilities go even further in searching out productive ways of thinking about politics and political injustice. As Barbauld says in a note to the poem, Priestley uses his mouse for "making experiments with different kinds of air" (35). She uses the same mouse that Priestley uses in his scientific experiment for her own experiment with a different kind of air: poetry. Taking the image of the mouse as her poetic starting point, she ignores Priestley's concern with the quantitative knowledge that the study of a mouse might make available, focusing instead on the qualitative character of the mouse's life in an effort to discover and present the means by which human consciousness and human society (and, by extension, nature and the world of the mouse) might be remade.

To glimpse Barbauld's effort in this direction, it is necessary only to consider the shift in the mouse's pleadings through the course of the poem. In the beginning, the mouse pleads with Priestley ("Oh! hear" [37]) much the same way that Percy Shelley pleads with the West Wind in his famous poem from 1819, as though Priestley possesses godlike power, except that whereas Shelley identifies with the West Wind and wants to become wholly one with its power, the mouse sees itself as threatened by Priestley's power. Indeed, through the better part of the poem, the mouse perceives itself as a victim—"For here forlorn and sad I sit" (37)—and it fears "th' approaching morn, / which brings impending fate" (37). In describing the mouse, one of nature's most vulnerable creatures, in relation to power in this way, Barbauld effectively exposes the limitations of pastoral, questioning its use even as a temporary retreat; the dire situation of the mouse throws into negative relief the lines at the conclusion of "Verses Written in an Alcove" in which Barbauld's narrator worships "the star of evening" and "this rustic temple" where she and Lissy temporarily reside. The mouse's rustic temple is not a retreat but a "trap," and the evening is nothing more than a bleak reminder of an "approaching morn" that promises harsh experiments that will result in death: pastoralism cannot explain or prevent this hard reality. Within the context of Barbauld's satire, the mouse's victimization exposes the gross injustice of the brute force controlling its life—it exposes the horrific reality of Priestley's "strong oppressive force" (38)—and deepens the reader's understanding of the immoral dimensions of this force by connecting its abuse of the mouse to a vision that stands at the center of Christian understanding: "Oh! do not stain with guiltless blood / Thy hospitable hearth" (38). If only for a moment, the mouse is Christ-like, an innocent victim of those who lack the ability to value life for its own sake.

But Barbauld's vision here is not purely Christian, nor is the poem only a satirical depiction, from a victim's perspective, of abusive power. As the mouse's petition unfolds, its pleading and tone modulate in such a way as to create a wide-ranging and subtle representation of the relations between the powerful and the powerless. For example, early in the poem the mouse argues that acts performed by the powerful against the powerless do not constitute the betterment of life; that is, Priestley's entrapment of the mouse for the purpose of experimentation has won "a prize so little worth" (38). While the sentiment here retains the Christian understanding voiced in earlier lines, the argument is essentially political, not religious, as it bears on principles of order among the living in the world and not simply on questions of moral guilt or innocence. The political dimension of the mouse's petition is elaborated further in Barbauld's use of the mouse to state that principles of order in relation to the exercise of power are directly connected to matters of economics and social class. As the mouse puts the matter, "Let nature's commoners enjoy/The common gifts of heaven" (38). Such a position rejects the conception of power as a binary relation between the great and small in favor of a nonhierarchical vision of a shared, communal existence that is unthreatened by arbitrary force, whether it is physical or economic in nature.

In subsequent sections of the poem, Barbauld gathers up these religious and economic principles into a larger set of concerns in such a way as to show the multidimensional character of her vision. The views promulgated in the mouse's petition extend into the areas of idealist and materialist philosophy. First, anticipating the Wordsworth of the "Intimations Ode," the mouse reminds Priestley of "the well-taught philosophic mind" that "to all compassion gives;/Casts round the world an equal eye,/And feels for all that lives" (39). Further, not only is the mouse's conception of the mind fundamentally sympathetic to all life; as a universal principle it may move through all objects, animate and inanimate, shifting "thro' matter's varying forms" (39). That is, for Barbauld's mouse, there is, as Coleridge puts it some years later in "The Eolian Harp," but "one Life within us and abroad" (101) and, for Barbauld, that one life is inherently good, compassionate, and bound by equality of feeling for "all that lives," and for all existence.[6] The failure to recognize this fundamental principle, the mouse says, allows for the sort of arbitrary exercise of power engaged in by Priestley, and, in turn, this single act of arbitrary power can potentially result in other such acts. The mouse warns Priestley about the dangers of creating other tyrannical minds like his own: "Tremble lest thy luckless hand/dislodge a kindred mind" (39). Finally, even if ancient philosophers are wrong about the universality of the compassionate mind, and if life is no more than a random admixture of particles, the argument against the exercise of arbitrary power does not change, because, the mouse says, in an arbitrary and existential world that will ultimately be swallowed by darkness, life holds special status as a fleeting presence that must be cherished:

> Or, if this transient gleam of day
> Be *all* of life we share,
> Let pity plead within thy breast
> That little *all* to spare. (39)

If there is no immortality, then life, however small, still constitutes *all* and, against a backdrop of darkness, deserves the same degree of compassion, pity, and sympathetic feeling *as if there were*. Whether one subscribes to a Christian, idealist, or materialist view of life, whether one views life as a perdurable reality or as a fleeting element in a purely material world, the only reasonable conclusion that can be drawn, if one assumes that life has any value, is that all of life has value and should be *revered as life*.

This line of argument is important for Barbauld because it makes available a radically different way of understanding power. If, as the mouse seems to claim, all life is to be valued, that means that the tyrant's life, too, must be valued. And, indeed, at this point in the poem (that is to say, after the mouse's flight of philosophical commentary) the mouse's petition turns from a self-interested plea for mercy into a blessing on Priestley's head:

> So may thy hospitable board
> With health and peace be crown'd;
> And every charm of heartfelt ease
> Beneath thy roof be found.
> So, when destruction lurks unseen,
> Which men, like mice, may share,
> May some kind angel clear thy path,
> And break the hidden snare. (40)

At last the mouse is able to see beyond its own predicament and to speak with love in its heart, even for the well-being of its oppressor. While the mouse remains trapped under Priestley's tyrannical authority and may face death once the sun rises, it has nevertheless broken free of the debilitating mindset that previously had reduced it to fear and pleading.[7] The blessing that the mouse bestows on Priestley is a liberating gesture that signifies the best of which the mouse—and life—is capable. For Barbauld, as the volume bears out, adopting this sort of positive and compassionate stance toward power is the only meaningful way to approach it if life and the world are to be transformed. Moreover, with respect to the volume itself, just as the mouse has liberated itself from the only true trap in which it was caught—"the hidden snare" of failed vision—so Barbauld must liberate herself from the temptation—seen in "Verses Written in an Alcove"—to succumb to the myth that pastoral idealism offers a viable alternative to the world in which the mouse and Priestley find themselves. Barbauld's view here eventually becomes central to her understanding of Christian belief, as "Hymns" demonstrates.

One final set of comments on "The Mouse's Petition" will help to clarify the nature of the vision toward which Barbauld is moving. While earlier poems feature epigraphs lifted from Virgil's eclogues, this poem's epigraph comes from the *Aeneid*, a fact that in itself may indicate her growing confidence in her poetic vision, as she moves from a pastoral to a prophetic source material to guide her thought. The specific line, in translation, reads as follows: "Spare the conquered, and subdue the proud." The line, spoken by Anchises, the father of Aeneas, is taken from book 6, which describes Aeneas's journey to the underworld to speak with his deceased father, who describes for Aeneas the future of Italy. The passage from which the line is taken is descriptively important because it sketches the future of Rome's history. But the passage also includes a prophetic warning in its insistence on relinquishing the use of brute force as a way of organizing society or dealing with people. Describing Rome's future rulers and noting the bloodshed that will accompany them, Anchises warns: "My sons, don't inure your spirits to such wars, / never turn the powerful forces of your country on itself: / You be the first to halt, you, who derive your race from heaven: / hurl the sword from your hand, who are of my blood!" He concludes:

> Others (I can well believe) will hammer out bronze that breathes
> with more delicacy than us, draw out living features
> from the marble: plead their causes better, trace with instruments
> the movement of the skies, and tell the rising of the constellations:
> remember, Roman, it is for you to rule the nations with your power,
> (that will be your skill) to crown peace with law,
> to spare the conquered, and subdue the proud.

The vision of power that is set out here lays the groundwork for the conception of power set out in "The Mouse's Petition," and it is distinct from the power associated with Priestley, insofar as its foundational principle is peace rather than self-interest or abusive treatment of others. That principle, in Virgil's poem, begins with Anchises' discomfort with war ("My sons, don't inure your spirits to such wars") and is accompanied by his understanding that courage means being willing to "be the first to halt." This sentiment anticipates a comment made by Liberty to Brutus in Yearsley's epic poem "Brutus": "To yield is to deserve a throne" (17). For Virgil, and for Barbauld, to yield is a sign that one belongs to heaven. As Anchises put it: "You, who derive your race from heaven: hurl the sword from your hand, who are of my blood!"

The epigraph and the context within it appears raise a number of issues that bear on the particulars of "The Mouse's Petition." Within the context of Barbauld's poem, Priestley is the proud one who mindlessly wields violent power and who therefore must be subdued. And that process of subduing the powerful, as

Barbauld states clearly, and as the lines from the *Aeneid* state as well, begins with a reimagining of how one can best position oneself in the face of tyrannical authority, if peace is one's ultimate goal. Barbauld's mouse figuratively follows the prophetic warning of Anchises: he hurls his sword from him. That is, he relinquishes the mindset that would position him in an immovable oppositional relation to tyranny—a position that would make him subject to pride and self-interest—until only the mouse or tyrant would be left standing. Rather than waiting on the tyrant to show pity or to surrender, the mouse (consistent with Anchises' prophetic insight) initiates its own liberation by expressing the fullness of its sympathetic heart and imagination, showing that it has learned the single most important lesson about power: subservience carries transformative possibility. Were the relations governing the operation of power reconceptualized along these lines, Barbauld suggests, it would then become possible to remake the world in such a way that pride, self-interest, and the exercise of tyranny would dissolve and peace would become the law of the land.

On this view, although the poem is a political satire that uses the conventional political means of the petition to state its case, at the same time it radically changes the idea of politics by a prophetic and visionary intervention into the modern conception of power. The poem's brilliance derives both from its use of the small mouse—and its different kind of air—to voice Barbauld's hopeful, universal vision and from its juxtaposition with the great epic of Virgil. From Barbauld's perspective, it seems, if visionary poetics is to carry transformative authority, it must engage all (to use the mouse's small word) of life, from its most (ostensibly) insignificant dimensions to its grandest dreams. And poetic practice must always be ready to cross the lines from small to large subject matter and from satire to pastoral and prophecy, as well.

CHAPTER FOUR

Personal Life and Visionary Poetics

Barbauld's cluster of satires and pastorals (or, perhaps more accurately, antipastorals) is followed by several poems that turn ostensibly to even smaller subjects, presumably in an effort to ground more securely the human focus of her visionary poetics. These poems—"To Mrs. P——," "Characters," "On a Lady's Writing," "Hymn to Content," and "To Wisdom"—address a range of issues dealing with personal life, individual imagination, desire, and, generally, the shaping realities of personhood. They are neither explicitly prophetic nor pastoral but rather personal, focusing on what John Stuart Mill would call in his *Autobiography* "the internal culture of the individual" (143). Much like Yearsley in the 1790s, Barbauld, in these poems, writes under the assumption that social and abstract philosophical notions are of little significance unless they make space for—indeed, embrace—the lived reality of individual people. Similarly, prophecy and pastoral are meaningful poetic modes only to the extent that their visions arise from and touch human experience. For Barbauld, intellect and poetry are a human endeavor, and visionary poetics, if it is to be truly transformative, must gather up all of the various threads of human life into this endeavor, including personal life. These explicitly personal poems are a reminder to Barbauld's reader, and (perhaps) to Barbauld herself, of this important fact.

Addressed to Joseph Priestley's wife, Mary, "To Mrs. P——" is, on its face, a rather lighthearted poem written simply to amuse Barbauld's friend and "to cheat the lonely hour" (48). But, as is often the case with Barbauld's poetry, the poem's lightheartedness is not indulged at the expense of serious thought or poetic sophistication. For one thing, the poem is an ekphrastic commentary on "some drawings of birds and insects" (41), and this commentary brings serious questions of a human and political nature to bear on a set of descriptive illustrations. This poetic strategy marks a considerable change of direction for Barbauld, who, earlier in the volume, had based her poems on historical, social, natural, fanciful, and personal situations. She now offers a poetic meditation on art (indeed, art from her own hand) by crafting a metalevel of imaginative observation, as it were, and constructing a framework for poetic, or artistic, self-reflection—for examination, that is, of the proper reach and focus of the creative imagination. On this view, "To Mrs. P——" is a poem that explores who Barbauld is as a poet and what her proper interests and subject matter should be.

Although the poetic strategy of "To Mrs. P——" suggests the seriousness and complexity of the poem, Barbauld also at the same time carefully sets parameters for her meditation that give direction to her imagination, and in so doing she discloses her conclusions about poetic and visionary endeavor. These parameters are seen clearly in that fact that she grounds her poem in a cherished dimension of personal life, from which she does not waver and that assures that her vision will not become lost in the outer reaches of imaginative flight. Returning to an idea that had been set out at the beginning of "The Invitation" (13) but had been lost through the course of that poem, "To Mrs. P——" is framed by the idea of friendship, beginning with the observation that "friendship, better than a Muse inspires" (41) and concluding with the insistence that she treasures the friendship of Mrs. Priestley above all else (49). Friendship is both an anchor and a guide for Barbauld's imagination, a sort of warm-blooded reminder (situated as bookends to the poem) to avoid visionary abstraction even as she ponders the nature and reach of her artistic talents. Any imaginative flight toward political or prophetic vision, Barbauld reminds herself, must be guided by the first and final governing principle of human experience; Barbauld here uses the word "friend" to represent that principle.

The epigraph to the poem, lifted from Alexander Pope's "Epistle to Mr. Jervas" and modified to make it an address to Mary Priestley, points the direction of Barbauld's interest in the relations between poetry and the visual arts.[1] Moreover, the larger context of Pope's poem helps account for the shape her conception of friendship and visionary poetics takes as well as for her choice of poetic strategy. The lines from Pope, in their original form, that Barbauld chooses for her epigraph—"The kindred arts shall in their praise conspire, / One dip the pencil, and one string the lyre" (41)—constitute a descriptive gesture toward the subject of her poem: the relations between poetry and the visual arts. But Barbauld's modification of the lines ("The kindred arts *to please thee* shall conspire") suggests a deeper concern as well: the importance of pleasure in matters of the imagination. Indeed, the significance she attaches to imaginative pleasure not only points to a theme in "To Mrs. P——" but also to a growing preoccupation in subsequent poems. Barbauld's immersion here in "the kindred arts," along with her reminder that art is about pleasure, seems to awaken her to an understanding that the core goal of art (even an engaged or transformative poetics) must be to give pleasure if it is to be humanly meaningful. Thus, she adopts a lighthearted tone (in the epigraph and in the poem) in her verbal descriptions of visual sketches of birds and insects, not to suggest that her poem is of little significance but rather to enact a vital artistic principle in which she is becoming invested.[2]

The broader context of Pope's epistle influences Barbauld's imagination as well, in ways both large and small. For example, just as Barbauld describes her art as an effort "to cheat the lonely hour," so Pope says to Jervas near the beginning of the epistle, "How oft' in pleasing tasks we wear the day,/ While summer suns roll unperceiv'd away?" (249). For Barbauld and Pope, art is a meaningful way to find, or create, purpose in a world and life that are constantly slipping away. Moreover, and perhaps most tellingly, Barbauld lifts from Pope the idea of friendship, which for both poets seems to signify the fundamentally social nature of human life, insofar as even the most personal endeavors, such as making visual and verbal art, require human contact and exchange. Just as Barbauld insists on the vital importance of friendship in her life ("friendship, better than a Muse inspires"), so Pope begins his poem with an appeal to friendship: "This verse be thine, my friend, nor thou refuse/ This, from no venal or ungrateful Muse" (249). The true muse resides with human social exchange; it is not an abstract spirit. With friendship and the imagination as secure foundational principles in life, the burdens of human experience become potentially lighter, and laughter and joy become possible. Referring to Jervas's work as an artist, Pope writes:

> New graces yearly, like thy works, display;
> Soft without weakness, without glaring gay;
> Led by some rule, that guides, but not constrains;
> And finish'd more thro' happiness than pains! (250)

An additional set of comments about the relations between "To Mrs. P——" and "Epistle to Mr. Jervas" may help to clarify the direction of Barbauld's vision in *Poems*.[3] Pope concludes the epistle with the comment that "the kindred arts" will happily work to keep alive the reality of beauty for future ages. But, he says, even if he and Jervas are wildly successful in their endeavors, in the end they will win little for themselves: "Alas! how little from the grave we claim?/ Thou but preserv'st a Face and I a Name" (251). These lines hint at an inescapable darkness, as they lament the ultimate triumph of time over the lives of Pope and Jervas. At the same time, however, the lines instruct that the arts and imagination are not to be pursued for the purpose of self-aggrandizement; rather, artistic endeavor ought to be an emblem of the social intercourse that makes life worth living, like Pope's celebration of Jervas in his epistle in which their "fate and fame" are vitally linked: "So mix'd our studies, and so join'd our name" (249). The resulting product of this social bond is beauty, found both in paintings and poems, as well as in friendship. Barbauld explains Pope's meaning in the conclusion of her own poem, expressing her hope that Amanda (Mrs. Priestley) will find pleasure in Barbauld's writing and drawings. If she does, Barbauld says, this will be reward enough, as her goal in pursuing the arts is not personal fame but rather creating a source of pleasure for another human being: "I envy not, nor emulate the fame / Or of the painter's, or the poet's name" (49). Even if fame were to come her way, she says, "Yet far, far dearer were the name of a FRIEND" (49). Pope and Barbauld celebrate idleness, art, pleasure, and imagination as social virtues capable of drawing people more closely and meaningfully into one another's company.[4]

Finally, in one important respect Barbauld stands at odds, tactically, with Pope. While Pope writes poetically to Jervas for the purpose of celebrating that artist's work and imagination, Barbauld (according to the subtitle of her poem: "WITH SOME DRAWINGS OF BIRDS AND INSECTS") focuses her poem only on her own drawings, thereby seeming to narrow, as it were, the range of her interest.[5] In fact, however, even as her poem is a sort of narrowing of vision to a consideration of her own creative work, at the same time it marks a broadening of visionary interest. In drawing upon Pope—including Pope's use of the heroic couplet—who in turn draws on John Dryden's translation of Charles-Alphonse du Fresnoy's *The Art of Painting*, which includes comments on the relations between poetry and painting, she relies on a broad literary and critical history to sharpen, deepen, and articulate her particular visionary principles. Just as she says near the beginning of her poem, for example, that "painting and poetry are near allied," so Fresnoy says (in Dryden's prose translation) by way of beginning his work that "Painting and Poetry are two Sisters, which are so like in all things, that they mutually lend to each other both their Name and Office" (3). The parallel here is not coincidental; Fresnoy's comments are the beginning of a meditation on visionary art that is central to Barbauld's imagination. In describing the sister arts, Fresnoy says that "both of them, that they might contribute all within their power to the sacred Honours of Religion, have rais'd themselves to Heaven, and, having found a free admission into the Palace of *Jove* himself, have enjoy'd the sight and conversation of the Gods. . . . From Heaven they take their passage through the World" (3–4). Barbauld is indebted to this visionary insight; it provides a confirmation of her own poetic convictions about the importance of visionary imagination, But she also draws on Pope as a kind of poetic point of leverage for transforming Fresnoy. While Fresnoy's understanding of vision begins with the artist's devotion to heaven, from where visionary insight is received and brought back to "the World," Barbauld offers a more materialist argument, beginning her visionary flight with the pleasures and warmth of friendship and moving outward from there toward heaven. In effect, she uses Fresnoy to enlarge Pope's vision, even as she uses Pope to localize Fresnoy's vision, and in the process she constructs her own unique vision.[6]

In beginning her account of the drawings that she has produced of birds and insects, Barbauld restates her opening comment that "the kindred arts two sister Muses guide" by saying that painting and poetry are "in friendly union join'd" (42). Now, however, despite this acknowledgment, she makes clear at the same time that, for her, poetry is the "deeper art" (42). Indeed, while painting "bids a gayer, brighter world arise" (42), thereby suggesting its capacity for simple idealism, poetry carries within it a power that touches the multiple layers of human experience. Poetry, she says,

> By well set syllables, and potent sound,
> Can rouse, can chill the breast, can sooth, can wound;
> To life adds motion, and to beauty soul,
> And breathes a spirit through the finish'd whole. (42)

For Barbauld, poetry is a potentially transformative medium of expression that is capable of enlarging or diminishing human experience, of aiding or harming life. The pursuit of poetry, therefore, carries with it great responsibility. But that responsibility is worth the risk that comes with writing poetry, because, she says, it is a potentially life-creating and life-affirming art that, without clouding over the hardships of experience, draws on rhythm and sound to awaken the slumbering body and soul to the potential reality of a unified beauty and spirit in life. Unlike painting, which is capable of sketching beautiful idealisms, poetry is a visionary force that carries within it the power to change the world. The challenge facing Barbauld in the volume is finding a way to capture and use that potential without falling prey either to limited vision, as she had done in "Corsica" and "The Invitation," or to simple description.

The caution with which Barbauld now proceeds in pursuing this "deeper art" is seen in her choice of subject matter in "Mrs. P——" (birds and insects) and in her poetic reminder to herself that, with this subject matter, she is turning to "humbler themes" (42). But if caution is needed to ensure that her poetry retains a meaningful focus, it does not mean that in the poem Barbauld sets aside her seriousness of purpose; indeed, she continues here to struggle toward a purposeful and transformative visionary poetics, though she does so in a different way, in a manner that seeks a proper balance between idealism and material circumstance. This task is made easier, presumably, by the subject matter, which does not require historical perspective and which, therefore, allows Barbauld to focus her attention more steadily on the visionary principles toward which she is working. By writing about birds and insects, she is able to think imaginatively about nations and violence and imperialism—about human experience—without becoming too weighed down by historical specificity, for which she would be obliged to account. Her task, moreover, is also made more meaningful by her connecting the representation of her subject matter to her friendship with Mary Priestley, which helps to ground her larger ideas on a particular and personally important human reality.

While in some respects Barbauld's poetic decision to write about birds and insects draws on a common literary strategy of the age, wherein writers often used creatures from the animal kingdom as a defensive and distancing mechanism as they wrote about society, politics, or history (for example, Bernard Mandeville's famous *Fable of the Bees* [1714], which uses bees as a way of talking about British politics), at the same time Barbauld takes this strategy an important step further by writing about drawings of creatures from the animal kingdom. This poetic strategy effectively locates her literary endeavor wholly within the realm of the arts, with the world, at least ostensibly, placed at a distant remove. Her defensive gesture is therefore not only more protective than, say, Mandeville's; more importantly, her concern with visionary poetics is fully distilled within the labors and products of the imagination: the poem, as it were, appears to be a meditation on art rather than on the world. At the same time, however, Barbauld pursues her interpretative intervention into the realm of art in such a way as to assure that her interest in the world is not compromised: although she is writing about pictures of birds and insects, her poetic interpretation of the drawings is explicitly political in nature. Immediately after describing her first subject as "the feather'd tribe" (42) of birds, for example, she refers to the different species of birds as "various nations" (42) that "plough with busy wing the peopled air" (42). These various species reflect all of the attributes and characteristics of human nations and individual people, as some scavenge for food, others "dip their crooked beak in kindred blood" (43), and still others "gather round [man's] hospitable door" to "find protection there / From all the lesser tyrants of the air" (43). On this view, Barbauld's decidedly strong move into the inner reaches of the arts is at the same time a strong move into the workings of the world, and this strategy helps to clarify and give direction to her interest in the visionary.

Barbauld's descriptions of birds are explicitly rooted in questions about society and the power relations that operate therein.[7] In describing her drawing of an eagle, for instance, she observes that "with cruel eye" he "premeditates the war, / And marks his destin'd victim from afar" (44), thereby verbally constructing the visual illustration of the eagle as something of a conquistador, carrying out violent and imperialistic actions in other lands for the purpose of enriching the homeland. As Barbauld puts it in her description, the eagle descends

> in a whirlwind to the ground,
> His pinions like the rush of waters sound;
> The fairest of the fold he bears away,
> And to his nest compels the struggling prey.
> He scorns the game by meaner hunters tore,
> And dips his talons in no vulgar gore. (44)

Unlike the vulture, which feeds on carrion, the eagle directs its killing power only against living creatures and thereby assures itself of the richest reward (warm blood). The violent horror that Barbauld associates here with imperialism is sharpened and complicated by her description of the harmless pheasant, whose glory is not associated with violence but with beauty: "With lovelier pomp along the grassy plain/The *silver* PHEASANT draws his shining strain" (44). When this bird is caught in a trap, she says, "he lowers his purple crest, and inly pines;/The beauteous captive hangs his ruffled wing,/Oppressed by bondage, and our chilly spring" (44). The pheasant, in effect, for all its beauteous glory, is the object of imperialistic violence, or oppression, rather than an agent of it, insofar as the pheasant is not native to Britain but rather was captured and brought to the country from Asia Minor to be used (initially) for food.[8] (In subsequent times, pheasants were also used in England for gaming purposes and were also captured and kept as pets.) The pheasant, like the mouse in "The Mouse's Petition," becomes, for Barbauld, an emblem of the beautiful, harmless, and helpless victim of an arbitrary power that resides at a distant remove from its natural home and its own kind.

In her portrayal of the eagle and the pheasant, Barbauld captures the violence as well as the jarring disregard for the native landscape associated with the brutal force of imperialism. While her initial description of the many types of birds suggests the richness and diversity of the avian species (43), her focus on the eagle and pheasant allows her to home in on the power dynamics at the center of the modern world of people. The eagle and pheasant occupy positions at the extremes of the social spectrum—at one end is the ruling elite that secures and extends its power without regard to the amount of blood spilt in that effort and at the other is the ruled that gently and submissively suffers the offenses against it—and the distance between them seems to promise nothing less than further bloodshed, sorrow, and oppression. Like "Corsica" "To Mrs. P——" exhibits the futility of resistance against an overwhelming force of oppression.

At the same time, the poem searches for a way beyond the binary extremes—aggressive power, submissive suffering—that seem to define large segments of both the avian and human worlds. And that search leads Barbauld to a consideration of poetry in the form of birdsong. In looking beyond the eagle and pheasant, she discovers "unnumber'd tribes" (45) of birds that are free rather than entrapped and happy rather than sorrowful; they "tune the lay" and "pour out all their little souls in song" (45). These birds, Barbauld says, are "a firm united band" (45); they are "congregated nations" that "wing their way / In dusky columns o'er the trackless sea" (45), extending their reach as far as Australia ("In clouds unnumber'd" the birds annually "hover o'er / The craggy Bass, or Kilda's utmost" [45]) as they "pursue the circling sun's indulgent ray" (45). The importance of these birds, as a corrective to the somber realities reflected in the lives of the eagle and pheasant, is that their flight and song reflect the possibility of freedom that may be associated with visionary poetry. Indeed, in concluding her description of the song birds by associating them with the sun, Barbauld evokes the spirit of Apollo, the god of poetry and prophecy, thereby suggesting the possibility of breaking through the binary and destructive structures of existence reflected in the experiences of the eagle and pheasant. Invested consistently with human significance (they are described as "tribes," "little souls," and "a firm united band," and they are given the power of agency when Barbauld says that they "tune the lay" [45]), the songbirds take on the identity of poets following the prophetic spirit of the sun, and in following that spirit they exemplify the freedom and joy that are the ideal of meaningful existence.

Had Barbauld concluded "To Mrs. P——" with the description of the songbirds, the poem could be viewed as her final step toward a prophetic vision that is defined by a purely idealistic sensibility. But, of course, the description of the birds constitutes only half the poem; in the second half Barbauld occupies her imagination with a consideration of lowly insects that do not follow the sun but rather hibernate through the winter months as they await the coming of spring. The picture here describes a different kind of darkness and difficulty from that which Barbauld associates with the eagle and pheasant. But, even here, she searches in the animal kingdom for a way to negotiate hardship and transform it into hope. The insects are "entomb'd" in a "dark retreat," sleeping among "their sordid spoils" (46). Still, their grim existence through the cold winter months carries a spiritual association. In Barbauld's characterization, the winter sleep is a "lazy sabbath" (46) for the insects; indeed, the insects themselves, in their tomb, are invested with a Christian significance, as Barbauld emphasizes the fact that they arise from their deaths to find new life. And, as she does with the songbirds, she describes the newly discovered lives of the insects in prophetic terms, though here there is a clearer emphasis (initially, at least) on the circumstantial hardships from which the newborn spirit arises; fighting against the darkness and cold of their winter death, "at length assur'd, they catch the favouring gale, / And leave their sordid spoils, and high in Ether sail" (46). Once freed from winter's dark gloom, the insects become very much like the songbirds: free and happy, embodiments of the joyous possibilities of life. To capture the grand scale of the insects' accomplishment and the spirit with which that accomplishment is associated, Barbauld compares the newly arisen insects to a scene from Tasso's *Jerusalem Delivered* ("So when Rinaldo struck the conscious rind / He found a nymph in every trunk confin'd" [46]), a comparison that not only humanizes the great feat that she describes in the insect world but also associates that feat with the powers of the poetic imagination.[9] The now-free insects, who live "their little hour" in "pleasure" and "play" (47), inspire, like the songbirds, a spirit of pure idealism; they are an entomological example of the sort of life of which the visionary imagination can only dream: "All spring their age, and sunshine all their day" (47).

Again, however, Barbauld suggests that pure idealism is a trap, or at best a partial truth, even if it is imagined in Christian terms. Thus, she is careful to explain that although she can imagine a life of pure joy and pleasure for insects, such a life of unmediated happiness is unavailable to man, who is "the child of sorrow": "His course with toil concludes, with pain began" (47). It is not that the pleasure of the songbirds and insects is a counterexperience to human reality or that human life is an experience of pure despair; rather, for Barbauld, human life is always an experience of conflict, which means that the struggle to discover and articulate idealistic principles is never neatly resolved. Once the insects find their way out of the tomb of winter, their lives are pure pleasure; the complicated circumstances of human life, with its dreams of unfettered joy constantly in conflict with the pressing reality of despair and hardship, guarantee that people never entirely leave the tomb and enter a sphere of pure pleasure. Like Keats after her, Barbauld views life as a school, wherein idealism is always shaped and mediated by material reality: "And in misfortune's school this lesson learn, / Pleasure's the portion of th' inferior kind; / But glory, virtue, Heaven for Man design'd" (47).[10] On this view, the example of the songbirds and the insects is crucial for showing the possibility of happiness and freedom in the natural world, for holding out to the human imagination, that is, an idealism toward which the poet might strive, even if that idealism will always be threatened by the harsh circumstances and difficult struggles that define much of human experience. Because the goals of human life are grander and more complex, the struggle is more difficult and riddled with hardship.

Following a brief description of several different types of insect (such as fireflies that "shoot like living stars athwart the night" [48] and others that are too small to be seen with the naked eye), Barbauld concludes her catalogue of insects with an account of the beetle, presenting it in such a way that it recalls the description of "the tawny EAGLE" (43) in the first part of the poem. Like the eagle, the beetle is driven by its imperialistic desire to conquer the world around it and to gather as much wealth for itself as possible. It is described as a vicious force prepared for battle with anything that might stand in its way:

> What shining arms his polish'd limbs enchase!
> Like some stern warrior formidably bright
> His steely sides reflect a gleaming light:
> On his large forehead spreading horns he wears,
> And high in air the branching antlers bears. (48)

If the insects described at the beginning of this section of the poem are like Christ arising from the tomb, destined to live, ethereal-like, in the open air above the world's natural limitations, the beetle, at least on initial consideration, seems to be likened to Satan with his "spreading horns," bound to the earth and destined to inflict violence on all around it. But two points suggest that the beetle is a complicated image for Barbauld, and that in fact it is perhaps the truest model for her visionary imagination. While it is described in military and even satanic terms, its imperialistic reach is laughably small—"O'er many an inch extends his wide domain,/ And his rich treasure swells with hoarded grain" (48)—suggesting the radical limitations of an imagination, or desire, that seeks to dominate the world by force. Furthermore, and paradoxically, the beetle's laborious endeavor does not require the use of military force and the display of satanic power, because the insect's goal is ultimately nothing more than the gathering of "grain"; in contrast to the eagle, the beetle does not seek the spilling of blood. The warlike demeanor and imperialistic goals of the beetle are rendered unnecessary by the material reality that its "rich treasure" is to be discovered in the natural world that is right in front of it. Unlike the songbirds, and unlike the flying insects, the beetle is anchored in the world, which, as it turns out, offers ample reward to the living. In the portrayal of the beetle, the idealism associated with the flying birds and insects is redirected into the rich physical landscape where life is actually lived. Barbauld's imagination and visionary poetics seem to have arrived at a new understanding, one that is energized by fanciful dreams of unmediated joy but that also is firmly grounded in the realm of lived human experience.

As the poem concludes, Barbauld returns to the idea of friendship, addressing it in such a way as to illustrate the position at which she seems to have arrived in the descriptive passages on birds and insects. She is caught within "the lonely hour" and tries "to cheat" that loneliness by exercise of the imagination, with its capacity for using "song or paint" to create "an insect or a flower" (48). While some artists may be imperialists of the imagination, seeking "fame" (49) by means of their artistic skills—using art, that is, to draw the world under their control—Barbauld's goal is simpler and, finally, more humane: rejecting fame as the proper goal of the artist's labors, she embraces friendship, or the community of people; art is a gift to others rather than a tool used to gain power over others. For her, at this moment, her idealism and her lived experience become one and the same; the closeness and caring regard of another human being is the highest ideal toward which she feels compelled to strive, no matter the dreams and possibilities that she may associate with flying birds and insects. Barbauld's idealism is not abandoned but is instead firmly grounded in the existential reality of human loneliness and its offsetting possibility of hope that comes from community. In "To Mrs. P——," Barbauld focuses on the sort of visionary poetics that she desires and successfully defines it, thereby helping to point the direction of her prophetic imagination. The challenge before her, of course, is to successfully reshape the understanding developed at the level of personal experience into a socially transformative and prophetic vision that will speak to humanity in general.

The poems immediately following "To Mrs. P——" constitute a sort of new beginning (one of several in the volume) for Barbauld, insofar as they are descriptions of principles rather than actions. If "To Mrs. P——" reflects Barbauld's effort to begin anew (with friendship) her quest for a meaningful foundational framework for her visionary poetics, the subsequent four poems begin to build on that foundation by considering the sorts of ideals that might sustain that vision and infuse it with transformative potential. At the same time, however, this endeavor is pursued in the full awareness (learned in the earlier poems) that idealism is difficult to sustain and is never entirely pure. The poems give full voice to idealism while at the same time offering a reminder that much work is required if the goals of that idealism are to be achieved.

In the two poems included under the title "Characters" and the poem following these ("On a Lady's Writing") Barbauld addresses unidentified females in such a way as to make clear that her purpose is to set out principles, or values, that might serve as a guiding spirit in a meaningful life. In the first "Characters" poem, for example, Barbauld associates the object of her address with principles of love and goodness (which, for her, are interchangeable), suggesting that these alone are capable of giving life meaning and nourishing its dreams of peace, security, and joy. As an embodiment of these principles, she says, her friend was "BORN to sooth distress, and lighten care, / Lively as soft, and innocent as fair!" (50); she is "so pure, so good, she scarce can guess at sin" (50); she is "the loveliest pattern of a female mind" (50).[11] These descriptions follow directly on the similar commentary in "To Mrs. P——," thereby enriching the idea of friendship presented in that poem by attaching it to ideals whose very excess is life affirming rather than debilitating, an idea of friendship that is self-generating, free of dependence on any sort of external power, political authority, or ideological system:

> Her charity almost becomes excess.
> Wealth may be courted, wisdom be rever'd,
> And beauty prais'd, and brutal strength be fear'd;
> But goodness only can affection move;
> And love must owe its origin to love. (50–51)

For Barbauld, love and goodness appear to be pure and unmediated ideals that can be trusted to guide one's life through the rough circumstances wrought by a blind pursuit (to cite her examples) of wealth, beauty, or strength. Trust in love, she says, is desirable because love is self-constituted and therefore unbeholden to the world. Further, though the world has all but banished the principles associated with love—for instance, "that sweet simplicity of thought / So rarely found" (50)—it is nevertheless freely and endlessly available at all times, as the character to whom the poem is addressed attests. Finally, as the one true embodiment, or realization, of goodness in life, it is the only principle that possesses truly transformative authority: "Goodness only can affection move." With friendship and love as anchors for her conception of the good, Barbauld suggests in this short poem that she is beginning to approach an important source of visionary power.

The brief poem immediately following, which is gathered under the same title, makes the identical point. In this poem, Barbauld describes a woman who is perfectly at ease with herself in the world, a woman who possesses "clear sense and truth" (51), whose feelings are "pois'd" and whose soul is "compos'd" (52), and who uses the "calm controul" (52) of reason as an anchor in her life. The only passion that upsets the balance of this woman's life is love, which "rul'd despotic in her breast" (52). But rather than diminish her life, this passion enriches it by its very excess: "Love delights to bless / the generous transports of a fond excess" (52). This little poem is important because it adds a new dimension to the preceding poem. Whereas the first poem included under the general title "Characters" describes love as self-generating, arising fully formed, as it were, from its own being, the second describes the boundlessness of love, wherein "fond excess" is a virtue rather than a liability in life. Without beginning or end, and yet fully humanly available (as evidenced in the objects of poetic address), love is shown to be the only truly meaningful human principle, superior to (and, indeed, subsuming) thought, reason, and feelings and thereby rendering meaningless the mad pursuit of wealth, wisdom, beauty, and "brutal strength."

These poems (simple, direct, confident) exhibit a new and vibrant spirit, but they are not sentimental or naïve in their celebration of love and goodness. As she often does in the volume, Barbauld anchors the poems with epigraphs that assure that idealism remains tethered to the world. The brief epigraph to the first poem, for example, is taken from the fifth ode in Horace's first volume of odes. The translation of the lines that Barbauld cites reads, simply, "still kind," or "always amiable," suggesting, perhaps, that the principle of love is ever desirable. But the larger context of Horace's ode complicates this idea by suggesting that love can be elusive and that one may mistake other passions for love. Horace's ode is about Pyrrha, the woman who (in Greek mythology) is the progenitor of all women, and a young man who has fallen in love with her. It reads in its entirety:

> What slender youth, besprinkled with perfume,
> Courts you on roses in some grotto's shade?
> Fair Pyrrha, say, for whom
> Your yellow hair you braid,
> So trim, so simple! Ah! how oft shall he
> Lament that faith can fail, that gods can change,
> Viewing the rough black sea
> With eyes to tempests strange,
> Who now is basking in your golden smile,

> And dreams of you still fancy-free, still kind,
> Poor fool, nor knows the guile
> Of the deceitful wind!
> Woe to the eyes you dazzle without cloud
> Untried! For me, they show in yonder fane
> My dripping garments, vow'd
> To Him who curbs the main.[12]

While Pyrrha may be the embodiment of pure beauty and love, she is not easily understood or fully embraced. As Horace observes in the ode, "Woe to the eyes you dazzle without cloud / Untried!," a statement suggesting that love is not a romantic or sentimental passion but rather a deep and difficult reality bound to the reality of "tempests strange" on "the rough black sea." Thus, while the woman to whom Barbauld addresses the first poem included under the title "Characters" may be the embodiment of love, and while Barbauld explicitly spells out the desirable traits of love, the difficulty of attaining love is embedded in the epigraph, which serves as a warning not to approach love too lightly.

The epigraph to the second poem included under the title "Characters" similarly complicates the idea of love. Turning this time to the Latin poet Albius Tibullus, Barbauld cites lines from one of his short poems ("Sulpicia's Garland") that translates as "Whatever she does, wherever she turns her steps, / Grace follows her secretly to prepare everything."[13] Once again, Barbauld is working from a literary source that challenges a simple reading of her poem. Although Sulpicia, the female subject of Tibullus's poem, is presented as an example of ideal beauty and love, she is at the same time placed within a context that bespeaks difficulty and even danger. The entire poem from which the epigraph is taken reads as follows:

> Sulpicia's dressed for you, great Mars, on your Calends:
> come from the sky yourself, to see her, if you're wise.
> Venus will forgive you: but you, violent one, beware
> lest your weapons fall, shamefully, in wonder.
> Cruel Love lights his twin torches from her eyes,
> When he would set fire to the gods themselves.
> Whatever she does, wherever she turns her steps,
> Grace follows her secretly to prepare everything.
> If she loosens her hair, flowing tresses become her:
> if she arranges it, the curls she's arranged are divine.
> She inflames, if she chooses to walk in a Tyrian gown:

she inflames, if she comes gleaming in white robes.
So, pleasing Vertumnus wears a thousand fashions
on eternal Olympus, and wears them gracefully
Sole among girls she's worthy that Tyre grants her
soft wool twice dipped in costly dyes,
and she possess whatever the rich Arab, the farmer
of perfumed fields, reaps from his fragrant lands,
and whatever gems the dark Indian gathers
from the red shores of the waters, near to the Dawn.
You Muses, sing of her, on the festive Calends,
and you, proud Phoebus, to the tortoiseshell lyre.
She'll carry out this sacred rite for many a year:
no girl is more worthy of your choir.

Sulpicia may be followed by grace, as the lines that constitute the epigraph note, and her very hair may be "divine" and her character "worthy" of songs of praise, as the poem itself observes, but the situation in which Sulpicia is placed exposes her to danger, as she is being presented to Mars, the "violent one," at the festival of Mars. Indeed, the poem is addressed to Mars, who, at the festival, is celebrated both as a war god and as the god of agriculture. Once this context is understood, it becomes apparent that Tibullus's poem is more of a prayer than a celebration, insofar as it is marked by a plea that Mars, on this occasion, will set aside his weapons in favor of the pleasures of love.[14] And the prayerful tone that guides Tibullus's poem is infused in the lines that Barbauld appropriates for use as an epigraph, guiding the spirit of her poem as well.

"On a Lady's Writing" is the first (though not the only) poem in the volume to be presented without an epigraphic introduction. It is also, at six lines long, the briefest poem in the volume. These facts are important because they suggest Barbauld's poetic arrival, after much starting and stopping and shifting between pastoral and prophetic poetic modes in the first third of the volume, at a reasonably clear and definable understanding of the sorts of poetic principles that matter most to her. The poem is a finely honed and self-supporting gem whose strength resides in its simplicity of statement. Drawing on the ideas presented in the preceding two poems gathered under the title "Characters," Barbauld here once again describes a female character, only this time focusing first on her writing skills and interests rather than her character. In two perfectly-executed heroic couplets, Barbauld describes the writing of her female subject as "even," "neat," "polished," "strong," "easy," "correct," and "regular" (53). According to Barbauld, these cursive features are a window into the physical and mental life of the person who has created them; her admirable "temper," "dress," "brow," "judgment," and "air" (53) are all captured in physical marks on a page, as though these marks were a cursive representation of the fullness and quality of her life. Like the writing, the writer whom Barbauld describes is "correct though free, and regular though fair" (53). The final couplet describes the relation between writer and writing: "And the same graces o'er her pen preside / That form her manners and her footsteps guide" (53). The poem draws together the physical and mental dimensions of its subject's life, offering something approaching an ideal picture of the relations between the material practice of writing and the values and hopes that might be registered and represented in that practice. In this way, this briefest of poems might be regarded as Barbauld's self-created map designed to guide her through the rough waters of visionary poetry, reminding her of the "graces" that will be necessary to assure that she is "strong" and "steady" as she pursues her important (and chosen) course of poetic action.

That "On a Lady's Writing" serves as a simple statement of poetic principle rather than as an example of poetic achievement becomes clear in "Hymn to Content," a poem that in effect tests the principle of steadiness of temper articulated in the preceding poem even as it keeps Barbauld's ideal of contentment, or happiness, in clear view. (It also anticipates the cluster of hymns that appear later in the volume.) The question that Barbauld seems to have begun to answer in "On a Lady's Writing" is not whether it is possible to arrive at the end of history, where all conflict is laid to rest, but rather whether it is possible to discover principles capable of sustaining one as one encounters the inevitable hardships and difficulties of history and to use these principles as a foundation for remaking human experience. In turning to "Hymn to Content," she does not fall into the trap of a sentimentalized notion of peace; instead she draws upon the features set out in "On a Lady's Writing" to engage the world on behalf of the ideals that she now, more confidently than in earlier poems, embraces.

Once again, Barbauld uses an epigraph to establish and enrich the central idea of her poem, lifting lines from the Roman poet Claudian to voice the idea that happiness is possible in this world. The lines from Claudian translate as follows (in prose): "Nature has given the opportunity of happiness to all, knew they but how to use it" (41). Two matters bear remarking on here. First, implicit in the view that happiness is available to all people is the lament that they have thus far failed to find it, suggesting that ignorance, rather than (say) fate or human nature, is the primary obstacle standing in the way of human happiness. Second, the poem from which the epigraph is taken, entitled *Against Rufinus* is an astonishingly violent narrative about a man whose greed knows no bounds, leading him to destroy everything and everyone in his path as he seeks to achieve greater wealth and power for himself. The poem is a cautionary tale about the human capacity for atrocity and the horrors that inevitably follow from acting on that capacity. Beginning with a description of a world that lives in relative peace, the narrative soon shifts to the underworld, where "the nether-world sisters" (29) begin to plot ways to disrupt that peace. The sisters decide to approach Rufinus, the most abominable of humans, who they think they might be able to tempt to wreak havoc on the world around him. Rufinus succumbs to the temptation put before him by the sisters and begins a series of horrific adventures that makes him powerful and feared, as well as wealthy: "He followed up one crime with another, heaping fuel on the inflamed mind and probing and embittering the erstwhile trivial wound" (39). As the horrors increase to an unimaginable level, the narrator of the story interrupts his story, crying out,

> Madman, what shall be the end? Though thou possess either Ocean, though Lydia pour forth her golden waters, though thou join Croesus' throne to Cyrus' crown, yet shalt thou never be rich nor ever contented with thy booty. The greedy man is always poor. Fabricius, happy in his honourable poverty, despised the gifts of monarchs; the consul Serranus sweated at his heavy plough and a small cottage gave shelter to the warlike Curii. To my mind such poverty as this is richer than thy wealth, such a home greater than thy palaces. There pernicious luxury seeks for the food that satisfieth not; here the earth provides a banquet for which is nought to pay. With thee wool absorbs the dyes of Tyre; thy patterned clothes are stained with purple; here are bright flowers and the meadow's breathing charm which owes its varied hues but to itself. There are beds piled on glittering bedsteads; here stretches the soft grass, that breaks not sleep with anxious cares. There a crowd of clients dins through the spacious halls, here is song of birds and the murmur of the gliding stream. A frugal life is best. Nature has given the opportunity of happiness to all, knew they but how to use it. Had we realized this we should now have been enjoying a simple life, no trumpets would be sounding, no whistling spear would speed, no ship be buffeted by the wind, no siege-engine overthrow battlements. (41)

For Barbauld, the importance of the tale of Rufinus and of the lines from the tale that she uses for her epigraph is twofold. First, the tale begins from the assumption that the natural state of the world is peace but that evils and horrors can be stirred up (in this case by the netherworld sisters) to disrupt that peace. Thus the foundational idea that she may take from Claudian (and that is reflected in the lines that she chooses for her epigraph) is that we must accept on faith that the basic nature of humanity is good. Second, Claudian's stake in the story of Rufinus is that of the prophet who interjects himself into the corrupt world on behalf of principles that, he believes, have the power to transform existence. Barbauld clearly aligns herself with this understanding, not only in this poem but throughout *Poems* and is doubtless drawn to Claudian's poem because of its view that humanity is not only peaceful by nature (although peace seems long ago to have been lost) but also can rediscover the path to a peaceful existence and thereby discover the most noble principles and virtues of human nature. As the narrative of Rufinus ends, Claudian describes the exchanges between one of the netherworld sisters and the goddess Justice:

Meanwhile Megaera, more eager now she has got her way, and revelling in this widespread calamity, comes upon Justice sad at heart in her palace, and thus provokes her with horrid utterance: "Is this that old reign of peace; this the return of that golden age thou fondly hopedst had come to pass? Is our power gone, and no place now left for the Furies? Turn thine eyes this way. See how many cities the barbarians' fires have laid low, how vast a slaughter, how much blood Rufinus hath procured for me, and on what widespread death my serpents gorge themselves. Leave thou the world of men; that lot is mine. Mount to the stars, return to that well-known tract of Autumn sky where the Standard-bearer dips towards the south. The space next to the summer constellation of the Lion, the neighbourhood of the winter Balance has long been empty. And would I could now follow thee through the dome of heaven."

The goddess made answer: "Thou shalt rage no further, mad that thou art. Now shall thy creature receive his due, the destined avenger hangs over him, and he who now wearies land and the very sky shall die, though no handful of dust shall cover his corpse. Soon shall come Honorius, promised of old to this fortunate age, brave as his father Theodosius, brilliant as his brother Arcadius; he shall subdue the Medes and overthrow the Indians with his spear. Kings shall pass under his yoke, frozen Phasis shall bear his horses' hooves, and Araxes submit perforce to be bridged by him. Then too shalt thou be bound with heavy chains of iron and cast out from the light of day and imprisoned in the nethermost pit, thy snaky locks overcome and shorn from thy head. Then the world shall be owned by all in common, no field marked off from another by any dividing boundary, no furrow cleft with bended ploughshare; for the husbandman shall rejoice in corn that springs untended. Oak groves shall drip with honey, streams of wine well up of every side, lakes of oil abound. No price shall be asked for fleeces dyed scarlet, but of themselves shall the flocks grow red to the astonishment of the shepherd, and in every sea the green seaweed will laugh with flashing jewels." (51–55)

Against Rufinus is filled with descriptions of wickedness and its propensity to disrupt (and even corrupt) the naturally peaceful cadence of human life. In the character of Rufinus Claudian's narrative also captures the human capacity for ignorance and violence. But at the heart of the narrative is a vision of common understanding, natural plenitude, peace, and laughter. The narrative, that is, articulates a vision perfectly consistent with Barbauld's idea that the ideals of peace and happiness do not, with a simple wish, sweep aside the complexities of the world, but these ideals can provide a meaningful foundation and goal for human life as people try to make their way through the world.

In "Hymn to Content," Barbauld, following the noble principles set out in *Against Rufinus*, constructs her own hopeful vision, and, like Claudian, she does so in such a way that situates her idealism amid the tribulations of lived reality. Even in its structure, in fact, her poem seems to be keenly aware that ideals (in this case, the ideal of "Content") are hard won and require constant protection and vigilance. For instance, while the poem is written under the title of a "hymn"—a song of praise—it is in fact also a prayer, a pleading that contentment might be found in this life. As the poem begins, the narrator describes "the Nymph" (presumably Content) as being "ever nigh" yet "seldom found" (54). The narrator hopes to discover the Nymph and persuade her to "receive my temperate vow," "bless my longing sight" (54), and show the way to a peaceful life:

> No more by varying passions beat,
> O gently guide my pilgrim feet
> To find thy hermit cell;
> Where in some pure and equal sky
> Beneath thy soft indulgent eye
> The modest virtues dwell. (55)

This prayer depicts the narrator as a devotee who desires—but who has not yet discovered—the "Simplicity," "Innocence," and "Hope" (55) that are associated with Content. Indeed, the narrator herself remains caught within "this vale of tears," eagerly searching for "a vista to the sky" (55). Moreover, this vale of tears, the narrator says, is characterized by violence, and great skill is needed to navigate that landscape of violence while keeping idealism and noble principles intact. According to the narrator, only with the aid of "Patience," the sister of Content, might one learn to face the challenges found in the world. But, for many, that aid is not easy to accept, because Patience insists that, in the face of violence and injustice, one must present a "mild unvarying cheek/To meet the offer'd blow" (56), much as "the Phrygian sage" learns to smile upon "a tyrant master's wanton rage" (56).[15] The narrator's prayer is that, like the sage, she might become "inur'd to toil and bitter bread" (56) and discover from such habit the "brown hamlet" (56) where Content resides.

In the final two stanzas of the poem, Barbauld focuses on Content as a "power" (57) that is located in time rather than in space, thereby deftly clarifying the nature of her idealism. While Content is a virtue to be sought, celebrated, and prayed for, it is not a virtue that by simple prayer or wishful thinking can push aside the hard circumstances of the world; nor is it a spatial reality that one can discover and stake a claim on. For Barbauld, Content is a spirit, or vision, that moves everywhere through life and that can guide one's conduct in the world in such a way as to make human betterment imaginable and therefore possible: it does not erase history or provide a substitute for history. She makes this point first by associating Content with "Autumn," who is "friendly to the Muse" and whose late-season features "shall thy own modest tints diffuse, / And shed thy milder day" (55). The description of Content in association with Autumn is followed immediately by a longer description of evening as the time when Content will appear:

> When Eve, her dewy star beneath,
> Thy balmy spirit loves to breathe,
> And every storm is laid;
> If such an hour was e'er thy choice,
> Oft let me hear thy soothing voice
> Low whispering thro' the shade. (57)

Perfect contentment, Barbauld seems to say, is discovered only when life itself draws to a close, just as autumn portends winter and evening marks the end of day. As a vision, however, contentment remains very much alive within history as a guiding principle that inspires human engagement with the injustices of the world. Thus, for Barbauld, contentment is an enlivening vision that provides a meaningful way of living in the world; it is not an avenue pointing toward an escape from the troubles of the world. In this respect, the poem is not simply a prayer; it is, as its title suggests, a song of praise.

"Hymn to Content" is a steadfastly visionary poem, and its vision is bound tightly to the existential and historical reality of human experience, even as it seeks to reimagine the world along lines similar to those described in the more idealistic sections of Claudian's *Against Rufinus*. Like Claudian, Barbauld knows that the world is a vale of tears inhabited by tyrant masters who take what they can get for themselves, no matter the cost to other people. But she also knows, again like Claudian, that the imagination, fueled by a spirit of justice and liberty, is capable of creating idealisms that are to be celebrated and followed even to the grave because they represent the possibility of life being remade in meaningful ways that will bring contentment and happiness within reach. Such a view brings Barbauld's visionary poetics forward quite a distance, as she shows here her ability to hold on to her idealism while no longer (as she had seemed to do in "Corsica") assuming that idealism requires the erasure or transcendence of history.

In "To Wisdom," Barbauld takes another step forward in shaping her visionary poetics by focusing on the qualities or characteristics that are most important to a meaningful life. Her confidence in this task is seen in her bold engagement with the concept of wisdom, which, she says, is of value only if it helps to create a place for joy and passion in life. And, for Barbauld, joy and passion require that fear be overcome and life be embraced fully and without restraint. As she puts it, if wisdom comes "with frown austere / To nurse the brood of care and fear" (58), then she wants nothing to do with it. For her, a wisdom defined by its association with restraint or reserve, even if it is intended to preserve the integrity of life, necessarily seeks its goal of integrity by also rejecting the better part of life, because the austerity created by an underlying fear of life's challenges makes openness and freedom impossible; on this view, wisdom becomes a power "to wither each poor transient flower / That cheers this pilgrimage of woe" (59). As she had done in "Hymn to Content," Barbauld here situates a prized human virtue or principle (in this case, wisdom) within the context of the circumstantial tribulations of human experience, and she states, more directly and forcefully than before, that, given the material constraints on life, the virtues that are most worthy of respect, and the ones that she insists on celebrating, are those cleansed of fear, not hardship, thus enabling or enriching the passionate and joyful possibilities of experience, even if large parts of that experience are a "pilgrimage of woe." Thus she says outright that if wisdom is simply another system of constraint, then "wisdom, thine empire I disclaim" (59).

Although the sentiment of "To Wisdom" in some respects echoes Horace's carpe diem view of the world, as voiced in his eleventh ode in his first book of odes, it is finally a complex and radical vision of the human capacity for happiness in life, even in the face of life's hardships, and of the desire to put wisdom in the service of that capacity.[16] That is, while the poem expresses Barbauld's unabashed commitment to "pleasure's frolic train!" (59), at the same time it gathers up and transforms the idea of wisdom, liberating it from its conventional associations with (puritanical) constraint and fear and thereby making it compatible with her worldview. As she puts it at the beginning of the poem:

> O wisdom! if thy soft controul
> Can sooth the sickness of the soul,
> Can bid the warring passions cease,
> And breathe the calm of tender peace;
> WISDOM! I bless thy gentle sway,
> And ever, ever will obey. (58)

Here is a wisdom that is soft, gentle, tender, and dedicated to the ideal of peace. This is a wisdom, Barbauld suggests across the larger sweep of the poem, that works in the service of "hope with eager sparkling eyes, / And easy faith, and fond surprise!" (59); it is a wisdom that is commensurate with "festive mirth, and laughter wild" (59). For Barbauld, true wisdom is defined by the understanding that the proper goal of human life is pleasure or happiness, not the building of blind defenses to fend off circumstance. Any form of wisdom not founded on this understanding is to be rejected. At the conclusion of the poem, in describing her vision of the world in relation of wisdom, she makes this point explicit, when she describes her embrace of hope, pleasure, mirth, laughter, and faith: "Tho' wise I may not be, / The wise themselves shall envy me" (59).

The complexity of the vision articulated in "To Wisdom" becomes evident when the poem is placed in the context of the ode from which Barbauld lifts her epigraph. The epigraph, which Sidney Alexander translates as "Gladly seize / the blessings of this moment / and let serious things slide by" (114), comes from the eighth ode in Horace's third book of odes. The ode is dedicated to Maecenas, who was an advisor to Caesar Augustus and who was known to be a wealthy and enlightened individual as well as a patron of Virgil and Horace.[17] While the ode is generally lighthearted, its expression of joy derives from a serious source: Horace's successful escape from a life-threatening situation. As Alexander comments in a note on the poem, the ode follows on the subject first addressed in the thirteenth ode of book two, where Horace describes the fall of a tree that nearly kills him, leading him to opine that "no man ever displays / sufficient caution from hour to hour" (76). Horace's invitation to Maecenas in the poem from which Barbauld lifts her epigraph is extended on "the first anniversary of the fall of the tree," as he takes it as "a sign of divine benevolence" that "the cursed tree" did not end up falling on his head (333). Horace's ode, therefore, is a celebration of life measured against the unforeseen and arbitrary forms of violence that can strike one down at any time. And it moves beyond the sentiment articulated in Horace's earlier poem by turning his attention away from caution and toward happiness. His brush with death, that is, in time brings a new sort of wisdom to him, one that makes him understand the beauty, value, and joy of life. In the face of circumstantial reality, Horace says, the best course of action is to "let tumult and anger / be far removed" (113), which is precisely the argument that Barbauld makes in "To Wisdom" and earlier in "Hymn to Content."

"To Wisdom," on the face of it, seems to lack seriousness, but in fact it is an important statement about Barbauld's effort to construct an idealistic vision that finds its hope and purpose within full view and with full understanding of the hard realities of experience. While, with Horace, she might advocate letting "serious things slide by," she does so with the full understanding that "serious things" do not simply go away, leaving in their place a purely edenic reality. After all, Horace's recommendation is deeply rooted in wisdom, in his understanding that life is fragile, that it must be cherished, and that the moments that offer the possibility of joy must be embraced. Barbauld takes this lesson from her literary forebear and uses it as the basis for beginning to imagine the possibility of a peaceful existence that is not austere but rather bold, confident, and filled with pleasure. Once this vision is formulated, of course, it remains to be seen whether she can devise a mode of poetic expression that is commensurate with its materially mediated idealism.

CHAPTER FIVE

Reflections on Writing

In the cluster of poems that follows on "To Wisdom"—"The Origin of Song-Writing," "Songs," "Delia," and "Ovid to His Wife"—Barbauld faces directly the problem of writing in an effort to determine the extent to which she is capable of creating a visionary poetry built on the principles set out in the previous poems. She also gathers up several major themes and modes of poetic expression from the earlier sections of the volume as if to test them against the deeper understanding that she has begun to develop across the range of previous poems. Finally, the poems here are marked by an elegiac tone that Barbauld constructs to ensure that her themes are not simply stated but also subjected to reflection. Thus, while her themes and modes are familiar—love, pastoral—her conception of the visionary is more sophisticated and nuanced than before.

That Barbauld would pause to reflect on the act of writing this far into the volume may at first seem to be a clumsy poetic move, insofar as one might expect that such reflection would precede visionary expression. Certainly the tradition of visionary writing prior to Barbauld suggests that she is not following the expected and necessary path toward becoming a visionary poet. To glimpse the unconventional turn that she takes in this cluster of poems, one need only consider the poetic trajectories of (say) Spenser, Milton, and Wordsworth (as well as Virgil), all of whom wrote visionary poetry only after having prepared themselves through lengthy apprenticeships in which they gathered the poetic tools needed for visionary expression.

But within the context of *Poems*, this interlude of poetic self-reflection is perfectly suited to Barbauld's visionary purposes. After all, her understanding of vision is inextricably tied to her understanding of the vital necessity of self-reflection. Just as her excursions into pastoral idealism provide a reflective space for meditating on the nature of idealism in relation to hard experience, so her reflection on writing serves as a check against becoming too comfortable and uncritical in her poetic endeavor.

Barbauld addresses "The Origin of Song-Writing" to her brother, John Aikin, who, in 1772, had published a well-received volume entitled *Essays on Song-Writing*, a collection of essays and various lyric poems (including several by

Barbauld) that, among other things, sought to intervene in contemporary discussions about literary taste.[1] As McCarthy notes of the collection, "The essays were to demonstrate literary taste and sensibility and also to assert some moderately original views—mainly the view that modern pastoral and love lyrics ('songs') deserve the same critical care and attention long lavished on ancient epic and tragedy" (106–7). Barbauld's reference to her brother's work helps to explain her own engagement with the pastoral genre in particular and the song in general as serious modes of poetic expression—or at least modes of expression that can be reimagined to serve serious poetic aims. For example, in his "Essay on Song-Writing in General," Aikin remarks:

> The term *song* may therefore be considered in a double sense—if the idea of music prevails, it signifies no more than a set of words calculated for adaptation to a tune: if poetry be the principle object, it is a species of poetical composition regulated by peculiar laws, and susceptible of a certain definition; still however retaining so much of the musical idea as to make it an essential circumstance, that by a regularly returning measure it be capable of being set to a tune.
>
> A song, as a poetical composition, may be defined, [as] a short piece, divided into returning portions of measure, and formed upon a single incident, thought, or sentiment. (10)

In the following essay, he then ties this idea of songwriting to pastoral, making explicit that British pastoral is a fiction rather than a form of expression that is *natural* to British culture. As he puts it:

> Pastoral Poetry is a native of happier climates, where the face of nature, and the manners of the people are widely different from those of our northern regions. What is reality on the soft Arcadian and Sicilian plains, is all fiction here; and though by reading we may be so familiarized to these imaginary scenes as to acquire a sort of natural taste for them, yet, like the fine fruits of the south, they will never be so far naturalized to the soil, as to flourish without borrowed warmth and forced culture. (27–28)

These comments emphasize the formal and fictional nature of pastoral (which Aikin defines as a kind of song) not for the purpose of suggesting that song writing in Britain is simply a mechanical exercise that lacks seriousness; quite the contrary, Aikin argues that the formal codes that define a song, and the artificiality of British pastoral, open up great possibilities for British poetry. Of the British pastoral, he remarks: "The simplicity of language gives it an air of nature and reality, though the fictitious character be entirely kept up; and throwing the subject into a little tale, gives an opportunity of novelty in description from the variety of incidents.... Perhaps the English alone, of all the moderns, have known how to unite the most perfect simplicity with real elegance and poetical expression" (34). The implication of Aikin's view, which Barbauld incorporates into her own writing of pastoral (in "Origin of Song-Writing" and subsequent poems), captures the importance of British song writing by suggesting that rather than constituting a hindrance to poetical expression, strictness of form and self-conscious artificiality can in fact sharpen a sentiment, or thought, and thereby raise consciousness. For Barbauld, as for her brother, the importance of pastoral artifice reduces to a simple conviction, which Aikin describes succinctly: "The passion of love is the eternal source of pastoral sentiment" (33).

While the sentiment that John Aikin describes seems to be simple enough, Barbauld knew that in fact it was extremely complex, just as the idea of artifice in songwriting is complex. And it is precisely this complexity that interests her. The particular cast of her interest in love, which, of course, she had examined in earlier poems as well, becomes clear immediately in "Origin of Song-Writing," when she once again places her verse under the guiding spirit of Tibullus, this time drawing her epigraph from the Roman poet's poem entitled "The Country Festival" (elegy 2.1), which Robert J. Ball calls "one of Tibullus's finest poems" (150). The epigraph is drawn from Tibullus's description of Cupid as a pastoral figure, who was "born in the fields / and among the flocks and the wild mares," where he learned his archery skills. Tibullus remarks of Cupid's youth spent among the rural landscape, in the lines that Barbauld uses for her epigraph, that "There he first practised with the untrained bow: / ah, what skilful hands he has now!" The lightness of spirit and simplicity of thought evident in this description suggest that Tibullus is constructing Cupid as a kind of artificial emblem of the vagaries of romantic love.

In fact, however, for Tibullus and Barbauld alike Cupid serves a different poetic function entirely. For one thing, however inviting and playful the spirit of Cupid may be in the lines that Barbauld cites, in the larger context of Tibullus's poem, he plays a relatively small role. The larger concern of "The Country Festival" is to describe the ceremony performed to purify the fields at harvest time and the celebrations that follow the cleansing ceremony. These descriptions are marked by an expressed desire for peace and purity, and they include (among other things) depictions of public and celebratory drunkenness ("no shame to be drunk on a day of festival"), the sacrifice of a lamb, and a salute to Messalles, the Roman general and patron of literature, all of which are recorded as part of Tibullus's desire to "give thanks / with my verse to the gods of the fields," that is to say, the "rural gods" of the pastoral world. Within such a context of social life, the romantic Cupid could be a hindrance rather than a social support. Indeed, If Cupid represents nothing more than a distraction from the serious matter of the harvest, then his power is to be lamented: "Ah wretched ones, whom the god bears down on fiercely!" Thus Tibullus's narrator pleads with him: "Sacred One, come to our festive meal: but set aside / your arrows I beg, leave your burning torch far from here."

The pastoral imagination of the Tibullus of elegy 2.1, with its expressed desire for peace and purity and its celebration of the gods of the fields, is aware that the pastoral dream always stands in close relation to the circumstantial hardships and realities of lived experience, the playfulness of Cupid notwithstanding. If, as Renato Poggioli argues, "the psychological root of the pastoral is a double longing after innocence and happiness, to be recovered not through conversion or regeneration but merely through a retreat," that longing is ultimately a visionary hope or "a sentimental or aesthetic illusion," at best, and not a material possibility (1–2). And pastoral poetry is aware of this fact. The narrative voice in Tibullus's poem speaks explicitly about the human labor that is required in drawing life-sustaining gifts out of the fields and hauntingly about the threats to the human endeavor to survive:

> Gods of our fathers, we purify worker and field:
> drive evil far away from our boundaries,
> let the fields not cheat us of harvest, failed in the shoot,
> let our slow lambs not be in fear of swifter wolves.

Such fears and anxieties are not replaced by the pastoral pleasures associated with young Cupid's shenanigans; they exist in tension with those pleasures, making Cupid's preoccupation with romantic love into a sort of wager over whether his principles can stand up to the "evil" that always awaits close by to destroy the dream of peaceful existence. That Tibullus is under no illusion that pastoral idealism might not win the day against the wolves and evils of the world becomes obvious at the end of the poem, where he suggests that idealism, in fact, will ultimately succumb to an ominous and inexorable darkness:

> Now Night yokes her team, and the golden stars
> follow their mother's chariot, playful dancers,
> and after them silent Sleep comes, furled in dark wings
> and ill-omened Dream with wandering steps.

Such a view, not surprisingly, complicates the character of Cupid himself, as Tibullus seems to question how a fanciful love of the sort often associated with the son of Venus is even possible.[2]

In "Origin of Song-Writing," Barbauld follows a similar line of imaginative representation, using Cupid as a vehicle for considering the role and possibility of love in a world that is marked by hardship and difficulty and resistance to human endeavor. The pastoral sympathies articulated in the epigraph are echoed immediately in the poem's opening lines, as Barbauld describes the young Cupid as loitering "in Arcadian bowers, / And his bow in wreaths of flowers" (60), much as Barbauld herself (perhaps) had loitered in the Arcadian bowers of Warrington Academy, when, like Cupid, she "was young," with "wings unfledg'd" (60). But the distinguishing feature of Barbauld's poem is that she regrets the purely Arcadian investments of Cupid, a young god concerned only with the emotional entanglements of romantic love. "Heroes scorn'd the idle boy," according to Barbauld, because "love was but a shepherd's toy" (61). The pastoral dream of retreat (exemplified by the exploits of Cupid) from the inexorable vagaries and threats that define human experience into a sphere of pure pleasure cannot be sustained. It becomes necessary, at some point, to relinquish the promise of pastoral and face the world as it is in reality. That necessity is described in the poem in the form of Venus, Cupid's mother, who seeks to turn her son away from the passing pleasures of erotic love toward a higher and deeper sort of love that might have a meaningful bearing on the world of politics and society. As Barbauld puts it, Venus wants her son to pursue "some nobler game, / Gods, and godlike men to tame" (61), by which she presumably means that she wants a higher form of love to subdue the coarser ambitions of men and gods alike. To this end, she presents Cupid to the Muses with the request that they guide him away from the sentiments of pastoral retreat and educate him about the importance of prophetic engagement with the world, where the young god's subject matter might become

> chiefs, and heroes old,
> In unsubmitting virtue bold:
> Of even valour's temperate heat,
> And toils, to stubborn patience sweet. (61)

Subject matter such as this, Barbauld says, constitutes the sort of "prophetic musing" that is more appropriate to serious poetry than the playful love songs with which Cupid is typically associated. The poetry that matters to the fate and character of human experience, she observes, is most properly identified with an "unconquerable hate / Of tyrant pride's unhallow'd state" (62).

In setting out her description of prophecy as a mode of poetry that is superior to romantic love songs but that nevertheless requires a spirit of love to guide its endeavors, Barbauld extends and complicates the views described in her brother's essay on songwriting. In doing so, moreover, she captures precisely the conflict between what sometimes may appear to be contradictory imaginative impulses with which she wrestles in *Poems*, illuminating her clear (if uncomfortable) understanding that the serious poet must ultimately find a way to resolve that conflict. The complicated poetic struggle in which she is engaged in the volume is glimpsed in her portrayal of Cupid, after the young romancer of pastoral fame has been made to listen to heroic and tragic stories told by the Muses. On hearing their descriptions of the sort of noble subject matter that Venus associates with "nobler game" and that the Muses associate with prophecy, Cupid is "abash'd, and half afraid" (62). Indeed, for him the subjects of those stories are off-putting, because they seem to lack the guiding spirit of love: Pallas is armored; Mars is "threat'ning"; Diana is characterized by an "icy look," which "with sudden chill his bosom struck" (62). Devoid of any attention to the principle of love, these characters and their stories, not surprisingly, leave Cupid resistant to his mother's desire that he be instructed by the Muses, whom she asks to "refine his air" and "teach him to spell those mystic names / That kindle bright immortal flames" (63).

Indeed, rather than taking guidance from the Muses, Cupid deceives them, effectively turning their powers to his own use. Rather than becoming their student, he takes over "the Muse's lyre" for himself, tuning it "to languid notes of soft desire" (64), thereby enhancing his already considerable skills as the authority in all matters relating to romantic love: "Now of power his darts are found / Twice ten thousand times to wound" (64). The result is that his power grows to the point where, in Barbauld's view, his poetic spirit becomes the standard of poetic expression everywhere:

> Now no more the slacken'd strings
> Breathe of high immortal things,
> But Cupid tunes the Muse's lyre
> To languid notes of soft desire.
> In every clime, in every tongue,
> 'Tis love inspires the poet's song. (64)

In Barbauld's telling, Cupid's successful evasion of the responsibilities that Venus and the muses would have placed on him has far-reaching consequences, shaping the entire course of Western poetry. Sappho, Otway, Shakespeare, Virgil,

Pope, Waller, and Petrarch to varying degrees all came under the sway of Cupid, setting aside (Barbauld seems to say) the nobler aim of visionary, or prophetic, expression in favor of the entanglements of private emotion.[3]

Barbauld's poetic maneuver in her portrayal of Cupid (and of the poetic line that flows from him) suggests the difficulty that poets often face in developing a visionary stance that reaches beyond personal life into the larger terrain of history, politics, and spirit. At the same time, the fact that illustrious poets have come under the sway of Cupid shows that an effort to construct a serious and visionary poetic strategy entails more than making a simple choice between love as a "shepherd's toy" (61) and "nobler game" associated with "prophetic musings." After all, the poets she names do not blindly follow the dictates of a "sly insidious child" (64), even if that child is Cupid; Virgil and Shakespeare, to name only two poets in her list, are writers of astonishing visionary reach, producing works whose imaginative portrayals capture the most vital and fundamental elements of culture, society, and history. The larger argument that Barbauld seems to be making is that poetry always runs the risk of falling too heavily under the influence of a narrow imaginative spirit that promises little possibility of personal and cultural transformation or redemption. As she demonstrates across the course of the poem, and particularly in her description of Venus's effort to school her son, the spirit of love that Cupid represents—and, more importantly, that Venus represents—must be integrated into the knowledge of history, poetry, tragedy, astronomy, and so on that the muses possess.

For Barbauld, the problem with Cupid involves a culturally specific concern: he has become too much the guardian of British poetry. As the master of "music and song" (65) dedicated to the pastoral pleasures found on "old Arcadian plains" (65), his spirit has effectively come to dominate the British imagination, deceiving Britain much as Cupid had deceived the Muses. Under the influence of this deception, Barbauld says, British poetry has become largely devoid of a prophetic impulse, leaving the reader to believe that personal romance or light distraction is the proper focus of poetic endeavor:

> The British pipe has caught the strains
> And where the Tweed's pure current glides,
> Or Lissy rolls her limpid tides,
> Or Thames his oozy waters leads
> Thro' rural bowers or yellow meads,
> With many an old romantic tale
> Has chear'd the lone sequester'd vale;

> With many a sweet and tender lay
> Deceiv'd the tiresome summer-day. (65–66)

These lines effectively capture the potential of the pastoral imagination to deceive as well as revive the spirit. The picture here is inviting and appealing, depicting a world of natural plenitude and historical adventure ("an old romantic tale"). At the same time, the picture is inaccurate. For one thing, as Barbauld demonstrates earlier in the volume, in "The Invitation" and "The Mouse's Petition," for example, Britain in the latter half of the eighteenth century was not quite so bucolic a place as the lines suggest. The industrial revolution and the struggle for democratic freedoms were very much under way, and, as she states elsewhere in the volume, the nation needed a visionary poetic voice to guide the way through these pressing realities. Under the pressure of such a historical moment, Cupid and pastoral retreat, while perhaps useful as a means of rejuvenating the spirit, are finally inadequate to the larger historical task at hand of transforming the nation. Being like shepherds, under such pressing historical conditions, is an ideal to be respected, but it is not enough.[4]

On this view, "Origin of Song-Writing" constitutes both an example and a critique of songwriting, and, as such, it also provides a poetic critique of John Aikin's commentary on pastoral poetics. The simplicity and fictional character of the song, as demonstrated in Barbauld's poem, elegantly make available "the passion of love" that her brother says "is the eternal source of pastoral sentiment." This passion is seen both in the activities and spirit of the young Cupid and in the tradition of Western, and specifically British, poetry that flows from them. At the same time, Barbauld asserts plainly that pastoral idealism, if left untested against the "nobler game" found in history and human struggle, is only an idle pastime. In the final lines of the poem, Barbauld seems to suggest that her brother has failed to grasp this fundamental dilemma posed by the idealism associated with pastoral. Indeed, after describing the limitations inherent in the alluring yet deceptive character of pastoral, she leaves the toilsome task of sorting out the value of love poetry to her brother:

> 'Tis yours to cull with happy art
> Each meaning verse that speaks the heart;
> And fair array'd, in order meet,
> To lay the wreath at beauty's feet. (66)

Barbauld offers no condemnation in these lines, but she implies that the task of sorting out the relative value of poetry "that speaks the heart" must be undertaken by others (in this case John Aikin) rather than by her. Her own poetic responsibilities, as she understands them, lie elsewhere, specifically with the quest to examine the relations between the principle of love and the tribulations of history. That quest does not entail an abandonment of pastoral altogether, and certainly does not entail an abandonment of the principle of love, but rather a deeper investigation of pastoral poetry and songwriting than her brother offers for the purpose of determining what elements might be redeemable from these for her larger engagement with the world through the sort of visionary poetics that she is pursuing.

Barbauld's strategy of deeper engagement is made evident in the collection of six songs that follow immediately on "Origin of Song-Writing." In these songs, she engages with the characteristics of pastoral and its defining interest in love in a manner that at first might seem to constitute something like a poetic interlude that, if only for a moment, provides a lighthearted break from the more serious poetry that has preceded. Certainly the absence of a guiding epigraph to the songs suggests that she has made a decision not to engage here in a complex intertextual line of poetic representation. However, these songs are connected closely to the direction of inquiry that she had begun in "Origin of Song-Writing," a fact that is stressed emphatically by the overlapping lines between it and the first song. Just as it ends with the line "To lay the wreath at beauty's feet," so the first song, in its description of love, states in its second verse that to love "is to be all bath'd in tears; / To live upon a smile for years; / To lie whole ages at a beauty's feet" (67). Although the various songs might not carry the intellectual weight of "Origin of Song-Writing," Barbauld's binding of the poems together in this way suggests that the songs are not as simple as they might at first appear and that, indeed, they stand in meaningful relation to the "prophetic musings" that are set out in "Origin of Song-Writing." At the very least, the songs are an echo of the earlier poem, providing a subtle and submerged reminder that her interest in Cupid's devious ways ultimately must be accounted for in the light of her larger poetic vision.

As a commentary on pastoral life and love, the songs leave little doubt that Barbauld's view of the poetic desire to be like shepherds is at least as much a delusion as an ideal. The first song, which is presented as a lecture (presumably spoken by Cupid) to a foolish young man who claims to be in love, is filled with images of despair and emotional fatigue that are meant to help the young man determine whether he really understands love. One's experience of love, the speaker of the poem insists, is properly defined by the extent to which one weeps, lives in fear, harbors feelings of jealousy, retreats into solitude, willingly subjects oneself to tyranny, and possesses hope that is finally synonymous with hopelessness. Nothing in the poem suggests that love possesses redemptive qualities or provides comfort to the individual; love is defined entirely in negative terms as "so wide a wound" (67) that it bleeds the very life out of oneself, and nothing more. While John Aikin, in Barbauld's view, may wish to research "verse that speaks the heart" for the purpose of laying "the wreath at beauty's feet," Barbauld herself envisions a life "at beauty's feet" as an experience akin to hellish self-abasement.

The second song, sung by a young man to Cupid, is not quite as offensive to visionary sensibilities as the first, presumably because the speaker is young, stubborn, and naïve. Even so, the poem contains its own peculiar commentary on love. The speaker, for instance, pleads with Cupid that the god make "Florella" love him as much as he loves her—a typical pastoral convention. But the speaker's mindset is so fraught with the tribulations of the historical moment that what is intended as an expression of desire for love is virtually transmogrified into a desire for material possessions. For example, he seeks "bliss" (71), which he understands in terms of Florella's love for him, but that bliss is imagined as a "mighty treasure," a "sterling love," a "sum" that Cupid is asked to "pay" (71). He reveals himself to be nothing more than a crass capitalist or a small-minded miser, for whom love and money are identical. While some of the imagery in the poem—for instance, the reference to the "white propitious hour" that is "pregnant with hoarded joys in store" (71)—might be interpreted to suggest purity and fullness of heart, the reality is that the speaker understands love in terms of self-interest and possessiveness. In fact, he goes so far as to say that if Cupid will not grant to him Florella's love, the god must at least assure him that Florella and he will remain unchanged, so that his sensation of love can be sustained even "when every gleam of hope is gone" (72), a wish that would effectively cut Florella off from the experience of life itself, thereby punishing her for not loving him.

These first two songs written from the perspective of Cupid and a young lover, respectively, are followed by a song that is presented as a dialogue and that in effect contests the discrete and autonomous poetic voices of the earlier poems. The shift to dialogue form marks a poetic step forward for Barbauld, insofar as it creates a formal social dynamic that replaces the narrow individualistic perspectives of the earlier songs. But the subject matter is the same, as are the conclusions. Sylvia does not love Corin, who is passionately in love with her, and she asks that the "simple shepherd" (73) "leave me; / Drag no more a hopeless chain: / I cannot like, nor would deceive thee" (73). While the sentiment that Sylvia articulates may echo the earlier poems, at the same time it constitutes a pastoral poetic vision that at least seems to recognize that deceit is not a good thing and that honest expression, while painful at the moment, is necessary to human dignity. In following the path of honesty, Sylvia goes so far as to tell Corin that "love that's forc'd is harsh and sour: / If the lover be displeasing, / To persist disgusts the more" (73). But the poem finally pushes the ways of Cupid and pastoral no further along toward a redemptive or transformative vision than the previous songs. As it turns out, neither Sylvia nor Corin is capable of self-reflection, and thus they lack self-understanding, leaving them both isolated at the end of the poem:

> But the fates had not consented,
> Since they both did fickle prove;
> Of her scorn the maid repented,
> And the shepherd—of his love. (74)

The ironic ending here once again points toward the inadequacy of the sort of love that is associated too narrowly with Cupid and pastoral. Such love is bound too tightly to individual passion, despite the appearance of social vision suggested by the dialogue form, lacking any connection to larger visionary ideals that might enable the deeper and more complex dimensions of human love to find reasonable constancy and to transform solitude and loneliness into redemptive hope.

The first three songs, then, demonstrate different sorts of limitations that are constituent features of a simplistic understanding of love and pastoral. Even if pastoral idealism is able to tap into certain necessary ingredients of human love—especially passion—and can provide a momentary retreat from the complexities of modern life, it cannot finally stand alone as a model of human behavior or desire, and in fact it too often leads into a volatile and dangerous trap of self-absorbed emotional turmoil. The characters and perspectives presented in the first three songs make this point emphatically clear.

That Barbauld understands this limitation inherent in the pastoral imagination becomes clear in the following three songs, which complicate the idea of pastoral, gradually casting off its limiting ideology and laying the groundwork for deeper understanding. The fourth song, for instance, appropriates the idea of inconstancy portrayed in the Sylvia and Corin poem, but here provides a critical commentary on the way that unchecked passion creates it, emphasizing, as earlier poems have not, the fatal risk inherent in succumbing blindly to passion. Central to this commentary is Barbauld's emphasis on the self-awareness of her speaker, who in surrendering to Chloris after giving up Celia says that "I know this beauty is false and vain" (76). Even if he is unable to alter the dangerous course that he is on ("Yet still I feel I love" [76]), he nevertheless knows that his passions—or at least *these* passions—should be resisted.

The speaker's self-awareness is articulated most fully in the final verses of the poem, which seem to abandon pastoral sensibility altogether and to move close to a visionary understanding of how human fate is determined by human actions in relation to the circumstantial realities of the world rather than by an external universal power alone. In speaking of his inability to control his private passions, which leads him to see the inevitability of his consequent demise, the speaker broadens his conversation beyond his personal situation to make a far-reaching statement about passion:

> But passion's wild impetuous sea
> Hurries me far from peace and thee;
> 'Twere vain to struggle more;
> Thus the poor sailor slumbering lies,
> While swelling tides around him rise,
> And push his bark from the shore.
> In vain he spreads his helpless arms,
> His pitying friends with fond alarms
> In vain deplore his state;
> Still far and farther from the coast,
> On the high surge his bark is tost,
> And foundering yields to fate. (77)

While Barbauld's focus here remains on passion, her vehicle for expressing her ideas is no longer the pastoral mode. The geographical focus of these lines turns away from the fields where shepherds tend their flocks to the open sea, which carries the speaker ever further "from the coast," to the point where he is entirely isolated and alone and therefore doomed, much like Coleridge's mariner twenty-five years later. Moreover, the pastoral promise of freedom is lost in these lines, as the destructive forces of "fate," which is both in the world (the sea) and in the human breast (passion), takes control of life and pushes it inexorably toward death.

This new geographical focus marks a decisive ideological shift for Barbauld, as she exhibits here more confidently than before her conviction that the pastoral imagination, if left unchecked, is insufficient, even as a place of momentary refuge visited for the purpose of restoring the spirit. Unconstrained by the material parameters of history and society, she suggests, the presumed restorative powers of the pastoral landscape allow individual emotion to grow into an uncontrollable and destructive force that compromises human dignity. What appears to be an idyllic retreat, on this view, is in fact a "high surge" that brings not life but death. Given the considerable investment that Barbauld has made in the ideals of pastoral earlier in the volume (however self-reflective and critical she may have been in deploying the pastoral mode), such a view constitutes a decisive moment in her effort to devise a visionary poetics that is grounded in both history and idealism, suggesting that pastoral idealism, at least, is limited as a force for engaging with material circumstance. In her treatment of pastoral subjects later in the volume, this understanding will serve as an important guide to her imagination.

When set alongside an earlier poem like "To Wisdom," this poem might seem to suggest that Barbauld is uncertain whether passion for life should be monitored or left unchecked. In fact, however, the poems stand in illuminating relation to one another, enabling her to distinguish the virtue of the fearless passion for life amid the tribulations of hard circumstance ("To Wisdom") from the naïve and self-indulgent passion associated with Cupid's erotic connivings. The self-absorbed characters portrayed in the first three songs show passion that is left unchecked by the world, thereby allowing them to become victims to their own egos. They do not exhibit an unchecked passion for life, which Barbauld (in "To Wisdom") admires, but rather an unchecked passion for themselves, and the result, as the fourth song shows, is tragic.

The fifth song deepens Barbauld's interrogation of pastoral idealism by picking up on the theme of betrayal and the self-interested nature of passion that has the potential to grow untrammeled within the pastoral landscape. Here, a young nymph (Araminta) laments the fact that she has been betrayed by a young man (Damon) whom she loves and that she, no less than Celia in the fourth song, is therefore forced to face the reality of "broken vows and alter'd truth" (78).[5] But the account of Araminta's pain differs from that of Celia's insofar as Barbauld introduces "an aged shepherd" (78) to instruct the young nymph on the ways of love within a pastoral landscape and to advise a course of action. The old shepherd is much closer in sensibility to a prophet than to a pastoral spokesperson because he never seeks to comfort Araminta with the illusion that lost love can be retrieved or that "alter'd truth" can be corrected. To the contrary, he says flatly that nothing can relieve "a breaking heart by love betray'd" (78) or restore "dying passion" (79), because the hard reality is that "in beauty's empire is no mean, / And woman, either slave or queen, / Is quickly scorn'd when not ador'd"

(79). According to the old shepherd, the only relief for the pain that Araminta feels is death: "For hearts o'ercome with love and grief / All nature yields but one relief; / Die, hapless Araminta, die" (80).

The pain experienced by the lovelorn in the first few songs and that is described in disturbing terms in the fourth is here portrayed as irredeemable suffering that can find no relief even in the most peaceful and sympathetic of natural landscapes. As the poem makes clear, suffering is entirely human in nature, not dependent on environment, however simple and idyllic that environment may be, and the inability or refusal to face the fundamentally human character of suffering means that death is the only reasonable avenue to take, if suffering is to be alleviated. Thus, Barbauld seems to suggest, whether an individual chooses to retreat from the world or engage with it is neither here nor there; what matters is how she or he deals with suffering. As the old shepherd understands, for Araminta, who, as a literary character, is entirely identified with pastoral idealism, death is the only possible relief, because the values that define the nymph are grounded in a binary opposition, namely that life is worth nothing unless one's self-interest is fully sated (a woman is "quickly scorn'd" unless she is "quickly . . . ador'd"). Unable to possess the love of Damon, therefore, death is her only recourse, a fact that, for Barbauld, seems to illuminate the reductive and therefore unsatisfactory character of pastoral vision as the sole foundation of human meaning. On this view, the final line of the poem constitutes a fatal blow to the pastoral vision, at least in terms of the way it has been understood to this point in the volume.

The final song turns away from pastoral altogether, focusing instead on the deeper and more complex challenge of developing an embracing prophetic sensibility. Here, the god in whom the poem is interested is not Cupid but rather Apollo, the god of prophecy, who is described as growing along with the narrator from youth to maturity. The account of the narrator's allegiance to the sun god reads almost like a description of the ordering of poems in Barbauld's volume, as the poet embraces prophecy from the beginning, though her understanding of prophetic vision is naïve, and continues to engage with the difficult demands of prophecy throughout, retreating periodically into the kinder landscape of pastoral for the purpose of self reflection. From the beginning, the narrator says, she "bow'd before your infant shrine" (80), associating the young god's character with "beauty's boundless empire" (80). Although neither the narrator nor Apollo fully grasps the importance that, in time, will be ascribed to the sun god, the narrator is certain that she must place herself in his company: "And ere your thoughts, devoid of art, / Could learn the value of a heart, / I gave my heart away" (81). At this moment of submission to Apollo, the narrator says, she remains at some distance from the young god, where it "'twas safe to gaze" (81); that is, while she makes her commitment to Apollo, she does so with some apprehension and without fully understanding the significance of what she has done. At this early moment in the poem, the expression of loyalty to Apollo seems to assume that prophecy and pastoral are equally idyllic and simple. As the narrator puts it, she did not think the innocence with which she first approached Apollo "could harm / The peace of future days" (81).

In reality, of course, as Barbauld makes clear, pastoral and prophecy are very different modes of poetic representation, and they exhibit a different conception of the visionary. If in the previous poems, Barbauld sought to shed herself of the values (of retreat, simplicity, and balance) associated with pastoral, here she wrestles with the difficulty and complexity associated with an allegiance to Apollo. When considered in the full light of understanding, she says, the god of prophecy is a demanding authority, who leads his followers along a path that does not seek to escape the threat of hardship or death but, indeed, faces them directly. Barbauld states directly the dangers associated with prophecy:

> But now despotic o'er the plains
> The awful noon of beauty reigns,
> And kneeling crowds adore;
> Its beams arise too fiercely bright,
> Danger and death attend the sight,
> And I must hope no more. (81)

The power associated with Apollo inspires awe, but it is also terrible in its reach and risk. Moreover, as the narrator says, one does not approach prophecy with hope (which, presumably, is the provenance of pastoral) but with dread. After many expressions of imaginative unrest, partial understanding, and indecision in the volume, Barbauld seems to grasp, at last, what must be waged in submitting to the demands of prophecy. But, even so, she does not say explicitly here that she is capable of committing herself wholly to the prophetic struggle to transform the world.

Indeed, as the song concludes, Barbauld restates the terrible power that comes with prophetic vision, only this time pushing further back in time to emphasize the long and difficult history of facing directly or accepting fully the principles and values of prophecy:

> Thus to the rising God of day
> Their early vows the Persians pay,

> And bless the spreading fire,
> Whose glowing chariot mounting soon
> Pours on their heads the burning noon;
> They sicken and expire. (82)⁶

The old shepherd at the conclusion of the fifth song regards death as the only solution to Araminta's distress, but here Barbauld sees the death of an entire civilization as requisite to transformation. The ability to look squarely into the glare of the sun, without turning away, and see (and accept) the collapse of a culture is a very heavy burden to bear, and it is a far cry from an idyllic pastoral landscape and the purely personal struggles therein with romantic love. The search to discover a path forward in the face of such a vision is a terrifying prospect. But, as Barbauld seems now to understand, this is the responsibility with which she is tasked. Although she does not now begin to move in a direct line toward an articulation of this new understanding, nor abandon entirely the pastoral imagination, she makes this understanding her first imperative.⁷

In "Delia: An Elegy," Barbauld returns to the pastoral mode, though she is no longer writing from within its guiding assumption that people can, or should, all be like shepherds. Nor does she write in the conventional elegiac mode (as the title suggests she will) that mourns the loss of a loved individual. Rather, her elegiac gesture is one of farewell to some of the pastoral and political investments that had marked many of her earlier poems. More importantly, as an elegy, "Delia" bids farewell to the dominant structures of modernity, not in a nostalgic turn to the past but in an effort to focus on the work of preserving and strengthening the sorts of values that, in her view, are vitally important to a new world marked by justice and freedom. That is, even as she abandons one piece of the pastoral imagination, at the same time she preserves and extends the pastoral interest in love, envisioning it (broadly conceived) as a fundamental human desire that can (and should) serve as a foundational principle in a reimagined world. On this view, her engagement with pastoral here is transformative rather than purely negative; rather than simply reject the pastoral imagination out of hand, she remakes it in such a way that is consistent with her maturing visionary sensibility. If in the fifth song, Barbauld says directly that death offers the only plausible resolution to Araminta's dilemma and in the sixth song she suggests that resolution to such a dilemma on a societal level might demand the death of an entire civilization, she now begins to imagine what principles might be worth preserving and cultivating in the wake of such loss.

The direction of Barbauld's maturing vision can be glimpsed in the epigraph to "Delia" and in the larger poem from which the epigraph is taken. Once again, Barbauld chooses Tibullus as her guiding spirit, just as she had done in the second "Characters" poem and in "Origin of Song-Writing," drawing her lines from elegy 3.3: "A long life's joy / With thee, and in old age to clasp thy hand" (98).[8] While these lines by themselves articulate an admittedly sentimental mindset, the larger poem from which they are taken places them within a social and cultural context that helps Tibullus to produce a remarkable statement about (among other things) the differences between love, on the one hand, and wealth and power, on the other, as guides or goals in life. And he makes clear that, as foundational principles in life, wealth and power are useless: "Wealth has no power to lift life's load of care, / Or free man's lot from Fortune's fatal chain"; "No! not dominion, nor Pactolian stream, / Nor all the riches the wide world can give! / These other men may ask":

If when my season of sweet light is o'er,
I, carrying nothing, unto Charon yield,
What profits me a ponderous golden store,
Or that a thousand yoke must plough my field?

What if proud Phrygian columns fill my halls,
Taenarian, Carystian, and the rest,
Or branching groves adorn my spacious walls,
Or golden roof, or floor with marbles dressed?

What pleasure in rare Erythraean dyes,
Or purple pride of Sidon and of Tyre,
Or all that can solicit envious eyes,
And which the mob of fools so well admire?

If wealth and power are useless in lifting "life's load of care," the poem says, then they are meaningless as grounding principles in life, and it becomes necessary to look elsewhere for purpose and direction. For Tibullus, the only trustworthy principle capable of grounding life in a meaningful way is love—"With thee, Neaera, poverty looks fair, / And lacking thee, a kingdom were in vain"—because it alone is (potentially) free of self-interested motivations.

Although Barbauld has already examined the idea of love in *Poems*, Tibullus's particular formulation helps to sharpen her vision because he places love firmly within the material context of political and economic reality, where it must find its way. Love, for Tibullus, is not a pure virtue that transcends the world, nor can it compete with wealth and power in material importance; rather it is a practice that infuses purpose into the life that is caught within the crosscurrents of human experience, making it possible (by bringing into view life's meaning beyond the solitary individual and beyond the principle of self-interest) to live meaningfully in the world. The abiding and ideal principle of love, that is, helps to elucidate the reality that the search for material possessions and the struggle for political power are transient, ever fading away and always under threat, and that only love is always available as an ever-present restorative power. Tibullus recognizes clearly the inescapable pressures, seductions, and temptations that the pastoral ideal of love seeks to transcend, as well as the impossibility of escape, but he insists that purposeful life is nevertheless possible.

In "Delia," Barbauld tilts her thought in the same direction, organizing her poem around the conviction that although the world is a troubled space, offering no true possibility of relief or retreat, love remains a living, vibrant, and deeply meaningful ideal that is capable of exciting life with a sense of purpose. Her affirmative comment in the first line of the poem—"Yes DELIA loves!" (83)—emphatically conveys her idealistic vision of life's potential for joy and happiness, and in the larger scope of the poem (as well as in subsequent poems) she attempts to extend her idealism across the broad range of human experience. As Tibullus's various elegies show, life is ever troubled, death is inevitable, and even the world is doomed eventually to collapse into ruin, but love can sustain life even in the face of these inexorable facts. In "Delia" and afterward, Barbauld follows a similar track, examining the proposition that love need not be viewed simply as an ideal associated with shepherds and nymphs on the pastoral landscape; it may be reimagined as an ideal that is directly relevant to living meaningfully within the constraints and crosscurrents of historical reality. Under the guiding spirit of such a possibility, she also gradually reimagines the idea of pastoral not as a place of retreat but rather as a way of thinking that keeps alive the principle of love.

The larger vision that Tibullus's poem encourages helps to clarify the deepening understanding at which Barbauld has begun to arrive. The possibility that love might serve as an anchor and guide in the face of human tribulation requires deep and unwavering courage and conviction, because it is also possible (and perhaps likely) that, as Tibullus knows, humanity will be unable to overcome the binary thinking that views love and experience as mutually and categorically distinct and that therefore under the pressure of circumstantial reality love will diminish into little more than a beautiful idealism that cannot be sustained. To counter this possibility, he uses his elegiac imagination to create a compelling poetic example of how love might stand firm in the face of affliction and loss, providing an essential insight into the very definition of life. As his narrator (who misses Neaera, the woman he loves) says earlier in the poem, love is more important than power and wealth; now he says directly in the concluding lines of the poem that love is of such vital worth that without it, life loses its purpose and death becomes a welcome companion; with love, all obstacles can be faced and all temptations to give into pure self-interest can be resisted, but without it, nothing possesses meaning:

> Saturnian Juno, to all nuptials kind,
> Receive with grace my ever-anxious vow!
> Come, Venus, wafted by the Cyprian wind,
> And from thy car of shell smile on me now!
> But if the mournful sisters, by whose hands
> Our threads of life are spun, refuse me all—
> May Pluto bid me to his dreary lands,
> Where those wide rivers through the darkness fall!

The prayer here (addressed to Juno, the queen of the gods, and to Venus, the goddess of love) states flatly the hard point that Barbauld is trying to learn, namely that, absent love, life may as well be cast into darkness and death.

But the lines hold an additional possible meaning as well, which would not have been lost on Barbauld. The absolute faith in love expressed by Tibullus's narrator carries within it such a magisterial authority that death itself loses its power to instill fear and dread. In the final lines of the elegy, the narrator shows himself to be emphatically less concerned about facing death than about living without love. Implicit in such a view is that life, under the auspices of love, can (and should) be built around entirely positive and hopeful sensibilities, sufficiently strong to resist even the most powerful temptation to despair: death. Whether human experience is troubled by politics, the mad ambition to secure wealth, or even the existential fact of death, love, fully embraced, relieves all fear and makes purposeful life possible.

The lesson that Barbauld seems to take from Tibullus's elegy 3.3—that love is an enduring and life-sustaining ideal and that its healing power is sufficiently strong to offset fear and dread—helps to clarify the relation between "Delia" and the ideas set out at the conclusion of the sixth song that immediately precedes it. As "Delia" begins, the narrator remarks that "one kind relenting glance has heal'd my breast, / And balanc'd in a moment years of pain" (83). That Barbauld aims to provide a redemptive picture to counter the visionary dread of the sixth song becomes clear when she appropriates from that poem the image of the sun and transforms it to fit her poetic purpose in "Delia." At the conclusion of the sixth song, Barbauld describes the sun as "the spreading fire" that "pours . . . the burning noon" on the Persians' heads, causing them to "sicken and expire." Here, however, Delia is associated with the sun in very different terms:

> O'er her soft cheek consenting blushes move,
> And with kind stealth her secret soul betray;
> Blushes, which usher in the morn of love,
> Sure as the red'ning east foretells the day. (83)

For the narrator, Delia is a benevolent and redemptive sun, identified by "simplicity" that "in native graces shine" (84). The narrator likewise describes Delia's hair in terms that evoke the beauty of the sun:

> When Delia's hand unlocks her shining hair,
> And o'er her shoulder spreads the flowing gold,
> Base were the man who one bright tress would spare
> For all the ore of India's coarser mold. (85)

Further, the associations between Delia and the sun, which suggest both her beauty and her capacity for love, eventually become an internalized principle in the poem, attesting to the power of love to change the human breast: "Yet if some youth, for gentler passions born,/ Shall chance to wander near our lowly cell,/ His feeling breast with purer flames shall glow" (87–88). Barbauld revisits and appropriates the imagery of the sixth song in order to transform its terrible association with death into a vision of hope through the enduring qualities of love that *shine* even more than gold in the physical features of Delia and that are stronger than the seductive appeal of imperialistic adventure and conquest.

The vision of love that Barbauld portrays in "Delia" is set against the same sorts of historical reality that Tibullus describes in elegy 3.3, embracing, as her Roman forbear does, the principle of love as the only human reality worth carrying forward through life and worthy of being embraced even till the end of day and the end of life, that is, "till the last ling'ring beam of doubtful light" (85). The love that Barbauld imagines here is simple and pure, unencumbered by the complexities of "the splendid feast" (84) and "the shepherd's lowly life" (84), which will require "the russet garment" (84) and a life of labor. And even when it is tied to a life of labor, Barbauld's conception of love remains an ideal, unthreatened by hardship, because it is happily wedded to rearing children (85–86), attending "the rural fair" (84), and tending to the natural landscape (86).

It is an ideal, moreover, that not only welcomes the burden of labor but that is also capable of withstanding the harshest historical realities that all too often are marked by struggle, violence, and mendacity:

> When beating rains forbid our feet to roam,
> We'll shelter'd sit, and turn the storied page;
> There see what passions shake the lofty dome
> With mad ambition or ungovern'd rage:
> What headlong ruin oft involves the great;
> What conscious terrors guilty bosoms prove;
> What strange and sudden turns of adverse fate
> Tear the sad virgin from her plighted love. (86)

The reading of history, in this instance, is not an example of human conduct to be followed but rather a warning against the principles that often threaten to corrupt human experience, and a confirmation that simple love is the highest ideal to which one might aspire:

> Delia shall read, and drop a gentle tear;
> Then cast her eyes around the low-roof'd cot,
> And own the fates have dealt more kindly here,
> That bles'd with only love our little lot. (86)

Barbauld here perhaps lapses to a degree into (for her) uncharacteristic sentimentality, but that sentimentality has a purpose: to provide a counterpoint to the culturally pervasive assumption that personal ambition and historical violence are the only, or most important, models of human behavior. For Barbauld, in this instance, the pastoral ideal is not a protection from history but rather the poetic (and prophetic) basis for a historical critique that laments the path that history has taken ("Delia shall read, and drop a gentle tear") while at the same time describing comfort that comes from knowing that human experience may be differently constructed. That is to say, the poem engages with the past as a way of commenting on the present and as a means of imagining how, under the auspices of love, the future may be transformed.[9]

Further, Barbauld's vision of love entails an appropriation and transformation of the vocabulary of history. For her, love, no less than the "made ambition" that has driven and structured past history, is a power, albeit a categorically different kind of power from ambition, that demands absolute subservience from its followers. As she puts it, "Love has sworn ... / the wav'ring heart shall never be his care / That stoops at any baser shrine to bow; / And what he cannot rule, he scorns to share" (87). Such a characterization indicates the extent to which, as a redemptive category, love must be divorced from the idea of withdrawal from the world and effectively inserted into history as a contender for the human soul. Such engagement requires taking over and remaking the very language of historical commentary and understanding. Further, while the landscape of the poem draws on the trappings and vocabulary of pastoral, Barbauld remakes pastoral along the lines of visionary poetics, thereby making the genre of pastoral into a space for textual and historical engagement and transformation. Once freed from the corruptions of "mad ambition," and transformed by the tyranny of mutual love, "rural peace," "cheerful leisure," and "poetic ease" (87) become possible: once love becomes the guiding principle of history, the distinctions between historical reality and pastoral idealism will dissolve, and the voice of the prophet will modulate into the softer voice of "poetic ease."

With the structural transformation of human history and understanding, the future—in the form of a youth visiting the lowly pastoral hut—can be confidently imagined in a new and more appealing way. This future, Barbauld says, will be defined by the absence of politics, conflict, and trouble and by the triumph of true equality of spirit and the selfless regard for others, which, finally, is the true meaning of love:

> Yet if some youth, for gentler passions born,
> Shall chance to wander near our lowly cell,
> His feeling breast with purer flames shall glow;
> And leaving pomp, and state, and cares behind,
> Shall own the world has little to bestow
> Where two fond hearts in equal love are join'd. (87–88)

The world that "has little to bestow," as Barbauld imagines it, is the world of "pomp, and state, and cares"—that is to say, the world of past history—and the future world that matters is one characterized by the lived ideal of "equal love." For Barbauld, it is possible for people to be guided by "purer flames" than those that have defined the broad course of human history, but that possibility requires an engagement with the records of the past, as well as self-reflection, both of which, properly studied, can purify the heart and imagination and lay the groundwork for a future that is marked by peaceful coexistence, justice, and freedom of imagination.

If "Delia" is an elegy, as its title says, clearly it is a complicated one, because it is neither a lament for the death of Delia (the titular character) or for the pastoral idiom per se. As an elegy, the poem is rather a somber meditation on the passing of one form of troubled human consciousness and on a past that has been lost—or, more properly, on a history that is marked thoroughly by patterns of human self-destruction. But the elegiac tenor of the poem is not characterized by a desire to revive the values and principles undergirding this past history. Indeed, the poem unblinkingly bids this history farewell, suggesting that it can never serve as a proper foundation for building a world that is infused with love and the spirit of freedom. Still, remembering the past, as Barbauld makes clear, nevertheless causes grief ("Delia shall read, and drop a gentle tear") because the troubled record of human experience is a record of human suffering and misunderstanding. At the same time, even as the poem describes Delia's grief over the troubled course of human history, it steps imaginatively and hopefully into the space left by the history that has destroyed itself, conceiving a new set of principles and values that might provide the necessary foundation for an enduring, meaningful, and hopeful human reality. The idea of pastoral retreat now becomes a retreat into the principle of absolute, selfless love, leaving the corrupt world to collapse, while a new vision of pure love arises to embrace all of lived experience.

That Barbauld's turn away from the principles underwriting "the storied page" of history and her complication of the idea of pastoral love constitute a decisive visionary choice becomes clear immediately in the following poem. "Ovid to His Wife: Imitated from Different Parts of His Tristia," written from the perspective of the Roman poet, is, in effect, the voice of one crying in the wilderness, as Ovid wrote *Tristia* (or "troubles") after having been banished from Rome by Caesar Augustus.[10] In her characterization of Ovid, Barbauld seems to suggest that the path she has chosen to follow will exile her from the dominant structures of thought governing her world and present her with a future of trouble into old age.[11] To the extent that Barbauld expresses her awareness that her visionary choice will leave her largely an outcast, this poem, more so than "Delia," is a personal elegy; indeed, unlike in "Delia," Barbauld here (following Ovid in *Tristia*) uses the elegiac couplet to express her sentiments, and the larger arc of the poem describes the loneliness of individual life lived outside the bounds of a loving and supportive community. But if Ovid's banishment from his native society suggests Barbauld's awareness of what may lie ahead for herself as a visionary poet, the poem itself is not a visionary statement, nor does it reflect her view on visionary poetry. It is, rather, a portrayal of what the individual and world look like when visionary hope has been lost. Indeed, the subject of the poem—Ovid's banishment—constitutes a darkly ironic commentary on the pastoral ideal of retreat, insofar as Ovid finds himself in a place of retreat away from the crowded city of Rome. But, for him, retreat is a punishment rather than a restorative ideal, suggesting that the simple fact of the rural landscape is no guarantee of pleasure in life. What matters are the principles by which one lives and the community within which those principles may be fully expressed. On this view, "Ovid to His Wife" marks a logical conclusion to Barbauld's studied effort, beginning with "Origin of Song-Writing," to sort out the underlying importance of a range of issues that are threaded through the earlier portions of the volume—love, pastoral, prophecy, visionary poetics—and to resolve, once and for all, the complex and troubling relations among them.

But, as these remarks suggest, the poem offers more than a logical conclusion to her examination of these issues. At the same time, it is a detailed consideration of the mode of poetic expression that Barbauld is abandoning as she embraces fully a poetic life of visionary commitment. The poem is something of a last look at a mode of poetic consciousness that must be allowed to pass if the path of vision is to be developed fully. To this end, it gives voice to a poetic understanding that is located entirely outside the possibilities promised by visionary idealism, focusing instead squarely on a reality in which human experience is bound inextricably within an untranscendable horizon of circumstance. In such a sphere of existence as this, where suffering rules and vision is irretrievably lost, change becomes impossible, life's meaning diminishes, and hope reaches an impasse, leaving one (in this case, the poem's titular character) forever victim to debilitating despair. For Barbauld, Ovid represents a different—and more tragic—version of the follies of solitude and self-absorption that she describes in her poems about Cupid and romantic love.

In a move that sharpens her interest in this direction, in "Ovid to His Wife" Barbauld examines the dimensions of personal trauma in an individual life as a way of understanding the extent to which troubles often block understanding and destroy hope. She captures Ovid's extreme psychological trauma by focusing on his physical severance from the world, a poetic strategy that enables her to demonstrate and explain the disproportionate attention the Roman poet paid to his personal life. In a turn that exhibits clearly Barbauld's decision to examine the limitations of a poetic mode that she is in process of abandoning, she takes her epigraph to the poem from *Tristia*, even as her poem is an imitation "from different parts of . . . *Tristia*." The effect of this poetic strategy is to create an enclosed, claustrophobic poetic space that emblematizes the psychological imprisonment that Ovid must have felt in his exile and that Barbauld must have known she, in time, eventually might experience as well. Anthony S. Kline translates the epigraph as follows: "My temples already take on the colour of swan's plumage, / and white old age is bleaching my dark hair." Insofar as Ovid's focus is turned inward, his understanding of community and any hope he may have possessed for orderliness in life become corrupted, and his enclosed sense of reality leads him to lament his growing old age and to question the way his life has unfolded. The proper course of life, he says elsewhere in the poem, should be marked by hardship in youth and leisure and peace in old age, but he has experienced the reverse. As he puts it, "The Fates were hostile, bringing ease / to my early years, pain to the later ones." Torn by personal trauma, he loses his understanding of the larger contours of life and is overcome by sorrow because he is growing old and by nostalgia for the way his life should have been passed: "It's time I no longer breathed foreign air, / or quenched my parched thirst at Getic fountains, / but retired now to the sheltered gardens I owned, / and enjoyed the sight of men, and the city, again."

If the lines that Barbauld lifts for her epigraph create an overwhelming sense of personal nostalgia for what might have been when placed alongside the larger concerns of the poem, at the same time they serve another important and critical poetic purpose. And in the context of Barbauld's volume, that purpose is pointed. Although Ovid's poem is marked by nostalgic longing, it also may rightly be seen as a commentary on pastoral idealism, suggesting that the city (society), after all, is the place where one remains young and where one's garden most properly should be cultivated. Life outside community, in the end, is a form of debilitating exile from what matters in life: loving and trusting relationships with people.

In addition to modifying her poetic course by choosing an epigraph from a poem that provides her subject matter, Barbauld takes another important turn into the sort of poetic mindset that she associates with Ovid by stating in her subtitle that her poem is "imitated from different parts of his *Tristia*" (89). By way of the word "imitated," she makes explicit the sort of poetic practice that she is in process of rejecting in the volume, insofar as visionary poetry is creative rather than imitative in spirit.[12] By momentarily short-circuiting the visionary spirit and giving voice to Ovid's imitative practice, she exposes the limitations of the earlier poet's sensibility in *Tristia*, a point that becomes clear when "Ovid to His Wife" is placed in critical relation to other poems in the volume, especially "Delia." The worldview of Ovid that she imitates is one (as her Ovid puts it) that is "averse to change" (89) and that desires "safe repose" and "a safe port" (90): sentiments radically at odds with the visionary recognition of risk and danger that accompany the brave call for the transformation of consciousness and the world. In Barbauld's characterization, Ovid is a tired old man, who is worn down by "stern winter," "the weary waste" of the "Scythian wilds," and "the savage mountains and the dreary shore" (91) and who spends his days shifting wearily between complaints about the sorry lot to which he has been condemned and nostalgic expressions of desire to return to his "native soil," where he might discover "long vacation from unquiet toil" (92). Such limited imagination leads him ultimately to condemn the mere existence of people:

> Society than solitude is worse,
> And man to man is still the greatest curse.
> A savage race my fearful steps surround,
> Practis'd in blood and disciplin'd to wound;
> Unknown alike to pity as to fear. (93)

In Barbauld's presentation, even if Ovid is correct in viewing the Scythians as a faithless people consumed by violent and militaristic motives—"The rage of battle works, when battles cease;/ And wars are brooding in the lap of peace" (93)—he is nevertheless ill equipped to serve as a vehicle meant to advance the idealistic interests and desires of visionary poetics.

With its emphasis on personal regret and nostalgia— which are captured perfectly by Barbauld's imitative strategy—the poem stands in marked contrast to "Delia," and, taken together, the poems constitute two sorts of elegy and two sorts of commentary on human consciousness. If "Delia" elegizes the passing of one form of human consciousness while at the same time imagining a new set of human possibilities, "Ovid to His Wife" serves as an example of the sort of consciousness—and the sort of conventional elegiac imagination—that must be allowed to pass if a transformed human consciousness is to arise. That is, "Ovid to His Wife" is imitative in nature for the purpose of elucidating the trap of conventional elegiac expression, the trap of conventional consciousness with which elegiac poetry is typically associated, and, at least implicitly, the inadequacy of the conventional pastoral imagination. Following immediately on the hopeful cast of "Delia," the poem seems doubly dreary in its capacity to imagine nothing more than loss and hardship. On this view, while Barbauld's poem is imitative it is also implicitly critical, insofar as it captures the impasse at which traditional poetic modes and interests ultimately arrive: to imitate is to dwell only in the world of lost hope. As the poem makes clear in its final paragraph, Ovid's imagination is focused entirely inward, as he can only imagine his continued exile ("Yet here, for ever here, your bard must dwell" [94]), which will end, ultimately, in his death ("The silent dust shall glow at thy command, /And the warm ashes feel thy pious hand" [95]). The world that is envisioned in these descriptions is unchanging and unchangeable. While Barbauld will continue to examine the possibilities of pastoral idealism for visionary poetics—and while she will continue to use elements of pastoral for her poetic purposes—she seems certain at last that a simpleminded view of pastoral and imitative poetry is unacceptable. In effect, in writing "Ovid to His Wife," Barbauld is taking one final look at the corpse of conventional poetic imagination before closing the coffin lid on it forever.

CHAPTER SIX

The Personal and Biblical Principles of Poetic Vision

The poems beginning with "Origin of Song-Writing" and concluding with "Ovid to His Wife" are among the most difficult and complex in *Poems*, insofar as they strive to work through many of the thorny issues—pastoral idealism, subjectivity, social engagement, the nature and function of the visionary imagination—that occupy Barbauld's imagination in the larger volume. That she seems to be successful in her effort, however, does not mean that the remainder of the volume can be interpreted as an untroubled expression of visionary idealism or prophetic proclamation. It remains for the poet to consider what it means, precisely and poetically, to "bless the spreading fire" (82), as she puts it in her sixth song. What does it mean, in other words, to dedicate one's poetic gift wholly to the difficult challenges of visionary idealism? How does the visionary poet transform human consciousness? How does the poet position herself productively in relation to the social and existential realities of human experience? To what extent might the teachings of the Bible serve as a guide for the visionary poet in the modern age? Barbauld begins to address these questions in what might at first appear to be a cluster of rather meek poems but that in fact is a cluster of carefully constructed pieces meant to restate some of the major ideas of the volume in a different sort of context. The poems here—"To a Lady," "Ode to Spring," "Verses on Mrs. Rowe," "To Miss R——," and "On the Death of Mrs. Jennings"—are, with the exception of "Ode to Spring," all addressed to women, and even in "Ode to Spring" Barbauld feminizes the season in setting out her vision: "Sweet daughter of a rough and stormy fire" (98). In this steadfast focus on female and feminized subject matter, Barbauld seems to be deploying a calculated strategy that concentrates her poetic attention on a socially subservient class of people in an effort to demonstrate the principles on which her vision relies and to test that vision against the hard realities of the larger and dominant forces of authority in the world. These poems, when set in relation to the hymns that follow, elucidate both the challenges and possibilities of visionary poetics in Barbauld's world.

The particular principle that Barbauld examines in these poems relates to the importance and possibility of establishing a transformative sensibility that does not rely on force or power to make itself manifest. Refusing to embrace any oppositional form of power to fight against a prevailing structure of authority on the grounds that doing so simply perpetuates an ideology of domination, she instead articulates her visionary ideals from a position of subservience and pacifist (and conscientious) refusal of conflict, believing that a wholehearted investment in her ideals without regard to struggles for domination is the only way to assure that those ideals remain uncorrupted and sustainable once a dominant structure of authority has disappeared. In developing the particulars of her visionary poetics along these lines, it becomes clear the extent to which she has divorced herself from what Wittreich calls "the Milton tradition" of vision, which is marked heavily by the idea that the transformation of human consciousness requires the visionary poet to enter explicitly and openly into to intellectual and imaginative warfare with prevailing forms of cultural and ideological authority (*Blake's Sublime Allegory* 25).[1]

The first of these short poems, "To a Lady," drew the ire of Mary Wollstonecraft, who, as noted, argued that the poem presents a stereotype of the female writer as a dainty and unthinking scribbler who assumes that women's primary responsibility in life (as Barbauld's poem puts it) is, like flowers, "to please" (97).[2] But Wollstonecraft is only partly correct in her criticism. While it is true that Barbauld draws connections between the nature of women and the softness and beauty of flowers, she does so in such a way as to capture the sorts of value that for her are necessary to imagining a transformed human experience and to capture the idealism that motivates her poetic aims. In the poem, Barbauld again turns to the pastoral tradition, drawing on those elements of the genre that point to the human desire for a meaningful and peaceful existence, describing flowers as "gay without toil, and lovely without art" (97). But she also integrates a biblical sensibility into Virgilian pastoral, stating that flowers "in Eden's pure and guiltless garden grew" (96), anticipating the literary and cultural tradition that she will explore in greater depth in the hymns that follow these brief poems. In Barbauld's imagination, pastoral idealism is no longer to be found only among shepherds and sheep but also in the biblical garden. In drawing this association, Barbauld makes explicit the risks entailed in imagining an ideal world. In Eden, after all, prohibitions are set, innocence is tempted, and corruption is only one poor decision away. That is, the allusion to the garden in effect brings to light the (often unseen) dangers that always threaten pastoral idealism.

Virgil's second eclogue, from which Barbauld takes her epigraph for the poem, helps to elucidate the relation between idealism and circumstance that is suggested by Barbauld's biblical reference. It also helps to elucidate the arc of Barbauld's vision of a transformed humanity. The epigraph translates as follows: "For you the Nymphs / Bring baskets, see, with lilies brimmed." These lines evoke a world of natural plentitude and beauty that nicely complements the "lady" with flowers, whom Barbauld is depicting. Yet the larger poem from which the epigraph is taken describes the unrequited love of Corydon for Alexis and records the shepherd's lament that he cannot win the heart of the person he loves. Further, the lines that constitute the epigraph are surrounded by long passages describing sadness, frustration, and danger. Following a tactic that she uses in some of her earlier pastoral poems, Barbauld here questions the possibility of idealism even as she idealizes the "lady" being described and imagines a world—an "empire" (97)—that is governed by the principle of service to others. According to Virgil's eclogue, Corydon is the victim, among other things, of power politics, insofar as Alexis's heart is ruled by another (a "master"), who, from Corydon's perspective, is a much less worthy partner than Corydon, a hardworking artist who is committed to living in service to Alexis. Moreover, Corydon is unafraid to face the dangers of his world—"Ay, and two fawns, I risked my neck to find / In a steep glen, with coats white-dappled still"—showing that he is not only creative and loving, but also strong.

Complicating Barbauld's poetic aims further, the poem from which the epigraph is taken explicitly describes homosexual desire. Homosexuality was acceptable in the Rome of Virgil's time as long as it was limited to relations between free Romans and the slave population.[3] As Virgil makes clear, Alexis is a slave and is "his own master's joy"; Cordyon therefore has no right to him and thus can never hope to win his affection. As he despairingly puts it near the beginning of the poem:

> Better have borne the petulant proud disdain
> Of Amaryllis, or Menalcas wooed,
> Albeit he was so dark, and you so fair!
> Trust not too much to colour, beauteous boy;
> White privets fall, dark hyacinths are culled.[4]

Corydon's frustration, too, leads him to state that Alexis's "scorn" will "drive me to my death." The unrequited homosexual love described in Virgil's poem was transgressive by the lights of British cultural standards and a capital crime under the laws of the eighteenth century.[5] Barbauld's selection of the second eclogue for her epigraph therefore raises difficult questions about her designs for the poem. William McCarthy has argued persuasively that "To a Lady" (among other of Barbauld's poems addressed to women) is a political poem by virtue of the fact that it expresses female pleasure, and it may be that there is at least a hint of lesbian desire associated with that articulation.[6] But, however one may wish to interpret the particular gender issues in the poem, it is likely that Barbauld is less interested in making a point about sexuality than about principles of human character that may provide a suitable foundation for a meaningful and benevolent existence. That is, the poem subtly challenges the dominant ideological structures of her age for the purpose of stating that love, desire, and pleasure—no matter their object—are ideals to be embraced without restraint, as long as they are freely given and received. Her interest is in the possibility that "consenting lovers" (96) hold the key to a passionate and peaceful existence.

Barbauld develops her idealistic principles by depicting flowers in such a way as to invest them with visionary symbolism. Several simple facts about the poem demonstrate her movement in this direction. First, it is a description of a gift of a painting of flowers freely presented by the narrator to a friend, thereby illustrating the principle of benevolence. Moreover, the flowers are not natural but rather painted; as the narrator puts it, the flowers in the painting are "emblems" (96). Thus the narrator is not providing her friend with a gift from the *natural* world but rather from the human imagination. These facts are important to Barbauld's visionary purposes because they capture the fundamentally human goal of her poetic practice. Working across creative media (poetry and painting), Barbauld presents a poem about a painting that, in turn, is given to a friend, thereby bringing her vision fully into the circle of human creativity and experience without compromising the idealism that she articulates. Her plea to her friend that she "nor blush, my fair, to own you copy" the flowers (97) is thus a plea that she recognize the ideal principles emblematized in the painting and that she find the inner strength to "copy" them. More specifically, insofar as copying these principles means pleasing others (as the final line, which drew the ire of Wollstonecraft, explicitly states), Barbauld is not saying that women are like flowers, whose purpose is simply to please in some sort of mindless or decorative sense; indeed, she is calling attention not to literal flowers at all but rather to the creativity and regard for others that are suggested by the painting of flowers that is given as a gift. Moreover, not only is a painting of flowers being given to the "Lady" but also the poem itself, as the poem's title suggests. On this view, the poem is about the role of art (poetry and painting) as a transformative power (it creates an "empire" [97]) on behalf of benevolence and the principle of subservience to love.

"Ode to Spring" appropriates several images from "To a Lady," as well as extending Barbauld's interest in gender and pastoral. For instance, the poem once again depicts flowers as the embodiment of beauty and delight, as Barbauld beseeches spring to "call those winds which thro' the whispering boughs / With warm and pleasant breath / Salute the blowing flowers" (100) and asks the spring dew to "feed the flowering osier's early shoots" (100). Pastoral imagery is also used to give thematic substance and poetic character to the poem, as Barbauld describes spring as being "More sweet than softest touch of Doric reed, / Or Lydian flute" (99).[7] These various images, in turn, are depicted within the context of a feminized spring, reflecting, as is often the case in the volume, Barbauld's effort to weave her poems together as part of a nuanced and embracing visionary stance. The ode articulates its own unique visionary theme, yet, at the same time, the meanings of the poem are inextricably tied to its surrounding poems and to the volume as a whole.

One aim of Barbauld's poetic strategy in this instance, it seems, is to unpack further the complicated relations between pastoral and visionary idealism. While the poem celebrates the beauty of spring, at the same time it acknowledges the hard circumstances from which the season is born: "Sweet daughter of a rough and stormy fire, / Hoar Winter's blooming child" (98). Inexorable difficulties in the natural world, the poem suggests, inspire in one a desire for a peaceful (pastoral) space free of hardship. As the poet states:

> Now let me sit beneath the whitening thorn,
> And mark thy spreading tints steal o'er the dale;
> And watch with patient eye
> Thy fair unfolding charms.
> O nymph approach! While yet the temperate sun
> With bashful forehead, thro' the cool moist air
> Throws his young maiden beams,
> And with chaste kisses wooes
> The earth's fair bosom. (100)

At the same time, Barbauld says, even if pastoral pleasures are possible, they are only momentary, at best; they can never constitute a permanent resolution of the problems born of circumstance. Just as spring arises from "a rough and stormy fire," so it will be destroyed by one. As she puts it:

> Sweet is thy reign, but short: The red dog-star
> Shall scorch thy tresses, and the mower's scythe
> Thy greens, thy flow'rets all,
> Remorseless shall destroy. (101)

This statement not only captures Barbauld's materialist poetic sensibility, her recognition of the inevitable course of seasonal change; it also evokes an apocalyptic vision of the destruction of all life, a vision that extends well beyond the understanding available to the pastoral imagination.[8]

The poem takes its visionary direction from the understanding that cataclysm is inevitable and that the meaning or value of life must be judged within the frame of that reality. Given this visionary stance, spring is most usefully viewed as a symbolic expression of how life might be interpreted within a larger eschatological reality. In Barbauld's characterization of the season, at least initially, spring suggests the possibility of a pastoral and bucolic moment in life. But as the poem moves toward visionary understanding, the pastoral understanding of spring gives way to a different sort of understanding, one that does not rely on an idea of retreat from the world into beauty but rather that imagines spring as a promise in the face of cataclysmic destruction. In the final stanza of the poem, Barbauld makes this point by stating that in spring one finds more of worth than can be found in the riches of summer or autumn:

> Fair Spring! [Your] ... simplest promise more delights
> Than all their largest wealth, and thro' the heart
> Each joy and new-born hope
> With softest influence breathes. (101)

Spring is a "promise," a "new-born hope"; it is not an alternative to the destructive realities of winter. Nor does it compete with the bountiful offerings found in summer and autumn. Such a view indicates the extent to which and the confidence with which Barbauld has left behind the sensibilities described in "Ovid to His Wife."

The idea of spring as promise or hope rather than as an emblem of pastoral retreat and triumph changes the meanings associated with the season throughout the larger trajectory of the poem. As an expression of promise or hope, spring is more desirable than an idea of "eternal youth" (98) and preferable to the pastoral preoccupations suggested by the references to the "Doric reed" and "Lydian flute." Spring, indeed, is characterized by sweetness, freshness, and most importantly, the possibility of free life being born: "Unlock thy copious stores; those tender showers / That drop their sweetness on the infant buds" (99). While its beauties ultimately surrender to summer, autumn, and winter ("Reluctant shall I bid thee then farewell" [101]), its promise and hope remain, and, for Barbauld, these are the basis for a meaningful life wherein love and benevolence become worthy principles to embrace despite the threat or even certainty of their destruction. Visionary idealism does not reject pastoral idealism altogether but rather subsumes it into a larger understanding meant to deepen the meaning of lived reality by mapping a possibility of hope that is found along a path that travels perilously close to death.

The direction of "Ode to Spring" is suggested by the poem's epigraph—"Hope waits upon the flowery prime"—which is taken from Edmund Waller's poem entitled "To a Very Young Lady" (1645). This poem was written during a tumultuous time in British history, as the struggles between the Roundhead supporters of Parliament and the loyalists who supported Charles I had pushed Britain into open civil war. Waller, loyal to the king and a member of Parliament, was something of a moderate in politics, though he organized a royalist uprising in 1643 (known as Waller's plot), and was eventually arrested, then banished from England until 1651.[9] In time, Waller made his peace with the new political order, even going so far as to write a poem in 1655 celebrating Cromwell entitled "A Panegyric to My Lord Protector," which he then followed, six years later, with a celebratory poem addressed to Charles II entitled "To the King, upon his Majesty's Happy Return."

Whether or not Barbauld chose her epigraph from Waller because of his political tribulations and his efforts to negotiate safe passage through difficult historical circumstances is impossible to know. But it is clear that his poem articulates a spirit of uncertainty and regret that may have arisen from the cultural moment in which he was writing. And it is clear, too, that in "Ode to Spring" Barbauld engages these features of Waller's poem in such a way as to construct a mindset for engaging successfully with hardship. Barbauld's imaginative efforts in the ode follow a path that is often seen in her poetry: she transforms Waller's poem even as she appropriates it for her poetic purposes. Waller's lament is that he has grown too old to hope that he may win the affections of a young woman, and the disparity in age between the poet and the lady is the basis for a sense of psychic dislocation articulated in the poem. This feeling of dislocation then causes the poet to wonder where hope in this life is to be found, and he concludes that it resides in youth:

> Hope waits upon the flowery prime,
> And summer, though it be less gay,
> Yet is not looked on as a time
> Of declination and decay.
> For with a full hand that does bring
> All that was promised by the spring. (1:57)

These lines articulate the key terms of Barbauld's poem: flowers, hope, promise, spring. But whereas Waller uses these terms to construct a general lament about the passage of time, Barbauld invests them with a different set of meanings suggesting that hope and promise are meaningful guides for moving forward through the inevitable hardships that life holds. Waller's poem looks to the past and laments the toll that life has taken on him; Barbauld looks to the future with a full understanding of what the passage of time means—death—and still finds purpose.

"Ode to Spring" is an intricate and powerful poem that transformatively engages literary tradition and confronts the problematic relation between pastoral idealism and visionary idealism. The poem cuts across metaphysical and (at least implicitly) cultural landscapes in search of a spirit capable of sustaining hope. The seasons are relentless in their course of change, Barbauld recognizes, and the lesson of their changing is not that spring always comes around again but rather that, in the face of "remorseless" destruction, hope and promise remain a viable option, indeed perhaps the only option, for meaningful life. And this is the visionary wager that she seems increasingly compelled to make in the volume: even as some form of apocalypse is inevitable (biblical or existential or metaphysical), hope and joy are the proper (even necessary) foundational principles for living meaningfully in this world. And the responsibility of poetic vision, she suggests, is to elaborate why this is so, without blinking in the face of the apocalypse.

In "Verses on Mrs. Rowe," Barbauld turns her attention to Elizabeth Singer Rowe (1674–1737), an early eighteenth-century Dissenting poet who was known for her pastoral lyrics on the subjects of friends, love, devotion, and death.[10] Barbauld's poetic choice enables her to examine the principles of religious dissent in relation to the larger themes that she has been exploring in the volume. Among Rowe's works are her first volume of poems, *Poems on Several Occasions* (1696)—which was published under the pseudonym Philomela, the name Barbauld calls her by in "Verses on Mrs. Rowe"—and *The History of Joseph* (1736), which presents the story of Joseph from the Book of Genesis. After her death, Theophilus Rowe (her husband's brother) published *The Miscellaneous Works, in Prose and Verse, of Mrs. Elizabeth Rowe* (1739) in two volumes, which includes an expanded ten-book version of *Joseph*. Of these volumes, *Miscellaneous Works* is perhaps the most relevant to a discussion of Barbauld, not only because the volume incorporates most of Rowe's previously published poems but also because Theophilus Rowe's long introduction provides a sketch of Elizabeth Rowe's Dissenting heritage, including, at the very beginning of the introduction, an account of the imprisonment of Walter Singer (Rowe's father) for religious reasons:

> Mr. *Singer* was not a native of the town now-mentioned [Ilchester], nor an *inhabitant*, before his imprisonment there for his non-conformity in the reign of Charles II. *Mrs Portnell* [Rowe's mother] thinking herself obliged to visit those that suffered for the sake of a good conscience, as a testimony of her regard, not to them only, but also to our *common* Lord, agreeably to the representation he himself makes of such kind and Christian offices: It was from hence that acquaintance first commenced between these two virtuous and well-pair'd minds, which afterwards proceeded to a union that only death could dissolve. (1:i–ii)[11]

Later in the introduction, Theophilus Rowe says of Elizabeth Rowe's husband (Thomas) that the "love of liberty" had always been one of his

> most darling passions. . . . [T]his made him, with so much anxiety for his native country, not very long after his return thither in the year 1708, observe that, a set of wretched principles, destructive of its liberties and welfare, were growing in fashion under the countenance of some in power. . . . Tyranny of all sorts he most sincerely detested, but most of all *ecclesiastical*, in every shape; deeming slavery of the mind, as the most abject and ignominious, so, in its consequences, more pernicious than any other. (x)

And in his description of Elizabeth Rowe, he includes a statement that goes to the heart of Barbauld's own Dissenting vision:

> *There is*, she says in a letter to a lady, written so early as in the year 1697, *an eternal propensity in my soul to love and beneficence. I received the generous principle with the breath of life, and find it inseparable from my existence.* (1:1)

These statements capture the foundation and framework of Rowe's Dissenting principles, helping to put into context the charge that the expression of her beliefs sometimes tended toward enthusiasm, as well as Barbauld's contrary observation that Rowe's character exhibited "the christian's meekness and the poet's fire" (102).[12] They also emphasize the fact that, in turning to Rowe as a poetic subject, Barbauld is expressing her full awareness of the literary and religious tradition to which she belongs, both as a woman and as a Dissenter.[13]

"Verses on Mrs. Rowe" combines commentary on Rowe's virtuous life with commentary on her poetic gift and expresses Barbauld's admiration of both, alongside her desire to emulate Rowe in her own life and work. In this regard, the poem is a straightforward celebration of the older poet's many accomplishments. As Barbauld puts it near the end of the poem,

> Bright pattern of thy sex, be thou my Muse;
> Thy gentle sweetness thro' my soul diffuse:
> Let me thy palm, tho' not thy laurel share,
> And copy thee in charity and prayer. (104)

These lines echo the sentiment articulated in "To a Lady," insofar as they describe Rowe as an ideal, or emblem, of a meaningful life, which, according to Barbauld's comments through the course of the poem, is exemplified by Rowe's confident and open-minded faith, her unconditional love for her husband, her many charitable works to help the poor, and her friendships with a range of people across religious lines (102–4). Rowe's life and work, Barbauld says, was the very example of human life and experience at their best: "Her whole soul was harmony and love" (102). Rowe's example even reinvests conventional political understanding with new meaning: "Virtue that breast without a conflict gain'd, / And easy, like a native monarch reign'd" (103).

But Barbauld complicates the poem in two ways beyond its descriptive interest. First, she takes her epigraph from Edward Young's *Night Thoughts*, a work that is anything but celebratory. In "The Complaint," which is the third night, Young describes the death of young Narcissa in the lines that Barbauld adopts: "How from the summit of the grove she fell, / And left it unharmonious" (44). Barbauld echoes and revises the sentiment of the epigraph early in her poem, when she notes of Rowe that "her whole soul was harmony and love." In lines immediately following his description of Narcissa's death , Young states that his poet is not capable of seeing the virtue of the deceased or of finding comfort in having known her: "Her song still vibrates in my ravish'd ear, / Sill melting there, and with voluptuous pain / (O to forget her) thrilling through my heart" (44). Even though Young's poet associates the dead Narcissa with many of the same characteristics that Barbauld associates with Rowe—"song, beauty, youth, love, virtue, joy!" (44)—they simply remind him of his own personal loss, not his blessing: "And these were all her own. / And she was mine; and I was—was most blest— / Gay title of the deepest misery" (44).

In the opening lines of her poem, Barbauld represents Rowe as being like Narcissa, though Barbauld also describes her as a "chaster Sappho," on whose tongue "every Muse drop'd honey" (102). These attributes are viewed as a blessing: "Blest shade! How pure a breath of praise was thine" (102). The tension between the epigraph and Barbauld's portrayal of Rowe in effect situates pastoral poetry (which both Rowe and Barbauld wrote), faith, and love within a poetic landscape that must find a way to negotiate conflict. Such a realistic recognition of the obstacle that love and beneficence must face, however, does not compromise Barbauld's idealism. Indeed, Rowe is not only described as a person of noble principles; she is constructed poetically as an ideal principle that can both inspire and guide Barbauld along her difficult visionary path. On this view, Barbauld's desire to "copy thee" is not a gesture toward poetic imitation but rather a statement of dedicated commitment to the sort of visionary idealism that she associates with Rowe, despite her understanding that such idealism may ultimately be defeated: "Tho' for the bard my lines are far too faint, / Yet in my life let me transcribe the saint" (104).

The other complicating factor in the poem also derives from Young's *Night Thoughts*. Like Barbauld, Young appended epigraphs to his poetry. The epigraph to "Narcissa" is taken from Virgil's fourth georgic, and it translates as follows: "Frenzy meet for pardon, did Hell know how to pardon" (231). The famous story from which the epigraph is taken is that of Orpheus and Eurydice, and the epigraph is taken from the passage describing Orpheus just as he rises from the underworld and makes the fatal mistake of looking back to Eurydice, an act that dooms her to eternal death. Several matters here bear on Barbauld's vision in relation to her portrayal of Rowe. First, Orpheus is a major figure in classical representations of poetry and song. Despite his artistic powers, however, he is unable to save his wife from the clutches Proserpine, a failure echoed in the doubt expressed in Barbauld's statement near the end of her poem that "for the bard my lines are far too faint" (104). Perhaps more interestingly, however, and perhaps a key reason Barbauld chooses Young as the source for her epigraph, is that Virgil's fourth georgic concludes with that poet's look back to a time when he was preoccupied with things pastoral, before he moved forward to his grand effort to write epic, with the *Aeneid*: "In those days, I, Virgil, was nursed of sweet Parthenope, and rejoiced in the arts of inglorious ease—I who dallied with shepherds' songs, and, in youth's boldness, sang, Tityrus, of thee under thy spreading beech's cover (237)."[14] Young's poem and his evocation of Virgil's fourth georgic thus carry considerable weight in Barbauld's poem about Rowe, serving as a kind of leverage point that forces recognition of the deep valleys of conflict and tribulation that are always present in life, even at those moments when one is able to see clearly the visionary path that must be taken.

While the description of Mrs. Rowe is fairly simple and straightforward, the poem nevertheless suggests that Barbauld's poetic strategy is becoming increasingly complex, as she not only uses her choice of epigraph to lay out her concerns, as she does in earlier poems but also appropriates and exploits the epigraphic choice of the author's poem (in this case, Young's choice of Virgil) from whom her own epigraph is taken. One effect of such a strategy is to create something of a bottomless well of cultural literary influence. The simultaneous presence and elusiveness of influence, however, does not so much align Barbauld's vision with a relativistic sensibility. Rather it ensures that she engages with the broader cultural and historical pressures on her imagination and serves to protect that imagination from the trap of reductive or imitative poetic expression. Without a restrictive or definitive set of influences to limit her poetry, Barbauld can acknowledge the unavoidable presence of these influences while at the same time appropriating and using them as she sees fit for her own visionary purpose.

The following poem in the volume, "To Miss R——, on Her Attendance upon Her Mother at Buxton," situates itself on a difficult path between satire and seriousness in its appropriation and transformation of satire for the purpose of commenting on family, death, and vision. Barbauld's interest in satire is manifested in two ways. First, she chooses her epigraph from Alexander Pope's "Epistle to Dr. Arbuthnot," a satirical commentary on poetry and politics in his day and a reflection on his own career as a poet. To be sure, the line from Pope that Barbauld introduces into her poem—"With lenient arts extend a mother's breath" (612)—comes from the final section of the epistle, where Pope speaks without any satirical distancing about his aging mother, who died in 1733, one year before Pope completed the composition of his poem, but the larger trajectory of the epistle is governed for the most part by Pope's satirical voice, the poet's aim being to use that voice as a way of constructing a dramatic persona that will help to create authorial credibility, so that when the reader comes to the final lines of the poem the voice in the poem is seen as being beyond reproach.[15] Second, like Pope, Barbauld writes her poem in the heroic couplet, thereby aligning herself even more closely with the sensibilities of this poem in particular and with Pope's satirical verse in general.

And yet Barbauld's poem is not satirical. Quite the reverse—it is a somber tribute to Sarah Rigby, who had traveled with her mother to the resort town of Buxton to care for the elder Rigby, who was suffering from health problems. And the seriousness of those health problems is seen in the fact that Sarah Taylor Rigby died in 1773, the same year that Barbauld's "To Miss R——" was published in *Poems*.[16] In retaining the sentiment from Pope expressed in the epigraph and in writing in heroic couplets, Barbauld in effect captures the form and content of Pope while at the same time effectively letting down the defenses and maneuverings that mark the direction of his satire: the virtues associated with respect, love, and family are exposed without regard to criticism or complaint. Indeed, the direction of Barbauld's poem is ultimately more closely aligned with the sentiment expressed in Pope's own epigraph, which comes from Cicero's *De re publica*, than with the sentiments expressed across the course of his epistle: "You will not any longer attend to the gossip of the vulgar herd nor put your trust in human rewards for your exploits; virtue herself, by her own charms, should lead you on to true glory. Let what others say of you be their own concern; whatever it is, they will say it in any case" (279). As Barbauld makes increasingly clear through the course of *Poems*, virtue (and its related principles of love, beneficence, and sympathy) is her one true pursuit, without regard to "the vulgar mob's gossip." In "To Miss R——," she celebrates one kind of virtue (familial) openly, effectively transforming, without criticizing, the literary formulations and strategies that define Pope and other writers from the preceding generation. And that transformation exhibits important dimensions of her visionary investments. She readily acknowledges the considerable accomplishments of poets from an earlier age, never speaking against these poets or their poetry, and she incorporates their accomplishments into a vision that is grounded in principles that serve the present and can live meaningfully into the future. As she says at the end of her poem, as she imagines the young Sarah Rigby growing old, after having spent the years of her "blooming beauty" (105) caring for her ailing mother:

> Some pious hand shall thy weak limbs sustain,
> And pay thee back these generous cares again;
> Thy name shall flourish by the good approv'd,
> Thy memory honour'd, and thy dust belov'd. (107)

These lines are not an imitation of "Epistle to Dr. Arbuthnot"; they are a tribute to one sentiment that Pope offers near the conclusion of his poem and a reconstruction of that sentiment so as to give it deeper meaning within a larger vision of the transformative power of benevolence and love.

"On the Death of Mrs. Jennings" picks up the theme of aging and death from "To Miss R——" by commemorating the death of Barbauld's grandmother, who died on October 15, 1770, at the age of eighty-three.[17] Here, however, Barbauld shifts her focus away from the caregiver to the deceased, recalling the many virtues that defined Anna Jennings's long life. Even as she shifts her focus in this way, she weaves the poem deeply into the fabric of the previous one, using the same strategy that she had deployed in "Verses on Mrs. Rowe." Here, Barbauld calls forward Pope's "Epistle to Dr. Arbuthnot" once again (a line from which she earlier had used for her epigraph in "To Miss R——") but not for the ideas in the poem itself; rather, like before, she engages with the epigraph to Pope's poem, specifically with his epigraph's emphasis on virtue. That Barbauld has Pope's epigraph in mind as she is writing about her grandmother is clear from the fact that, like Pope, she takes her own epigraph for "On the Death of Mrs. Jennings" from Cicero (section five of his essay *On Old Age*), which observes that not all meaningful lives are lives of action. As the epigraph to Barbauld's poem puts it, "But there is also the tranquil and serene old age of a life spent quietly, amid pure and refining pursuits," a statement that closely resembles Pope's epigraph, which says, in effect, that virtue is its own reward. Cicero writes:

> And yet, not every one can be a Scipio or a Maximus and call to mind the cities he has taken, the battles he has fought on land and sea, the campaigns he has conducted, and the triumphs he has won. But there is also the tranquil and serene old age of a life spent quietly, amid pure and refining pursuits— such an old age, for example, as we are told was that of Plato, who died, pen in hand, in his eighty-first year; such as that of Isocrates, who, by his own statement, was ninety-four when he composed the work entitled *Panathenaicus*, and he lived five years after that. His teacher, Gorgias of Leontini, rounded out one hundred and seven years and never rested from his pursuits or his labours. When some one asked him why he chose to remain so long alive, he answered; "I have no reason to reproach old age." A noble answer and worthy of a scholar! For, in truth, it is their own vices and their own faults that fools charge to old age. (23)

The sentiments inherent in Barbauld's description of her grandmother's life follow directly from this line of reasoning, though she recasts the intellectual emphases of Cicero's commentary in such a way as to stress the quiet and sure principles of love and care for family that defined Anna Jennings's life even into the last days of her life.

At the center of Jennings's life, Barbauld says, were two abiding virtues— piety and love—that guided her through her quiet existence. "Religion had her heart, her cares, her voice; / 'Twas her last refuge, as her earliest choice" (109), and even as she grew old, she never wavered in the beliefs that gave her life meaning, a fact that Barbauld interprets in religious terms: "Heaven prolong'd her life to spread its praise" (109). Her piety was accompanied by an equally powerful—and deeply intertwined—love, not only for spiritual life, but also for her family: "Her spreading offspring of the fourth degree / Fill'd her fond arms, and clasp'd her trembling knee" (109). For Mrs. Jennings, quiet religious faith and service to family were enough to make her life full and meaningful: "Her hopes all bright, her prospects all serene, / Each part of life sustain'd with equal worth, / And not a wish left unfill'd on earth" (109). And, for Barbauld, it is enough that Mrs. Jennings lived her life in this manner, because such a life not only brings self-fulfillment; it also provides warmth, meaning, and comfort to others. As she puts it near the end of the poem: "Farewell! Thy cherish'd image, ever dear, / Shall many a heart with pious love revere: / Long, long shall mine her honour'd memory bless" (110). Barbauld's poetic memorial to her grandmother provides an important insight into the larger visionary character of the volume, which has consistently sought to find a set of principles that hold transformative possibilities without falling prey to the risks of debilitating or compromising conflict. For the moment of this poem, at least, Barbauld seems to give full voice to the idea so eloquently articulated in Milton's sonnet 19: "They also serve who only stand and wait." According to Barbauld, humanity can be served not only through public engagement (which Barbauld, as a poet, has chosen) but also by the quiet practice of virtue. Jennings is an emblem of a life well lived, a perfect example of one dimension of the ideal toward which Barbauld strives in her visionary poetics, which through the course of the volume embraces all of life from grand events ("Corsica") to the small, private habits of daily experience ("On the Death of Mrs. Jennings").

In describing her grandmother's piety, Barbauld draws on biblical vocabulary to a degree that is unusual for the volume up this point. She observes, for example, that heaven has blessed her grandmother "with a patriarch's length of days," calls her "an Israelite indeed," and notes that "to holy Anna's spirit not more dear / The church of Israel, and the house of prayer" (109). One reason for this choice of vocabulary, perhaps, is that it is intended to reflect, and show respect for, her grandmother's personal attachment to biblical knowledge and understanding. But the vocabulary also looks forward to the hymns that follow immediately after "On the Death of Mrs. Jennings," suggesting an area of investigation that Barbauld has not yet directly taken on. In particular, her use of words like "patriarch" and "Israelite" are evocative, calling to mind Barbauld's periodic engagement in the volume with prophecy during the course of her efforts to construct a meaningful visionary poetics. To this point, in examining the nature and demands of prophecy, she has worked largely with epic, pastoral, satirical, and lyrical modes of expression (the one exception being "Hymn to Content").[18] In turning to face directly the force of biblical authority and coming to it through the character of her grandmother, Barbauld displays both respectful caution and her sense of purpose as she moves toward a more direct and sophisticated engagement with the prophetic imagination.

That the group of poems gathered under the general heading of "Hymns" carries special importance for Barbauld is seen, among other ways, in the fact that in the 1792 edition of the *Poems* she added three hymns (hymns 6, 7, and 8) to the five that had appeared originally in the 1773 volume. These additions, along with the addition of *Epistle to William Wilberforce*, the final poem in the in the 1792 volume, constituted the largest single revision Barbauld had made since the first publication of *Poems*, suggesting that, for Barbauld, the collection of hymns is instrumental to the visionary trajectory of the volume as a whole. In particular, they extend the reach of the poems immediately preceding, retaining the personal interests of them while at the same time showing the importance of personal life to the larger social investments of visionary poetics. That Barbauld felt compelled to expand the original group of hymns by five and a half pages demonstrates her apparent need to elaborate more fully on why hymnal poetry was important to her.

The hymns, collectively, are placed under an epigraph taken from Horace's ode 1.12 that helps to define their direction. The epigraph translates as follows:

> Whom praise we first? the Sire on high,
> Who gods and men unerring guides,
> Who rules the sea, the earth, the sky,
> Their times and tides.

Taken out of context, these lines seem to fit perfectly with the biblical interest of the ensuing poems, even to the point of providing an Old Testament picture of a stern and demanding deity. But the poem from which the epigraph is taken, of course, has nothing to do with the Old Testament God. Rather, the poem begins with an address to Clio, the muse of history ("What man, what hero, Clio sweet, / On harp or flute wilt thou proclaim?"), and the "Sire" being addressed, as subsequent lines of the poem make clear, is Jove. Further, the poem itself is motivated by a political concern, namely that Jove protect Caesar Augustus and the power that he wields over the world:

> Dread Sire and Guardian of man's race,
> To Thee, O Jove, the Fates assign
> Our Caesar's charge; his power and place
> Be next to Thine.
> Whether the Parthian, threatening Rome,
> His eagles scatter to the wind,
> Or follow to their eastern home
> Cathay and Ind,
> Thy second let him rule below.

In drawing her epigraph from a poem that is both pagan and political in its expression Barbauld makes clear that although she intends the hymns to be meditations on subjects of a biblical nature, she does not mean to simply echo orthodox views on God or the Bible.[19] As the epigraph from Horace foretells, in the hymns she will put herself in critical tension with orthodoxy, adopting an interventionist and transformative stance toward the Bible, much as Blake does, and in a way that is entirely consistent with her own Dissenting heritage. And, reflecting the radically independent nature of her own mind, in "Hymns" she also puts her conception of the visionary in tension with the ideas articulated in the epigraph, thereby revealing her desire to escape the temptation to choose between the binary opposites of pagan and biblical belief systems.

The first hymn opens with a tribute to "Jehova" (111) that returns to Barbauld's preoccupation in the volume with the relations between spirituality and lived experience. And the opening lines indicate the visionary path that she intends to follow. In these lines, she establishes an important distance from both the narrowly drawn political sentiments articulated in Horace's ode (the plea that God will protect Caesar) and British nationalist assumptions about the alignment of God and nation, even as she draws on both for her subject matter. For Barbauld, God possesses "absolute command" (111) capable of instilling fear in people, but his power is not exercised on behalf of one person, or one nation: "Jehovah reigns: let every nation hear, / And at his footstool bow with holy fear" (111). Rather than being a god of the moment, of the nation, or even of history, Barbauld's is cast as a universal authority who rules all, from nations to ocean to land to hell itself, and who "reigns alone" (112): "Let no inferior nature / Usurp, or share the throne of the Creator" (112). While Horace pleads that Caesar's power will be "next to Thine" in godlike stature, Barbauld pleads just the reverse; for her, God is an impenetrable and unfathomable "Creator" (112) who resides entirely beyond the reach of human comprehension as a sort of perfect spiritual and authorial nebulous point that can only be imagined and against which all human experience—not simply British experience—must be measured. As she puts it near the end of the poem, God is "his own unfathom'd essence" (114), not a puppeteer directing the course of human and universal events.

Barbauld's deity is at first strikingly similar to Blake's, especially as the embodiment of a universal creative spirit. Across four stanzas, Barbauld describes the creation of the universe, from "the struggling beams of infant light" (112) to the final "new-born world" (113), all of which God looks on as "good" (113). But, unlike Blake, who constructs a cosmological system for the purpose of dramatizing the struggles of a fallen humanity to find its way back to eternity, Barbauld describes the creation of the universe mainly as a means of showing that God is not a personal savior. In fact, all of creation, as Barbauld presents it, is only a moment in time, and, as such, is destined for destruction: "Yet this fair world, the creature of a day, / Tho' built by God's right hand, must pass away" (113). When that moment of passing arrives, individuals, nations, and human accomplishments will all be lost forever:

> And long oblivion creep o'er mortal things,
> The fate of empires, and the pride of kings:
> Eternal night shall veil their proudest story,
> And drop the curtain o'er all human glory. (113–14)

Barbauld's statement here not only anticipates the vision she will sketch in "A Summer Evening's Meditation" later in the volume; it also looks forward to Byron's apocalyptic vision offered in "Darkness" in 1816.[20] Without contesting the idea of a universal creator, Barbauld steadfastly rejects the proposition that the creation is part of a design centered on the personal and species needs of humanity. Her view of life and reality is thoroughly materialist in nature, a position that compels her, just as it will compel Byron in the second decade of the nineteenth century, to reimagine the limitations and possibilities of human experience.

That Barbauld's materialist intellectual tendencies do not entirely compromise her idealism is suggested in the final stanzas of the poem, which, after the destruction of the world is described, return to a consideration of God, stressing once again the point that she makes early in the poem, namely that the conception of God, for her, is a conception of a pure essence who "reigns, a universe alone" (114). Whether imagined as "collected, or diffus'd" God "is still the same" (114): an absence who "fills all space with his unbounded presence" (114). The view here reflects neither orthodox Christianity nor animism. Rather, it reflects a hard-nosed materialist understanding that nevertheless insists on the purposefulness of life. Indeed, for Barbauld, the removal of God from the material operations of existence, which her intellect seems to require, preserves for her the possibility of a spiritual force beyond intellect that is present in the imagination even as it is absent from the world. Such a position enables her to extend her visionary reach across the entire span of history, science, religion, and philosophy without falling into the trap of simpleminded religious belief or of a cynical mechanistic materialism. It also leads her toward a clearer understanding and fuller embrace of the sort of stance in the world toward which she has been moving through the course of the volume.

The final stanza of the first hymn marks a critical juncture for Barbauld because it constitutes her first effort in the volume to articulate directly her vision of how she might best situate herself in the world that is both realistic and prophetically meaningful. The stanza reads as follows:

> But oh! our highest notes the theme debase,
> And silence is our least injurious praise:
> Cease, cease your songs, the daring flight controul,
> Revere him in the stillness of the soul;
> With silent duty meekly bend before him,
> And keep within your inmost hearts adore him. (115)

The very act of praising God, she says, is a debasement of God, perhaps because praise is a personal act that can never be entirely selfless, as it necessarily calls attention to personal need or desire. As such, calling on God, or even praising God, is an effort to negotiate power to serve a personal end. The proper response, the most respectful response, to the idea of an "unfathom'd essence," therefore, is silence. Barbauld suggests that God cannot be directed or controlled by vocal calls on his power; therefore, people should turn their attention, instead, toward discovering the workings of their own "inmost hearts," letting meekness, duty, and self-understanding represent their love for God. Barbauld is not making a deistic claim to the effect that God is removed from human affairs and can only be discovered through the application of human reason to the things of this world. Rather, she is articulating what she thinks should be the central principle in religious belief: the practice and expression of unconditional love, which, she says, is to be discovered in "the stillness of the soul." The question that remains for her to reflect on in the remainder of the volume is whether by analogy with ceasing to appeal to God to intervene in human experience, one should cease calling on humanity to engage in political struggle for the purpose of changing the world and instead seek another spiritual path, more consistent with the view expressed here, that might lead to a world organized more securely around the guiding principle of love.

The second hymn is structured much like the first, insofar as it begins with a joyous exclamation of God's love and the "blessings" (116) that he bestows on humanity, only to shift direction toward to middle of the poem to imagine a time when the blessings of the world may no longer be found. The tension that is created between these two moments of religious sensibility becomes the structural center of Barbauld's effort to clarify her thinking about the relations between people and God. The guiding biblical text behind her hymn, according to a note at the bottom of it first page (115) is the book of Habakkuk, written by a minor Old Testament prophet. The passage that Barbauld cites from Habakkuk is from chapter 3, verses 17 and 18, and it reads as follows:

> Although the fig-tree shall not blossom, neither shall fruit be in the vines, the labour of the olive shall fail, and the fields shall yield no meat, the flocks shall be cut off from the fold, and there shall be no herd in the stalls: Yet I will rejoice in the Lord, I will joy in the God of my salvation. (115)[21]

These verses appear near the very end of the book (only one more verse follows them), effectively picking up the sentiment that Barbauld articulates in the previous hymn, suggesting that when love is pure, it is not predicated on a quid pro quo. Imagining a blighted world, that is, a world devoid of all fruitfulness and pleasure, is important to her because it provides the basis for a vision of pure and unconditional love, defining the nature of her idealism. As she puts it in the final lines of the hymn, after having described a blighted world:

> Yet to thee my soul should raise
> Grateful vows, and solemn praise;
> And, when every blessing's flown,
> Love thee—for thy self alone. (117)

McCarthy observes that in this hymn Barbauld is following Elizabeth Rowe, both in the choice of Habakkuk as a biblical guide and in portraying faith as a virtue that must be able to withstand the worst sorts of tribulation.[22] But even as she looks back to an earlier Dissenting poet as a model, she uses that poet, along with the book of Habakkuk, as a way of mapping a visionary course for the future, one that faces the darkest realities and possibilities of lived experience without forfeiting the sustaining hope that resides at the center of her idealism.

While in the first two hymns Barbauld relies on the Old Testament in constructing her religious voice, the third hymn, entitled "For Easter Sunday," is explicitly Christian, celebrating the resurrection of Christ. And with this hymn, Barbauld begins a poetic course of reflection that distinguishes a remote deity from Christ, who is fundamentally human and the embodiment of the highest virtues and principles toward which humanity might strive. The poem follows logically on the previous hymns by depicting an individual (Jesus) who has withstood the worst tribulations imaginable in the world (having been subjected to "the powers of darkness" [119]) and come through them with his capacity for love fully intact. The humanity of Barbauld's Christ is seen clearly in her comment that he is "the friend of human kind" (119) and "a brother," who, even after having been subjected to the worst sorts of torment on behalf of humanity, still can pity "erring, guilty man" and feel "touch'd / With memory of our woes" (120). For Barbauld, Christ, in this instance, is the perfect model of human character, one who lives the principle of love even in the face of suffering and death. He is therefore the fullest embodiment of the principles by which she desires to live:

> To thee, my Saviour, and my King,
> Glad homage let me give;
> And stand prepar'd like thee to die,
> With thee that I may live. (120)

If the first two hymns depict a world subject to blight, famine, and destruction and voice Barbauld's desire to stand firm in her faith when faced with such catastrophes, the third hymn provides an example of the capacity for such faith to transform the world. The example of Christ, she says, is meaningful not only on a particular Easter Sunday or to a single group of worshippers; the meaning of Easter morning is that it "scatters blessings from its wings, / To nations yet unborn" (119). For Barbauld, unconditional and unwavering love is the very definition of faith, and it is transformative. And it is one key source of Barbauld's visionary poetics.

The fourth hymn, which provides a commentary on charity, picks up directly on "For Easter Sunday," imagining Christ as the embodiment of pure love, giving his last commands to the world just before the moment of his death. The hymn is founded on the Psalm 41 and parts of it have been incorporated into the

Hymns of the Protestant Episcopal Church.²³ Barbauld's purpose in the poem is to begin shifting her spiritual interests away from questions of pure faith toward the relations between faith and lived experience. Indeed, in issuing his command to the world, Christ states that

> blest is the man, whose softening heart
> Feels all another's pain;
> To whom the supplicating eye
> Was never rais'd in vain. (121)

Christ's lesson is thoroughly human, instructing people how to live in the world of people. As he directs his commands to people, he speaks of feeling, kindness, mercy, peace, subservience, and, most importantly, love. If in the Easter hymn Christ was depicted as a "brother" to humanity, here he calls on humanity to embrace its noblest—and attainable—virtue:

> To him protection shall be shewn,
> And mercy from above
> Descend on those who thus fulfil
> The perfect law of love. (123)

The sympathetic social character of the larger trajectory of the poem shows emphatically that, for Barbauld, vision is not about personal salvation but rather about social transformation. And the definitiveness of her statement here suggests that she has begun to arrive at the conclusion that only love is capable of redeeming the world.

If the fourth hymn begins to direct the reader's attention toward lived experience, the fifth hymn (along with the three hymns that follow) turns fully to the world, considering explicitly the human relevance of the spiritual matters described in the earlier poems. Her search for that relevance, not surprisingly, begins with a plea for self awareness, as she calls to herself to "awake" and "see where thy foes against thee rise" (123). She seems emboldened at last to put on fully the mantle of the prophet, calling attention to her need for personal strength and clear conscience if she is to carry the principle of unconditional love forward into the world in a meaningful way. As she speaks to herself in the poem, the vocabulary resonates with biblical prophetic certainty:

> Here giant danger threat'ning stands
> Mustering his pale terrific bands;
> There pleasure's silken banners spread,

And willing souls are captive led.
See where rebellious passions rage,
And fierce desires and lusts engage. (123)

These lines could have been written by Blake, and their tone and sentiment are carried forward through the remainder of the poem, voicing dire warnings and mapping out a course of proper action in the world:

Thou tread'st upon enchanted ground,
Perils and snares beset thee round;
Beware of all, guard every part,
But most, the traitor in thy heart.
"Come then, my soul, now learn to wield
The weight of thine immortal shield." (124)[24]

Barbauld announces her full awareness of the danger and trials that lie before her, and she reminds herself that the only protection she will have—and will need—in making her visionary poetics public are "heavenly truth and heavenly love" (124), the very protections that enabled Christ to triumph: "The Man of Calvary triumph'd here;/Why should his faithful followers fear?" (124). For Barbauld, Christ, no less than Habakkuk, is a prophet, and Barbauld, in following Christ, is also a prophet, carrying forward the principle of love into the strife and turmoil of the world.

The final three hymns in this section were added in 1792, and they seem intended to complete the description of Barbauld's hymnal journey through three moments of biblical and historical time, each of which tests her vision of love as the only appropriate and durable principle on which to build a meaningful personal life and to guide her engagement with the world. The direction of her thought can be seen by considering the nature and direction of the first five hymns: the first two hymns present an Old Testament sense of the world doomed to destruction; hymns three and four turn to the figure of Christ, portraying him as the embodiment of pure love capable of withstanding immense turmoil and suffering; and the fifth hymn is an act of self-assessment, in which Barbauld reminds herself to carry the principle of love forward into the world. She then follows these three moments with the final three hymns, which turn directly toward humanity, bringing forward the darkness and hope of the earlier hymns with the aim of situating confidently the visionary aims and conclusions of the volume. Unlike the first five hymns, each of the three hymns that were added to the 1792 volume is introduced either by an epigraph or descriptive statement that provides a point of entry into the poem. Further, each introductory marker derives from a different source or tradition, a poetic strategy that effectively brings the poems, collectively, into the orbit of a broad range of social and historical experience.

Hymn 6 is prefaced by the words "Pious Friendship," calling attention to the poem's interest in the way that the close ties between two people can enrich the course of life. As Barbauld puts it in the hymn, those "whose hearts, whose faith, whose hopes are one" are "blest" by a "sacred tie that binds" (125). This tie constitutes a "generous flame within" that helps to "cleanse" individuals "from sin" (125). That is to say, the warm and authentic regard for another human being—the turn away from selfishness toward sympathy—is the key to virtue. This liberal social sensibility enriches and sustains life, even to the point of death, when Barbauld says, those individuals blessed with friendship "meet in realms above / A heaven of joy—because of love" (126). At the center of Barbauld's poetic claims about friendship is her vision of the fundamental necessity of a social bond, and at the center of her conception of the social bond is love. To put the matter more strongly, the blessing, the "heavenly course" (125), the dream of a reward "in realms above" are not simply the goal of human life; they are also the *product* of love embraced as a social reality.

Barbauld's prefatory statement that the poem is about pious friendship arguably indicates that she is not restricting herself to a biblical authority in exploring this theme in the hymn. Throughout the volume, she has called on various traditions, cultures, and historical moments—as well as various modes of poetic expression—as part of her investigation and articulation of a visionary poetics. While hymn 6 clearly draws on the Bible as a source of inspiration (she not only references heaven in the poem but also God [26]), it also gestures toward the classical past, as the reference to friendship almost certainly echoes Cicero's essay *On Friendship*, which among other things, draws a necessary connection between friendship and love.[25] As Cicero's Laelius says to Scaevola, "it is love . . . , the thing that gives us our word for friendship . . . , that provides the first impulse toward mutual regard" (58). Moreover, Cicero's comments on the soul and immortality sound very much like Barbauld's views on heaven. Not only does Laelius tell Fannius that "I cannot agree with those who in the last few years have begun to . . . say that the soul dies with the body and that death is the end of all things"; he also endorses Socrates' view "that the souls of men were divine, and that when they had departed from the body, they found the road back to heaven lying open before them, and that, the better and more just a man had been, the smoother and easier this road was for him" (51).

Friendship, justice, virtue, goodness, the soul, heaven: for Barbauld and Cicero alike, these principles are bound together into a single identity, and that identity is defined by sympathy rather than selfishness as the necessary condition of a meaningful life: "It is not so much what we gain from our friend as the love of the friend itself that gives us joy, and what we get from a friend gives us joy since it comes to us with love" (69).

The echoes of Cicero in this hymn of course do not suggest that, for Barbauld, the Bible is an inadequate guide to life. Rather, it suggests that her poetic vision is highly flexible, running across a broad span of Western thought, and that she is not wedded to a narrow or reductive orthodoxy in her effort to understand and articulate love. Her stance here is entirely in keeping with her Dissenting heritage, which embraced the principle of free inquiry. As her Dissenting contemporary Richard Price explicitly puts the matter in *A Discourse on the Love of Our Country*, all individuals must possess "the right to liberty of conscience in religious matters" (34).[26] While many Dissenters recognized "the supremacy of Christ as the only head of his church, and the sufficiency of holy scriptures as the rule of faith and practice,"[27] Barbauld's views do not seem quite so pat, especially at those moments, as in hymn 6, when she places biblical and Christian sentiments alongside perspectives from other traditions, using all to construct her vision of a meaningful life.[28]

The deeply human qualities sketched in hymn 6 are carried over in hymn 7 and applied to Christ, who is depicted as a friend to humanity, motivated by a selfless desire to bring rest and peace to the world. The epigraph to the poem, taken from Matthew 11:28, shows the human Christ reaching out to those who are troubled by the trials and tribulations in the world: "Come unto me all ye that are weary and heavy laden, and I will give you rest." The Christ seen here is, as the following biblical verse says, "meek and lowly in heart" (11:29), very much a fellow traveler with humanity, a friend and guide rather than master. Barbauld draws on this sentiment in her poem when she has Christ say to the world:

> I will guide you to your home;
> Weary pilgrim, hither come!
> Thou, who houseless, sole, forlorn,
> Long has roamed the barren waste,
> Weary pilgrim, hither haste! (126–27)

Christ's comments here reflect his willing submission or subservience to the needs of humanity, much in the way that Cicero's Laelius describes the selflessness of friendship: both the terms "love" and "friendship" "after all are derived from the verb 'to love' . . . , and 'to love' means nothing but to cherish the person form whom one feels affection, without any special need and without any thought of advantage" (88). Cicero's friendship and Christ's love are humanly the same thing: the embodiment and lived experience of virtue.

Hymn 7 uses a biblical word—"sinner" (127)—that might suggest that Barbauld's Christianity is not quite so broad minded as I am arguing and that, indeed, she exhibits a conventional Christian view of humanity as fallen and in need of redemption, which only Christ can promise. Without disputing such a view, I would argue that, if the poem operates to an extent within the framework of conventional Christian thought, it is also more complex than an orthodox view. Christ's desire, after all, as Barbauld imagines it, is to guide humanity "to your home" (126), that is to say, to a home that naturally and properly belongs to humanity. Moreover, Christ's love is fully human, leading him to seek comfort for people who are "tossed on beds of pain," who have "swollen and sleepless eyes," who are "by fiercer anguish torn," who experience "strong remorse" (127). In an important respect, the sin of the world is not individual moral failing but rather pain, grief, and hardship that arise in the course of daily life. The home to which Christ wishes to guide humanity, and which promises "peace, that ever shall endure, / Rest eternal, sacred, sure" (127)—the *heaven* that Barbauld imagines—is defined as life built on the principle of love (or friendship), which is sufficiently strong to dissolve weariness and enable humanity to face without fear or regret both life ("beds of pain") and death ("rest eternal"). On this view, the sin that weakens humanity, and which Christ teaches that humanity must resist, is the failure to love.

That Barbauld's "Hymns" do not hew to an orthodox biblical (specifically Anglican) understanding is made explicit in hymn 8, which is prefaced by a surprisingly heterodox epigraph: "The world is not their friend, nor the world's law." A quick glance might seem to suggest that Barbauld is here simply extending the ideas articulated in her earlier hymns on the topics of friendship and human experience, and that, indeed, she is calling on her readers to look past the hardships of the world (described in hymn 7) toward heaven. The hymn itself supports such a view. But the source and circulation of the epigraph suggest a more complex set of possibilities. A version of the epigraphic line appears first in act 2, scene 1, of Shakespeare's *Romeo and Juliet*, where Romeo, negotiating with the apothecary to buy poison, remarks sharply that "the world is not thy friend nor the world's law." But Barbauld does not use this precise wording. Rather, she uses the wording found in the *Rambler* no. 107, where Samuel Johnson presents a commentary on prostitution and prostitutes. The full passage from which Johnson's statement is taken is as follows:

> It cannot be doubted but that numbers follow this dreadful course of life, with shame, horrour, and regret; but where can they hope for refuge? "The world is not their friend, nor the world's law." Their sighs, and tears, and groans, are criminal in the eye of their tyrants, the bully and the bawd, who fatten on their misery, and threaten them with want or a gaol, if they show the least design of escaping from their bondage.
>
> "To wipe all tears from off all faces," is a task too hard for mortals; but to alleviate misfortunes is often within the most limited power: yet the opportunities which every day affords of relieving the most wretched of human beings are overlooked and neglected, with equal disregard of policy and goodness. (208)

Even as Barbauld's prayerful poem directs attention to "Emanuel's land" (129), the epigraph reminds the reader of the horrific injustices of the world, which condemn many people, through no fault of their own, to poverty, loss of integrity, and hardship.

The epigraph from Johnson serves as an anchor for the poem, reminding Barbauld's reader that the ideals governing human experience must pass along the vale of death and that this fact is forgotten at the peril of those who seek the support of heaven. Indeed, the "stranger" (128) in the poem who calls out for others to follow the "crowd of Pilgrims" as they "toil" (128) to find their way to "heaven" (130) understands clearly the difficulties, pain, and suffering that are necessarily associated with heavenly desire. Yet he is equally confident that "ecstasies of love" (130) will give him and his fellow travelers the strength to engage meaningfully with the sorts of tragedy that Johnson describes, much as Christ was able to look with open eyes at life's ills, work tirelessly to transform humanity along the lines of virtue, and bear the torments of crucifixion, finding strength in the redemptive power of love.

In the stranger's comments, three important points become apparent that are relevant to the position at which Barbauld seems to be arriving in *Poems*. First, the pilgrims in the poem view themselves as being Christ-like, and they view Christ as being like themselves:

> We tread the path our Master trod,
> We bear the cross he bore

> And every thorn that wounds our feet
> His temples pierced before. (129)

This description restates the sentiment expressed in earlier hymns that Christ was human and exemplified the (potential) spiritual character of all humans. Second, Barbauld suggests in the poem that she is now leaving behind her earlier investments in pastoral idealism, because this poetic mode is inadequate to the responsibilities that she feels compelled to take on as a visionary poet:

> The flowers that spring along the road
> We scarcely stoop to pluck,
> We walk o'er beds of shining ore,
> Nor waste one wishful look. (129)

Barbauld's view of the relations between time and eternity has now taken on a sense of urgency, making it impossible for her to retreat any longer into the pastoral shades to deliberate a proper course of action in the world. Finally, the stranger's authority, understanding, and sense of purpose reflect a fully developed prophetic sensibility, which has at last come to maturation after Barbauld's lengthy and detailed reflections of what prophecy is and how one who aspires to prophetic vision might best situate herself poetically and spiritually as well as in the world. The goal of the prophet is heaven for all of humanity, and that goal requires the foundational principle of unconditional love, the fortitude to "walk o'er beds of shining ore," and the certainty that "we [can] purge our mortal dross away, / Refining as we run" (130). Prophecy, that is, is a form of engagement with the world, and it accepts the proposition that death on behalf of the world (as Christ's example shows) is consonant with finding heaven: "But while we die to earth and sense, / Our heaven is begun" (130). Much of Barbauld's vocabulary is conventionally biblical, and yet the hymn holds within its sights, with a deeper understanding than before, her earlier pastoral and political sensibilities, as well as her abiding commitment to those mortals (described both in the poem and in its epigraph) who suffer in the world.

The "Hymns" are a remarkable achievement for Barbauld, as they exhibit her developing visionary sophistication, as well as her astonishing courage in addressing the complex relations between spiritual and material life. While the various hymns are rooted in biblical texts and understanding and follow the Judeo-Christian tradition of prayerful expression, they draw their inspiration from other texts and traditions as well (specifically classical) and turn the reader's focus toward the role of spiritual understanding in everyday life. In so doing, these poems reshape the very ideas of heaven, sin, faith, life, and death, insisting that all spiritual matters are in fact social realities that must be brought into alignment with lived experience, because, ultimately, spirituality is nothing more than love for humanity, a fact clearly exemplified in the life of Christ.

CHAPTER SEVEN

God, Vision, and the Political Moment

The biblical and religious interests of "Hymns" provide the spiritual foundation for the two following long poems, "An Address to the Deity" and "A Summer Evening's Meditation," which, in turn, prepare Barbauld's reader for a return to politics in the final poem of the volume, *Epistle to William Wilberforce*, which addresses with newfound confidence and conviction the problem of politics in the modern age. In "An Address to the Deity" and "A Summer Evening's Meditation," Barbauld writes boldly as she gives full voice to her prophetic and visionary interests that have evolved over the course of the volume. The hymns focus largely on the nature and function of belief in the world of lived experience, particularly on the possibility of a credible belief system that is situated within the frame of human events, and they conclude that the example of Christ affirms the spiritual dimension of mortal existence. Christ's ability to love humanity in the face of insufferable torment by those who opposed him is evidence, for Barbauld, that faith is capable of sustaining her in the world as a human and historical example of the human capacity for love. While God may be removed from the world, Christ is in and of the world. And Christ's faith is unshakable and his love boundless. Barbauld models her own understanding of love and faith on him. However, for her, faith and love also entail free enquiry and free expression: if faith and love (as exemplified by Christ) know no limits, then the investigation and articulation of the mind's visionary character—its capacity for faith and love and its place in the world—should know no limits either. Thus, "An Address to the Deity" and "A Summer Evening's Meditation" do not simply describe the rewards of belief in God; they push the idea of God as far as Barbauld's imagination is capable, using the intellectual and imaginative freedom discovered in this effort to guide her toward the political and visionary conclusions set out in *Epistle to William Wilberforce*.

That "An Address to the Deity" is more than a simple prayer to God is seen from the very beginning, in the title of the poem. While Barbauld casts herself as a supplicant standing before God ("Permit my feeble voice to lisp thy praise" [131]), and while in various passages the poem voices her desire for God's guidance, her title states her intention to name God and to speak to him directly, reporting to him the power and reach of her visionary imagination, which, she says, is capable of surpassing even the efforts of the seraphim: "Yet here the brightest Seraphs could no more / than veil their faces, tremble, and adore" (131).[1] The boldness of this statement is reflected in subsequent lines, where Barbauld describes a visionary flight that discovers God everywhere and that brings her into a perfect association with him:

> My hush'd spirit finds a sudden peace,
> Till every worldly thought within me dies,
> And earth's gay pageants vanish from my eyes
> Till all my sense is lost in infinite,
> And one vast object fills my aching sight. (132)

While such visionary flights cannot be sustained and must be reignited after periods of quiet, they capture Barbauld's confident poetic understanding that, if only for a moment, she can become one with God, sharing in his power, much as Shelley wished to share the power of the West Wind:[2]

> Thus shall I rest, unmoved by all alarms,
> Secure within the temple of thine arms;
> From anxious cares, from gloomy terrors free,
> And feel myself omnipotent in thee. (135)

Barbauld here describes her ability, in effect, to see existence much as Blake would see it only a few years later: "To see a world in a grain of sand, / And a heaven in a wild flower, // And eternity in an hour" ("Auguries of Innocence" 493). The "mystic characters" that people her imagination accompany her through the world as sustaining and protective guides.

The visionary flights of "An Address to the Deity" bring into view two important matters that are relevant to Barbauld's visionary poetics. First, the poem revisits, for a final time in the volume, the pastoral imagination, not because Barbauld either wants to dismiss it or retreat fully into it but rather because she wishes to situate it within the larger context of her visionary poetics. In the poem, Barbauld imagines that her faith might lead her "by living waters, and thro' flow'ry meads, / When all is smiling, tranquil, and serene, / And vernal beauty paints the flattering scene" (133–34). Such pastoral scenes, as Barbauld has shown elsewhere in the volume, might be suitable places for reflection. But she also understands (as she had acknowledged in "Ovid to His Wife") that their beauty can be a trap, luring one away from the world of human events, and yet the world of human events (as the example of Christ affirms) is where

Barbauld belongs. To make her understanding plain, she focuses on this more negative side of pastoral, asking that God "teach me to elude each latent snare, / And whisper to my sliding heart—beware!" (134). Rather than retreat into a bower of bliss to contemplate God or to map a course of conduct in the world, Barbauld now wishes to test herself directly against the many temptations in life. Drawing on the biblical tradition of prayer, language from Homer, and religious skepticism alike, she says to God, "With caution let me hear the Syren's voice, / And doubtful, with a trembling heart, rejoice" (134). Rather than tying herself to the mast of a ship to protect herself from temptation, as Ulysses did, she weds herself to God in preparation for facing the world in whatever form it might present itself.

The second matter that Barbauld examines in "An Address to the Deity" is implicit in various poems across the volume (for instance, in "The Mouse's Petition"), though it is only here that she considers it in detail: pantheism.[3] Her attention to this issue helps to formulate more precisely her views, set out in the hymns, on the relations between God and the world. Specifically, she articulates with greater clarity than before that God should be understood as both "a universe alone" and an "unbounded presence" (114). For her, God is not an approachable and identifiable authority who possesses human characteristics and the power to redeem or condemn individuals in the world. Rather, he is an irreducible spirit that is present only through lived experience in the world. He is an essence unto himself that cannot be discovered in any singular form but can be found through the gift of imagination everywhere in the world. Thus, while he is removed from everyday life, at the same time he is everywhere *as* life; he is immanent in the world, not only in "the illumined sky" (134) but also "in each flower," "in every tree," "in every leaf that trembles to the breeze" (135). And Barbauld presses this pantheistic vision even further, almost to the point of animism, as she asserts that God is also present "in shady solitudes," "in busy crowded cities," "in every creature," and "in each event" (135).

Barbauld's position here, which proclaims that God is both empirically resistant and ever present in the world, is critical to her visionary poetics, because it asserts, in effect, that the conventional distinction between spiritual and material reality, and even between holy and unholy things, is mistaken. Barbauld's claim, indeed, anticipates the view that Blake will articulate some years later in "Song of Liberty" that "everything that lives is Holy" (45). Such a monistic vision locates Barbauld, like Christ, not only in relation to eternity but also in the midst of lived experience—nature, solitude, political reality—including in the midst of "each event" that may arise "in busy crowded cities," making her personal conduct and her call to a transformed reality, along with her appeal to God for protection and guidance, a material practice carried out within the world of circumstance.

Not surprisingly, Barbauld's pantheistic articulations bring with them a degree of uncertainty, even as she states her convictions regarding the relations between God, the natural world, and society. It is also not surprising that Barbauld "addresses" God, that is, directs his attention to her aims and identity as a visionary poet, even as she pleads with him to guide her course of action in such a way that brings her to him:

> When trembling on the doubtful edge of fate
> I stand, and stretch my view to either state;
> Teach me to quit this transitory scene
> With decent triumph and a look serene;
> Teach me to fix my ardent hopes on high,
> And having lived to thee, in thee to die. (136)

Unlike Blake, Barbauld embraces an ethic of subservience, even as she embraces an unorthodox view of God and the world. Her visionary conclusions compel her to speak boldly and directly about God and the world, but her foundational visionary principles—love, benevolence, virtue—direct her away from a confrontational or oppositional mode of address, and call on her instead to articulate her interventionist and transformative vision from a position of humility and deference. While this orientation to visionary poetry (intertwining confidence and deference into a single principle) may at first seem paradoxical, if not contradictory, its aim becomes clear in the final poem in the volume.

Barbauld's thinking about God in relation to life in the world is reflected in her choice of epigraph, which is taken from Lucan's *Pharsalia*, a ten-book poem that Lucan, a young poet who committed suicide at the age of twenty-five after falling into disfavor with Nero, wrote about the civil war between Julius Caesar and Pompey the Great. The passage from the poem that Barbauld lifts for use in "An Address to the Deity" is from book 9, which describes events after the death of Pompey, and it translates as follows: "God is whatever you see and every move of your being" (230). This statement is made by Cato the Younger, a Stoic and supporter of Pompey, who has been asked by Labienus to consult the oracle at the temple of Jupiter Hammon. In refusing to consult the oracle, Cato provides a lengthy statement on the nature of God, which, in part, reads as follows:

> The deity
> Needs no audible voice: the general author of all things
> Opened up to us men at our birth time, once and forever,
> All that he means us to know. Did he choose this desert from which to
> Prophesy to a few, and bury his truth in the sand drifts?
> Where can he make his abode except in the elements, land, sea,
> Air, and the sky above, and in virtue wherever he finds it?
> Why extend our search for deities further beyond that?
> God is whatever you see and every move of your being.
> Prophecies I leave to men who are doubtful and always
> Anxious about the future; I look for certainty not from
> Oracles, but from death, that one thing certain. The hero,
> Like the coward, must die, for so has Juppiter spoken:
> That is enough for me. (229–30)

This remarkable passage shows just how deeply Barbauld was influenced by Lucan, and especially by Stoicism, in writing "An Address to the Deity." The "elements, land, sea, / Air, and the sky above" are a constellation of images on which Barbauld draws directly in her poem, and the line she selects for her epigraph shows the decision she has clearly arrived at about the *place* of God in relation to human experience. Moreover, according to Barbauld, the only thing certain in life—certain even when definitive knowledge of God is lacking—is death, which is the existential reality against which all else must be measured. In the light of Cato's comment about death, the meaning of Barbauld's own statement about death at the conclusion of "An Address to the Deity" becomes clear: the only thing worthy of pursuit, while living in the world, is the practice of virtue in all things; metaphysical questions about the nature of God are meaningless.

Cato's statement also raises another issue that is important for Barbauld, namely the character of prophecy. Cato does not wish to become a prophet himself, who would tell the story of the future. Unlike a biblical prophet and unlike Blake, Cato does not see himself as the voice of one crying in the wilderness.[4] Nor does he believe that God speaks to only a few select individuals. Rather "men are bound to the gods, and, with all their oracles silent / Nothing we do is done without their direction" (229). Cato, that is, does not look to God for inspiration or guidance; rather, in determining his course of action and his system of values, he looks to the one inexorable reality that all human beings, from the hero to the coward, must face: death. Divine intervention, in the form of prophetic vision, serves no purpose in the face of this reality.

Barbauld's visionary poetics takes its direction from Cato's statement, not so much for the purpose of rejecting prophecy outright as for situating herself away from the biblical idea of prophecy that was appropriated and developed by Milton. Her visionary model, after all, is not the remote and stern God described in her first hymn but rather the human Christ described in the fourth hymn; in the face of unbearable torment, this Christ is still able to express sympathy and love for humanity. Hers is not the voice of one crying in the wilderness, a position that would not only leave her standing alongside the tragically distraught Ovid but also would commit her simply to imitating rather than engaging with the field of vision; it is rather the voice of one who embraces the troubled reality of society and discovers the transformative capacity of love within that reality. In thus situating herself squarely in the world, she in effect maps out a new sort of prophetic stance for herself, claiming that rather than searching for God or waiting on word from God to guide our actions, we must dedicate ourselves to searching for the great potential of our own humanity and, once that potential is discovered, work to make love and virtue triumphant across the span of human experience. We cannot, like Blake, embrace the isolation of the wilderness or, like Ulysses, tie ourselves to a mast for protection from the sirens of the world: we must find the courage and faith within our own lives to speak truth to the world. In mapping out such a visionary ground, Barbauld becomes a very different sort of poet from the prophetic Milton, insofar as she rejects the idea that it is her responsibility to "justify the ways of God to men"; instead, she is like Cato, using death as the definitive measure of experience (see the final lines of the poem) and, in the face of this reality, urging the world to live according to the best principles that can be found in the human breast.

In "An Address to the Deity," Barbauld begins to test the character and reach of her conception of the visionary, and in so doing she discovers that poetic vision is not an imitative art but rather a discovery of new paths that are full of risk and possibility. The greatest risk, of course, is that hope may be threatened and defeated by the hard recognition that life is filled with pain and ends in death. But the possibility is that, by fully embracing that reality, one might discover the rich and deep beauties of human love, sympathy, beneficence, and virtue; by facing the world without fear, one might become enlightened. The poem is both a plea (a prayer) and a visionary proclamation in which Barbauld carefully checks the direction of her imaginative flight ("Teach me") even as she steadfastly follows her vision toward the destination where it leads, bringing her to the "doubtful edge of fate." With this poem, Barbauld steps fully into the zone where doubt and hope intermingle so closely as to be indistinguishable from one another.

Barbauld concluded the 1773 edition of *Poems* with "A Summer Evening's Meditation," the most compelling and metaphysically challenging poem in the volume. Its confidence and reach seem to bring to a close Barbauld's relentless and often circuitous search for a visionary stance that is true to her understanding of the beauties of this world, the foibles of humanity, the redemptive power of hope, the dangerous temptations of despair, and the salvific possibility of love and virtue. In the poem, she exhibits her conviction that, if divinity is to be discovered in its highest and truest form, the imagination must be free to express itself openly, with courage and faith and without fear of consequences. And to this end Barbauld builds on the expansive vision set out in "An Address to the Deity" and pushes to the very borders of her imaginative capacity. In doing so, she voices emphatically the visionary position at which she has now arrived in the volume, expressing her poetic confidence and the sureness of her conscience in relation to the course of action she has chosen for her personal conduct.[5]

As several scholars have observed, the reach of the poem calls to mind various moments in *Paradise Lost*.[6] And, indeed, Barbauld's visionary flight in the poem reflects the sort of expansive visionary idealism found in Milton. But the nature and character of Barbauld's vision are finally distinct from her predecessor's, not least because Barbauld focuses less on justifying God's ways to man and less on the prospect of the redemption of humanity by an objectively real, if remote, divinity, than on the freedom and meaning of the imagination's ability to push beyond all boundaries or limitations that would restrict its freedom. Her vision, in this respect, more closely approximates Blake's monistic vision of God as a resident of the human breast; in fact, she says that, when she "turns inward," she discovers "an embryo God" (140).[7] Still, even here she marks her own unique course of visionary expression, as she draws together the interests of her earlier poems and directs her attention not to God's promise of light but rather to the certainty of death and darkness. Indeed, Barbauld sets the poem during evening as a way of calling attention to the darkness that she (like Cato in *Pharsalia*) sees in the future for everyone. Her vision does not aim to not push beyond God or to reject God, but it does claim that human beings are capable of knowing one important reality that God himself knows: human beings are destined to face an ultimate "eternal night":

> What hand unseen
> Impels me onward thro' the glowing orbs
> Of habitable nature, far remote,
> To the dread confines of eternal night,
> To solitudes of vast unpeopled space,
> The deserts of creation, wide and wild. (142)

While Barbauld's statement here does not mark her as an atheist or even point her in the direction of the sort of spiritual crisis that marks so much poetry of the nineteenth century, it does position her as a radical free thinker whose theology and poetic vision alike are constrained by and shaped within the inexorable realm of material reality. Just as in "Hymns," poems that turn away from a remote and unapproachable God toward a suffering and human Christ, Barbauld finds her poetic terrain to be marked everywhere by human footsteps, which trace a path through the vale of death bolstered (hopefully) by the support of love, benevolence, and virtue toward an eternity whose meaning lies beyond her human visionary reach.

One way that Barbauld establishes a poetic context for her unorthodox meditation, making it more than simply a commentary on conventional Christianity, is by intermingling classical literary subject matter and Enlightenment philosophical understanding with biblical allusions to mark the direction of her visionary path. She places references to Saturn, Jupiter, Mars, Dian, Venus, and Hesperian gardens alongside biblical and Miltonic references as a way of breaking down barriers between pagan and Judeo-Christian understanding, thereby opening a window onto eternity and free thought through which her imagination might pass.[8] The trajectory of her imaginative flight toward eternity carries her (not despairingly, it should be noted) directly into the face of that "eternal night" that classical pagan thought before her had discovered. Only when she has meditated on the complexity and full reality of the universe, in all its remoteness and darkness, can she speculate on her own place in the face of eternity and express her vision of hope and faith. And even here, her conclusions are not conventionally biblical in nature. Her expression of hope does not require that she blink in the face of "this transitory scene" (as she put it in "An Address to the Deity"), nor is it built on the expectation that she will find a personal savior when she dies. Her prayer is, in effect, built on the principles of Presbyterian Unitarianism, and it constitutes a direct stare into the abyss of the universe and a proclamation that, in the face of that abyss, she will hold on to the principle of hope through life and into the moment of death.

Recognizing the radical character of the poem, Jonathan Wordsworth observes that it "is surely the most adventurous poetry written by a woman before the later nineteenth century" (25). Wordsworth is wrong on only one point; he need not have restricted his claim to poetry written by women.

In "A Summer Evening's Meditation," Barbauld no longer requires the bucolic surroundings of the pastoral landscape for her meditations. Rather than seeking a place within "the cool damp grotto, or the lonely depth / Of unpierc'd woods" (138), she now situates herself in the darkness of evening, beneath "the living eyes of heaven" (138), and in the face of

> ten thousand trembling fires,
> And dancing lustres, where the unsteady eye,
> Restless and dazzled, wanders unconfin'd
> O'er all this field of glories. (139)

The world on which she directly gazes now is limitless and complex, unable to be contained within a single system of thought. Drawing on a cultural understanding beyond what is to be found in the Bible, Barbauld says that the stars are not only a sign but also the place of God, "whose hand / With hieroglyphics elder than the Nile / Inscribed the mystic tablet" (139) of the heavens. Although God can never be deciphered, rationally explained, or known in any way beyond what faith and imagination allow, he is nevertheless present in all living things; in the stars, Barbauld sees "the finger of thy God" (139). Her pantheism here is clear, as she discovers "a tongue in every star that talks with man, / And wooes him to be wise" (140). This moment of meditation, for Barbauld, anticipates Coleridge's own meditative spirit, insofar as both poets find the evening and utter silence to be most conducive to free thought and imagination; but, unlike Coleridge, Barbauld never questions that the darkness and silence within which she stands is a place of "wisdom" wherein "the self-collected soul / Turns inward" (140) and discovers its own greatness, a greatness that cannot be certain that it is subject to any limits whatsoever: "Here must I stop, / Or is there aught beyond?" (142).[9] Barbauld's vision stretches beyond the world and even beyond the known universe to the point where it is compelled to question whether new realities lie beyond the present reach of the human imagination. As she puts the question, do "embryo systems and unkindled suns / Sleep in the womb of chaos?" (142–43).

The apparent limitlessness of Barbauld's visionary reach, however, does not overwhelm her interest in the world and its personal, social, and political complications but rather intensifies it. As she sails "on fancy's wild and roving wing" (141) and "launch[es] into the trackless deeps of space" (142), she imagines herself passing "solitary Mars" and "the vast orb / Of Jupiter" (141), that is, passing the great heavenly symbols of war and power that marked a previous historical moment, until she reaches

> The dim verge, the suburbs of the system,
> Where cheerless Saturn 'midst his wat'ry moons
> Girt with a lucid zone, in gloomy pomp,
> Sits like an exiled monarch. (141–42)

Barbauld's visionary flight to the "suburbs of the system" marks not only her ability to imagine infinity; it also indicates her systemic understanding of power politics and her view that the collapse of a system of power is neither inherently evil nor a sign of inevitable and irreversible chaos. The mythological Titan, Saturn, is defeated and "exiled" by his son Jupiter, whose power also ran its course and ended in defeat. As I have argued, at the time when the first edition of *Poems* was published, Barbauld was an outspoken supporter of democratic government (see her poem "Corsica," for instance) and, as McCarthy observes, she had been influenced in her thinking by two important political events in England, the Seven Years' War and the accession of George III (*Anna Letitia Barbauld* 98–99). Moreover, she was deeply influenced by her friends and by the tutors at Warrington, especially Priestley, who was fearless in his critique of monarchy. Viewed through the lens of her intellectual life, and within the context of *Poems*, the description of Saturn in the passage from "A Summer Evening's Meditation" is likely a description of the sort of Britain that Barbauld imagines for the future, wherein monarchy (perhaps even the monarchy of George III) has failed. Even the opening line of the poem, describing sunset, suggests as much, as Barbauld proclaims " 'Tis past! The sultry tyrant of the south [the sun] / Has spent his short-liv'd rage" (137). Certainly, the depiction of England in *Eighteen Hundred and Eleven* makes clear Barbauld's ability to envision an entire monarchical history reduced to ruins. Further, Barbauld states explicitly that, in the face of Saturn's demise, she is "fearless" (242), an astonishingly bold statement that prepares for her antimonarchist comment that she neither requires nor desires the guidance "of our terrestrial star" (142) as she pursues her visionary flight.

But Barbauld's political radicalism is now tempered by new understanding, one significantly different from that reflected (say) in "Corsica." This new understanding emerges from the trajectory of her religious and intellectual, as well as poetic, maturation, which is mapped out across the course of the volume. While her visionary poetics remains rooted in the idealistic hope and faith that the world can be transformed in such a way as to make love, benevolence, and virtue triumphant, she seems less dedicated to developing a conventionally prophetic stance that derives its shape and authority from scripture. In fact, she explicitly states her wish to break free from the sort of prophetic vision articulated by Milton (and that would subsequently be articulated in Blake). After her visionary flight ends with a question about whether the identity and authority of the biblical God depend on the classical and pagan tradition—"Or does the beamy shoulder of Orion / Support thy throne?" (143)—she offers a telling prayer:

> O look with pity down
> On erring, guilty man; not in thy names
> Of terror clad; not with those thunders armed
> That conscious Sinai felt, when fear appalled
> The Scatter'd tribes. (143)

The fear, terror, and life in the wilderness that mark biblical prophecy do not here appeal to Barbauld or seem useful to her in her visionary aims. Rather, she now imagines a God who "hast a gentler voice, / That whispers comfort to the swelling heart" (143). It is this softer voice, the voice of the thoroughly human Christ, who speaks to her in her "longing to behold her Maker" (143). Barbauld does not abandon prophecy but rather transforms it according to the principles that she discovers through the larger trajectory of the volume, and at last she arrives at a point of conviction, namely that the arc of history can best be bent toward a purposeful life when it is faced with a loving vision that says to the world "let all things be" (143). This vision does not operate by force to subvert and transform conventional and corrupt modes of thought or systems of reality. For Barbauld, it constitutes the one true "perfection" (143).

Barbauld's prophecy, such as it is, is not strictly biblical, though it is marked by an understanding of Old Testament theology and is deeply rooted in her understanding of Christ's pacifist lesson to the world. Through the course of the poem, she draws on classical and Egyptian sources, and, like Milton, she uses science and astronomy to give shape to her visionary space. Most importantly, while she expresses her desire to "behold her Maker," she does not live and hopes not to die in expectation of doing so; indeed, in drawing as she does on so many sources and in pursuing an exercise of unconstrained free thought and visionary flight, she acknowledges that the Bible may not fully or properly account for human reality. And she is not disturbed by that possibility. Her prayer at the end of the poem is simply that she will remain strong enough to live by the principles that define the character of Christ and that she may, upon death, come to understand the purpose and meaning of existence. As she puts it in her description of the prospect of dying:

> Let me here,
> Content and grateful wait the appointed time,
> And ripen for the skies: the hour will come
> When all these splendors bursting on my sight
> Shall stand unveiled, and to my ravish'd sense
> Unlock the glories of the world unknown. (144)

No god is the object of Barbauld's prayerful desire in these concluding lines. While she voices her conviction (hope?) that she will come to witness the "glories of the world unknown" when she dies, her expression of such conviction is much less reflective of a biblical understanding or expectation of an afterlife than it is of her earlier astronomical speculation that "embryo systems and unkindled suns" may "sleep in the womb of chaos." Free thought and meditation guide her on her course through biblical understanding into the fields of many other modes of understanding, from astronomy to classical mythology to Egyptian hieroglyphics, until she arrives at a position that is consistent with her view of the human Christ, whose divinity is manifested in his unwavering expressions of love, faith, and benevolence in all areas of experience, including thought and death.

For her epigraph to "A Summer Evening's Meditation," Barbauld returns to Edward Young's *Night Thoughts*, this time selecting a line from night 9, the final poem, entitled "The Consolation." Here Young portrays the beauty and expanse of the night sky as proof of God's existence and grandeur. The line from Young—"One sun by day, by night ten thousand shine" (277)—that Barbauld appropriates for her poem perfectly captures her wonderment at a universe that is only barely glimpsed by someone whose vision is guided solely by the sun, the singular light of day. But it is likely that Barbauld has larger visionary poetic purposes in mind as well in invoking this line, especially since Young not only portrays the night sky as a sign of God's greatness but also because, for him, the night sky likewise inspires reflection on the power of the human mind. The larger passage from which the epigraph is taken makes this point clear in its description of the evening sky, God, and the mind of man:

> This gorgeous apparatus! This display!
> This ostentation of creative pow'r!
> This theatre!—what eye can take it in?

By what divine enchantment was it rais'd,
For minds of the first magnitude to launch
In endless speculation, and adore?
One sun by day, by night ten thousand shine;
And light us deep into the Deity;
How boundless in magnificence and might! (277)

"A Summer Evening's Meditation" begins from and extends the visionary imaginings voiced in Young's lines. Just as God's grandeur is "boundless," so the human mind is capable of "endless speculation," which of course is exactly the emphasis of the poem, though Barbauld engages more fully with the implications of endless speculation than with the authority of the deity. For Barbauld as for Young, the deity is "deep," but for her the divine theater of the evening stars gains its importance from the fact that it inspires visionary flight into the free and unconstrained zone of infinity. To this extent, "A Summer Evening's Meditation" does not so much imitate as transform the thematic concerns of Young's "The Consolation."

In "A Summer Evening's Meditation," Barbauld pushes her visionary imagination to its apparent limit, going so far as to collapse conventional categorical distinctions within and between the conceptual and spiritual dimensions of reality. The glorious light of the stars shows Barbauld that before her lies "eternal night"; meditation on God creates in her the understanding that "the self-collected soul" is itself "an embryo God"; the prophetic proclamations in the Bible lead her to wish herself away from the isolationist elements of biblical prophecy; a truthful consideration of the biblical God and the gods of classical mythology show her that both are equally relevant to spiritual meditation; examination of her desire for meaningful life leads her to understand that death must be openly accepted and embraced; and so on. Although, at first glance, such paradoxes might seem to suggest that Barbauld has lost all visionary clarity in the poem, in fact they point to the unavoidable conclusion that she has at last arrived at a perfectly clear understanding of her purpose, because they capture and express her confident belief in the necessity of absolute freedom in all things social, intellectual, and spiritual. Moreover, they point toward her acceptance that the world cannot be changed by forceful intervention into its confused and corrupt power dynamics and her understanding that a peaceful and virtuous life and poetic voice are the proper principles on which visionary poetry must be grounded.

While Barbauld may have viewed "A Summer Evening's Meditation" as a proper conclusion to the 1773 edition of *Poems*, the subsequent course of political and social history—which witnessed most obviously the American and French revolutions and the many social disruptions and corruptions associated with the industrial revolution—doubtless led her to rethink the shape of the original volume.[10] "A Summer Evening's Meditation" offers an implicit commentary on monarchy, but it is largely a philosophical poem that does not consider closely the ways in which her visionary poetics may be brought to bear on lived experience. Thus, when she reissued the volume in 1792, she added *Epistle to William Wilberforce, Esq. on the Rejection of the Bill for Abolishing the Slave Trade*, a poem founded on the principles that she has constructed through the course of the volume and states directly in "A Summer Evening's Meditation" and that she uses as a vehicle for addressing directly one of the major political debates of her day. The poem, that is, brings Barbauld's visionary poetics into the direct light of the world.[11]

The epistle is distinguished not only by the length of its title but also by the fact that it is one of the few poems in the volume that is not prefaced with an epigraph from a literary source ("On a Lady's Writing" is another). Abandoning the practice that had guided her through the course of the volume and abandoning the blank verse that she used to give voice to her conception of the visionary in "A Summer Evening's Meditation," Barbauld here uses the poetic epistle (which reaches back to Ovid and was popular in eighteenth-century Britain among such poets as Pope) and heroic couplets as the formal framework on which she constructs her understanding of a contemporary political situation.[12] While it is impossible to know why she made these formal decisions, it is likely that her thinking was both literary and political in nature. In literary terms, her reliance on the epistolary form allows her to effectively recreate its largely personal associations while at the same time turning the form toward a visionary purpose; in Barbauld's hands, the form of the letter now speaks not only to the person but to the world with the aim of transforming collective consciousness. Politically, the direct address of the epistle creates a sense of immediacy and active engagement; in fact as a letter, the poem constitutes an intervention into the life and mind not only of Wilberforce but also of those members of Parliament before whom he had pleaded his case. Further, Barbauld's couplets have the effect of imposing a firm sense of order on her vision and bringing poetic precision to her topic, both of which, again, fuel the urgency of her purpose. It is possible as well that her choice of a poetic form—especially the closed heroic couplet, which, in its very nature, is marked by restriction—is meant to reflect the restrictions that British society has placed not only on Wilberforce but also on the African slaves, whose cause he champions.

In "A Summer Evening's Meditation," Barbauld takes her final and definitive leave of the sort of prophetic poetry that derives its shape and principles from the Old Testament. But she does so for the purpose of imagining a new sort of prophecy, one based on a "gentler voice" that is able to "let all things be." In *Epistle to William Wilberforce* she brings her new understanding of prophecy forward directly into the arena of public affairs, showing exactly how unorthodox her visionary poetics has become. Speaking to Wilberforce, but with her eye at the same time fixed directly on the "Country," "the Preacher, Poet, Senator," and "the Negro," she calls on him—indeed, she instructs him—to "cease . . . thy generous aim!" (145), which was to pass a bill in Parliament outlawing the slave trade. While this view may seem morally suspicious or even repugnant to someone who believes that it is imperative to take up the struggle against injustice, wherever injustice may be found, Barbauld is certain of the rightness of her view that no effort should be made to pass legislation that would make illegal the trading of slaves; she twice repeats her conviction that Wilberforce's efforts are "vain" (146) and that he should therefore abandon his effort to bring about a political solution to the injustice: "Forbear!—thy virtues but provoke our doom, / And swell th' account of vengeance yet to come" (147); "seek no more to break a Nation's fall, / For ye have sav'd yourselves—and that is all" (152). For Barbauld, Wilberforce's struggle against British injustice cannot defeat that injustice; in fact it only promotes it by propping up a fundamentally corrupt nation that is beyond redemption and that, therefore, should be allowed to collapse into ruin.

Barbauld's stance here is neither cynical nor quietist. Her condemnation of the savagery inherent in trading human lives for profit is clear in every line of the poem. But, for her, the slave trade is not an abstractly moral or metaphysical issue. It is, rather, a material reality that is inextricably tied to the larger political and social situation in which Britain finds itself in the 1790s. The problem with the slave trade, for Barbauld, is systemic in nature, bound up with British imperialistic and economic practices that extend across the globe; thus, a purely moral intervention that seeks to change national trade policy leaves intact the principles underlying the slave trade and that gave rise to it. Her insistence on a broad, materialist (rather than purely moral) understanding is made plain when she connects the slave trade to the extension of British commerce into "the gay East," from where "on essenced wings" "contagion springs," spreading its "soft luxurious plague" across the British landscape from "the marble palaces" to "rural shades" (150). By identifying its historical mission as the extension of its reach across the globe for the purpose of accruing and consolidating economic and national power, which necessarily entails the exploitation of peoples and cultures, Britain has planted the seeds of its own destruction. As Barbauld puts it, "Corruption follows with gigantic stride," until it becomes a "spreading leprosy" that "taints ev'ry part" and "infects each limb, and sickens at the heart": "By foreign wealth are British morals chang'd" (151).

For Barbauld, the slave trade is not a singular problem whose eradication will restore Britain to its former greatness as a nation of principle and virtue. It is, rather, a symptom of a problem that runs to the very core of the national identity, a problem that can never be resolved, because it lives too deeply, like a cancer, in the body of the nation, preventing virtue from gaining a toehold for effecting meaningful change. In a difficult set of lines on the relation of the slave trade to the broader reality of British society, Barbauld describes how such corruption expands outward from a single social situation until it infects an entire people:

> Injured Afric, by herself redrest,
> Darts her own serpents at her Tyrant's breast.
> Each vice, to minds depraved by bondage known,
> With sure contagion fastens on his own;
> In sickly languors melts his nerveless frame,
> And blows to rage impetuous Passion's flame:
> Fermenting swift, the fiery venom gains
> The milky innocence of infant veins;
> There swell the stubborn will, damps learning's fire,
> The whirlind wakes of uncontrouled desire,
> Sears the young heart to images of wo,
> And blasts the buds of Virtue as they blow. (148)

On such a view, it makes little sense to stand on principle against the slave trade. Across the course of modern British history, the mad imperialist drive to conquer the globe and gather wealth and power laid the cultural and political groundwork for converting human lives into commodities to be traded on the open market. Then the corrupt action of trading in human lives corrupted those lives that were victimized. In turn, the destruction of those victims of bondage further corrupted the slave traders themselves. This awful reality in time created a "rage" that could not be contained within the tyrant and slave dynamic; rather, it quickly cycled outward, gathering other people and institutions into its orbit until corruption was infused into "the milky innocence of infant veins" and all moral clarity was destroyed. In such a world, where might one usefully begin a course of interventionist action if the problem of corruption is spread equally across every facet of the nation and lies at the very core of every institution?

The problem of addressing the slave trade, according Barbauld, is made even more difficult by the fact that the corrupt and pervasive power dynamic on which it is grounded and the social body through which that dynamic courses covers its *systemic* tracks with rhetorical proclamations of virtue and liberty, proclamations that promise the reconciliation of all discordant elements under a single idea of beauty. Like Blake's Urizen, Barbauld's tyranny is defined by the principle that a uniform and tightly ordered reality is a good reality, despite the fact that empirical evidence exists everywhere demonstrating that this is not the case. This point becomes clear in the passage immediately following her description of how, in Britain, virtue is destroyed by the unjust exercise of power. Observe beauty, she writes,

> in monstrous fellowship, unite
> At once the Scythian, and the Sybarite;
> Blending repugnant vices, misally'd,
> Which *frugal* nature purposed to divide;
> See her, with indolence to fierceness join'd,
> Of body delicate, infirm of mind,
> With languid tones imperious mandates urge;
> With arm recumbent wield the household scourge;
> And with unruffled mien, and placid sounds,
> Contriving torture, and inflicting wounds. (149)

In these lines, Barbauld pushes the British conception of the good to its logical—and absurd—conclusion, showing that ultimately beauty, when tied to unjust forms of power, becomes synonymous with torture. The moral and political corruption created by the slave trade in Britain is not limited to the fact of bodies in chains that are sold for money; the real problem is the cultural and social reality that British values have become perverted to the point where the nation no longer possesses a clear, humane, and meaningful moral core. When such a moment arises in a nation, Barbauld says here (and two decades later in *Eighteen Hundred and Eleven*), the nation is weakened to the point of collapse—and it should be allowed to collapse. This conclusion constitutes the hard reality of Barbauld's prophecy, which is announced in her plea to Wilberforce that he "seek no more to break a Nation's fall."

As she comes to accept the necessity of letting Britain die, she also becomes more convinced than she was in earlier poems that the pastoral imagination is inadequate to her visionary task. She glances one last time at the features of the pastoral imagination to drive home two points: first, that the pastoral imagination is incapable of providing a meaningful way of transforming the complex and resistant circumstances under which human experience is constructed and, second, that Britain, in particular, is not now and can never be a pastoral landscape of peace and beauty, because its soul has become defiled by acts of violence and injustice.[13] Her rejection of pastoral is stated explicitly:

> Nor, in their palmy walks and spicy groves,
> The form benign of rural Pleasure roves;
> No milk-maids' song, or hum of village talk,
> Sooths the lone poet in his evening walk:
> No willing arm the flail unwearied plies,
> Where the mixed sounds of cheerful labour rise;
> No blooming maids, and frolic swains are seen
> To pay gay homage to their harvest queen:
> Not heart-expanding scenes their eyes must prove
> Of thriving industry, and faithful love:
> But shrieks and yells disturb the balmy air,
> Dumb sullen looks of wo announce despair,
> And angry eyes thro' dusky features glare.
> Far from the sounding lash the Muses fly,
> And sensual riot drowns each finer joy. (149–50)[14]

In earlier poems in which she calls on the pastoral imagination, Barbauld (like her classical forbears) often situates the pastoral landscape alongside the obstacles and hardships in the world that afflict human experience, and, indeed, in "Ovid to His Wife" she speaks harshly about the inability of pastoral to deal productively with those obstacles and hardships. But only here does she call the pastoral world into view solely to describe its inadequacy in the face of the "despair" that Britain has created by its involvement in the slave trade. And only here does she state directly that the ostensible beauties of Britain that have underwritten the nation's unique status in world history are entirely without redemptive power, as they lack "the form benign of rural Pleasure." The final dismissal of the pastoral imagination as a useful tool for transforming Britain marks Barbauld's definitive visionary step into the world as it is and her clear acceptance of historical collapse as the necessary consequence of corrupt human actions.

I want now to expand on my earlier observation regarding Barbauld's view of the economic dimensions of the slave trade. Her position arises from her understanding that the necessary landscape on which human experience unfolds—including the slave trade—is historical in nature. Such a materialist view does not reject moral temperament as an epiphenomenal aftereffect of human behavior in the world but rather assumes that the content of morality is mediated by and found within as well as arises from historical reality. In positioning herself firmly within the framework of historical understanding, she stands apart not only from Wilberforce but also from Hannah More and other abolitionists of the day. While More, for instance, in her famous poem "The Black Slave Trade," prays that God will intervene and enlighten Britons so that they will abandon their practice of trading in human flesh—"LET THERE BE LIGHT!/Bring each benighted soul, great God, to Thee,/And with thy wide Salvation make them free!" (121)—Barbauld begins from the assumption that no prayers can change a situation whose source is to be found not in the moral character of individual slave traders but instead in the prevailing structures of value and in the material practices that govern the nation. Those values and practices are imperialistic and capitalistic in nature, organized around the assumption that people are economic units and nothing more and that some people—Africans—are not even human. While an individual, or group of individuals, may be persuaded through moral pleading to abandon a given immoral practice, an entire society cannot be. When a nation reaches such a point of warped character, it cannot be saved: "Where seasoned tools of Avarice prevail,/A Nation's eloquence, combined, must fail" (147).

Further, for Barbauld, the abolitionist movement can never be successful because it fails to understand that history is expansive rather than local and particular. That is, the systemic nature of British injustice—of which the slave trade is but one manifestation—has been a long time in the making and has not yet run its historical course, as evidenced by the fact that the nation has been made fully aware of the injustice of the slave trade and yet persists in refusing to change policy. The weight of history cannot be moved by moral appeal. As she says to Wilberforce of his political efforts,

> The Muse, too soon awaked, with ready tongue
> At Mercy's shrine applausive peans rung;
> And Freedom's eager sons, in vain foretold
> A new Astrean reign, an age of gold:
> She knows and she persists—Still Afric bleeds,
> Unchecked, the human traffic still proceeds;
> She stamps her infamy to future time,
> And on her hardened forehead seals the crime. (146)

These lines go to the very center of Barbauld's visionary poetics, suggesting the reach of her historical understanding and the largeness of the context in which she places the events of the moment. Wilberforce's efforts will fail, she says, because the historical moment is not right for his arguments. While Wilberforce's motives may be pure and his dream of a new age of freedom and justice may be noble, the circumstances—economic, historical, cultural—under which he carries out his efforts are, for now, implacable; even if some individuals may be brought to moral clarity, the nation itself is unable to change its course of conduct because its very identity and character are corrupt.

Barbauld's vision brings into view the complexities of the historical situation of the 1790s. Britain had arrived at a moment when many of its citizens recognized that their nation was on a dangerous and self destructive path, and yet that moment, defined by the not yet full maw of "avarice" (to use Barbauld's term), also drove the nation inexorably further down that path toward destruction. Britain, therefore, was caught in a historical bind, aware in isolated moments (suggested, for instance, by Wilberforce's legislative action) of its destructive behavior and yet unable to change it. In fact, in Barbauld's view, the nation had begun to reach a tipping point, wherein no group of people could leverage the nation away from the eventual destruction that was becoming increasingly certain, a point that she restates twenty years later in *Eighteen Hundred and Eleven*. Hence her plea to Wilberforce to cease in his efforts that are simply stalling the inevitable and creating further conflict in the interim.

If *Epistle to William Wilberforce* presents the nation as irrevocably doomed, it nevertheless acknowledges the virtue of Wilberforce's desire to speak on behalf of Africans who have been victimized by British policy, and in doing so it exhibits Barbauld's conviction that personal character, not less than national identity, is historically meaningful. While Wilberforce's efforts will be marked by failure, they will nevertheless become part of the historical record of those individuals who are driven by a nobility of purpose: "In Virtue's fasti be inscribed your fame, / And uttered yours with Howard's honour'd name, / Friends of the friendless" (152).[15] The importance of Wilberforce's actions, despite their failure, is that they provide a foundation and inspiration for virtuous action at a future time, after Britain has fallen into ruins and a new society has begun to emerge:

> Succeeding times your struggles, and their fate,
> With mingled shame and triumph shall relate,
> While faithful History, in her various page,

> Marking the features of this motley age,
> To shed a glory, and to fix a stain,
> Tells how you strove, and that you strove in vain. (152)

Historical reality is complicated, just as a given historical moment is complicated ("this motley age"), and it cannot be sifted down to one explanation or singular understanding. Wilberforce's "struggles" to help the nation will be remembered alongside the "shame" of the nation, a shame that will forever be a "stain" on the historical record. And the failure of Wilberforce's virtuous actions will nevertheless also be regarded as a "triumph," because they provide a principled human guide for future understanding.

The historical vision set out in the epistle recalls Barbauld's efforts to treat similar issues in "Corsica." Not only does it bring the volume full circle by returning explicitly in its choice of subject matter to the realm of public and political experience. It also provides something of a corrective to the earlier poem's failures of vision by drawing into the realm of politics the various visionary themes of the volume. For example, while "Corsica" is constructed on the principles of nationalism, celebrating Paoli's efforts to free the island nation from Genoa and then France, *Epistle to William Wilberforce* abandons nationalist investments altogether, even though it is a poem about Barbauld's own country. She now understands what she did not in the earlier poem, namely, that history cannot be understood or shaped by focusing on a single moment in time or on a single nation. As she puts it in "Corsica" after the nationalist liberation movement has failed, in her belief that liberty was in process of being born she had "read the book of destiny amiss" (12). But whereas in "Corsica" she is left bewildered by her discovery that nationalism is an insufficient basis for imagining liberty, and she can imagine no place to redirect her visionary poetics except into "the freedom of the mind" (12), in the epistle she imagines a much larger frame of reference, beyond nationalism and personal character, for addressing matters of liberty and human experience, a frame of reference that allows her to engage with the public world rather than withdraw into the solitude of her own mind. Here she takes a very long view of the historical course of human experience, one that takes its direction from her spiritual explorations in "An Address to the Deity" and "A Summer Evening's Meditation" and returns to the material world with a largeness of vision that was missing in "Corsica." The complexities of history, she now understands, are not sorted out and settled in a day or even in a "motley age" such as the 1790s. The sort of transformative vision to which she is now wedded demands patience, and it requires looking steadily at the world through the lens of the distant past and the distant future, not simply the present.

Epistle to William Wilberforce is a public and prophetic poem, but it is of a sort radically different from the prophecy that Barbauld had attempted in "Corsica" and different as well from the sorts of prophecy that Blake would write later in the 1790s. Here she discovers a way to address the world not from the position of the moment but from the expansive reach of history. When she calls on Wilberforce to cease his efforts to pass his abolitionist bill through Parliament, she does so not because she finds fault with his character but because she finds fault with his understanding of history. Her prophetic vision states forthrightly that the nation—Britain—must fall, and her call for the future is for people to work toward cultivating the sorts of virtue found in Wilberforce's actions, so that the understanding of human virtue and moral purpose can mature and make itself manifest in a new world, built from the ashes of the old. This prophecy is not presented from the perspective of eternity; it is rather given from the perspective of history, which, for all intents and purposes, in Barbauld's vision, is as expansive as eternity.

Conclusion

At the conclusion of *Visionary Poetics,* Joseph Wittreich remarks that "for Blake and for the other Romantics, Milton is a type of the *renovator mundi,* a liberator rather than an oppressor, who, like other such figures, appears under a number of guises—as *Corrector, Reparator, Reformator.* Milton, for these poets, is the great prophet who stands between the ancient and the modern world" (214). This statement calls to mind two important considerations bearing on the study of eighteenth-century women's poetry in general and the poetry of Barbauld in particular. First, Wittreich's implication that there is a gap in the writing of visionary poetry between the periods of Milton and Blake needs to be reconsidered in the light of recent studies on women poets of the eighteenth century; as I have tried to show, almost twenty years before Blake began his visionary project, Barbauld (among others) had developed a systematic and sophisticated visionary poetics.[1] Second, while Barbauld certainly knew the work of Milton, as William McCarthy makes clear and as various allusions in her own poetry show, she does not easily fit within a Miltonic line of vision.[2]

Barbauld draws from multiple sources, including Milton, and shapes these sources to fit her own purposes. Not only do her purposes (arguably) differ from Milton's but her poetic strategies and conclusions about how to achieve salvation and liberty depart markedly from the strategies deployed by Milton before her and Blake afterward. Barbauld does not engage in any sustained way with Milton's vision in an effort to correct it; Milton is but one of many sources—classical and Christian—on whom she draws in mapping out her vision for eighteenth-century Britain. Her visionary poetics, that is, derives from broad and diverse sets of cultural interest rather than from a singular set of literary engagements. The result is a poetry that needs to be examined within contexts beyond those that inform the conventional understanding of British visionary poetics.

As an expression of the reach and depth of the visionary imagination, Barbauld's *Poems* is perhaps the most important poetic document of the later eighteenth century. Her poetic interests embrace various eighteenth-century preoccupations with history and politics, speculative philosophy, and religious dissent; she also looks beyond the interests of her own day, pushing back into ancient literary history for the purpose of bringing earlier literary views to bear on contemporary social relations, and she appropriates Milton and biblical writings and ideas when they suit her visionary purposes. Drawing upon epic, satire, lyric, hymns, songs, pastoral, and other modes of poetic expression, she constructs over the course of the volume a coherent and compelling visionary statement about the most important and durable principles of human experience and about how to bring these principles to bear on the public world in such a way as to transform it. Her visionary reach takes in personal life and public life, the present and the past, and the spiritual and secular dimensions of the human situation, which she interweaves to demonstrate the singular reality of experience that, under the pressure of contemporary British history, has become divided and corrupted to the point of collapse but that can be remade along the lines of humane and just principles.

While the early reception of *Poems* was largely positive, Barbauld's good reputation became tainted over time as readers and critics came to understand more fully the implications of her visionary charge to the public, sketched in *An Epistle to William Wilberforce*, then stated explicitly and in detail twenty years later in *Eighteen Hundred and Eleven*.[3] These poems explicitly set out the political meaning of her pacifist vision. However, other poems in the volume lay the foundation for the political conclusions she ultimately arrives at, beginning, for instance, with "Corsica," which acknowledges that in interpreting the Corsican nationalist movement she had "read the book of destiny amiss" and concludes with her retreat into the "freedom of the mind." In subsequent poems, she explores with great patience and in considerable detail the possibility of situating oneself meaningfully in the world so as to preserve one's personal integrity, and at the same time she shows how structural transformation of the world might be possible. Over the course of the volume, she engages with classical and contemporary traditions of literary expression, meditates on the ways of science and the limitations and possibilities of religion, considers the role of friendship in life, examines the existential reality of death, speculates on the reach of the mind's knowledge and imagination, and more. Quite simply, no subject and no ideas lie beyond the reach of her poetic interest. And she approaches her visionary task with a restless energy, never succumbing to any set of doctrinaire truths that she may encounter but instead constructing a fluid and organic worldview that grows and takes shape across the range of the volume. The result is a vision that is firm yet tentative, sure of its claims yet marked by a readiness to engage new forms of knowledge and understanding.

At the center of Barbauld's visionary poetics, as I have shown, are several abiding principles, all of which help to define her pacifist view of the world. Foremost among these principles is love, which is expressed often in poems about friends, God, and (more generally) life. For Barbauld, the full human reach of love is to be found most explicitly in the character of Christ, whose unsurpassed capacity for love is marked by courage, generosity, and subservience. Love is not a sentimental emotion, and it is not a personal feeling; it is rather an orientation toward the world and life and is therefore a social imperative. It is a principle of global significance, insofar as love, for Barbauld, proceeds outward into the world in the face of even the harshest of circumstances and strictest of oppositions, following an ethic that places care and regard for the world before self. Barbauld's conception of love, on this view, requires the courage to stand strong in the face of any efforts to restrict freedom of conscience, joy, or intellectual life. Vitally related to the principle of love are the principles of friendship, faith, and public service, as Barbauld steadfastly resists any assumption that the personal and social dimensions of life are distinct from one another. These principles are grounded on her conviction that matters of personal life, spiritual life, and social and political life are inextricably interwoven and must be recognized as equally vital parts of the human condition. Combined, these principles constitute a stance toward the world that is fully positive; that is, rather than engaging in any sort of oppositional endeavor to dismantle those parts of human experience that are limiting or debilitating, Barbauld focuses wholly on those values and ideals that, in her view, are necessary to a meaningful, just, and free life.

The visionary dimension of Barbauld's poetics can be found in her patient and loving insistence that, by focusing steadfastly on the highest ideals of life, it becomes possible to transform the world along the lines of those ideals. While her poems move across various modes of expression and across multiple types of subject matter, they are steady in their warm regard for humanity, and collectively they create a picture of experience that is not compromised by religious doctrine, limiting forms of nationalism, debilitating forms of political struggle, or the unavoidable existential reality of death. In her poems, Barbauld recognizes the hard realities of human experience, but at the same time she envisions love and kindness as guiding spirits, welcomes subservience as a transformative possibility in the face of injustice, and expresses faith that freedom is possible and life purposeful. For her, the world cannot be remade through conflict or violent engagement but only by embracing and living fully those values and principles that stand at the center of one's idealism.

Other poets of the age followed the direction of Barbauld's visionary poetics. For instance, in her final volume of poems, *The Rural Lyre* (1796), Ann Yearsley, the laboring-class poet from Clifton, explicitly acknowledges the transformative power of subservience when she has Liberty say to Brutus that "to yield is to deserve a throne" (17). Subservience is combined with the virtue of sympathy when Brutus later tells the mourning Hermia that "I'll mourn with thee, indulge thy tedious grief, / And, sympathizing with thee, give relief" (25). Once Brutus puts himself in the service of Hermia, she immediately surrenders to him—"Accept, brave chief, my arrows and my bow—/ I follow thee" (25)—as he does to her, and the result is a loving and sustainable relationship. Further along in the volume, in a poem entitled "Remonstrance in the Platonic Shade," Yearsley echoes Barbauld again, speaking of "universal love" (67) and, more fully, of the "trinomial pow'r" of "love, friendship, virtue" (68), all of which occupy the center of Barbauld's vision. These sorts of subjects and interests run through the entirety of Yearsley's volume, along with poems on the politics of the age, showing that Yearsley, like Barbauld, was dedicated to the visionary task of changing the world by way of love rather than political force. And like Barbauld's *Poems*, *Rural Lyre* is a systematic whole, working out the complications and dimensions of change in its various poems but never straying far from its central visionary concern with the power of love to change the world.

The link between the central principles of Barbauld and Yearsley's visionary claims—and some of the differences between the two poets—about how to live in the world can be seen most explicitly in "The Indifferent Shepherdess to Colin," the final poem in *Rural Lyre*. In this poem, Yearsley, like Barbauld, draws on the pastoral mode for the purpose of meditating on life, experience, and human purpose. And, like Barbauld, she observes that her interest is not in the specific details of the political or social moment but rather in "the soul entire" (140). Only when the human situation is considered in its entirety, she says, does it become possible to imagine that the real goal of life is liberty—not political liberty per se but human freedom in all respects. As she puts it:

> For my eternal plan
> Is to be calm and free.
> Estrang'd from tyrant man
> I'll keep my liberty. (141)

Yearsley retreats to the margins not because she rejects mankind in general—she is not a misanthrope—but because she seeks to gain perspective beyond that found within the constraints of "*tyrant* man." For Yearsley, there is no difference between the threat to liberty brought on by political force (as in "Bristol Elegy") or by romantic love (as in "Indifferent Shepherdess"), and in every case, she says, it is necessary to "guard my liberty" (142). And her recommendation for learning how to guard one's liberty rejects the idea of opposition and force, adopting instead the pacifist stance of indifference, as the title of the poem suggests.

Joanna Baillie, too, follows a path similar to Barbauld, though her poetic strategies differ markedly from those found in *Poems* and *Rural Lyre*. In *Metrical Legends* (1821), for example, a collection of three long "chronicles," followed by four shorter gothic tales, Baillie identifies subservience as an abiding virtue and socially transformative power. In the first chronicle, describing the history of William Wallace, she says that the young Wallace put himself, body and mind, in the service of his country—his "nightly thought for Scotland's weal, / ... clothed his form in mimick steel" (8); this willing and complete commitment to Scotland's freedom later leads the various clans of Scottish soldiers to submit, in turn, to Wallace's leadership: "They William Wallace there proclaim'd; / And there, exultingly, each gallant soul, / Ev'n proudly yielded to such high controul" (17). Unlike Napoleon, who, according to Byron in *Childe Harold's Pilgrimage* 3, came to view himself as "a god unto thyself" (2.90), Wallace Wallace derives his power from the people, just as the nation's power derives from his own subservience to the nation. Even as she recognizes and even celebrates the accomplishments of great individuals, Baillie redefines greatness, rejecting the idea of purely individual and self-interested distinction and offering in its place a vision wherein individual greatness is understood as a form of service to the social good, presenting in historical terms the values that Barbauld associates with Christ.

Other poems in Baillie's volume offer a similar view of greatness as a function of service to others. In "Lady Griseld Baillie," for example, Baillie traces the conduct of her heroine through a series of difficult and dangerous episodes, showing how at every turn she puts self-interest aside in favor of helping those in need. Lady Griseld is, for Baillie, the ideal model for individual and social conduct. At the conclusion of the poem, indeed, Baillie extrapolates the broad lesson of Lady Griseld's life for the women of the early nineteenth century, expressing her confidence that, like Lady Griseld, modern women can accomplish greatness through social service: "Leagued for good they act, a virtuous band, / The young, the rich, the loveliest of the land, / Who clothe the naked, and each passing week, / The wretched poor in their sad dwellings seek" (259). In concluding passages of the poem, Baillie steps directly into the midst of the arguments over gender in the nineteenth century, doing much what Barbauld had done almost fifty years earlier by stating directly and evenly that oppositional political engagement is an inadequate strategy for effecting meaningful social change.

Even Christopher Columbus, in Baillie's tale about the great explorer, despite his many failings, is someone who, in the final analysis, was driven by an interest larger than personal ambition. Even as he leads his fellow mariners on an exploratory voyage of great danger, he expresses his willingness to yield to their wishes, should they lose faith in his leadership; should his followers decide that he is unworthy of them, Baillie says, he is willing to be "cast . . . to the main" (137). Not only does Baillie recognize the greatness of Columbus; she also describes the noble character of the indigenous people who occupy the newly discovered lands across the Atlantic, idealizing them for their willingness to share their wealth, an act that inspires in Columbus and his followers "humble, timid rev'rence" (143). For Baillie, the story of Columbus matters not only because it reflects the human capacity for great deeds but also because it embodies the sorts of noble ideals of which all humans are capable.

Baillie, however, does not simply offer a nostalgic and sentimental view of Columbus. Indeed, she understands that, whatever his motives (and, for her, these motives were complex and conflicted), the consequences of his actions were played out under the circumstances of historical reality, which was deeply defined by imperialistic conquest. For instance, the narrator of the poem says of the explorer that after he arrived in the New World "there did he possession claim, / In Isabella's royal name" (141). Further, Baillie recognizes the human cost of European greed; although the indigenous peoples of the New World freely offer their treasures to Columbus and his followers, they are ("O foul disgrace!") "repaid with cruel wreck of all their harmless race" (143). But, for Baillie, historical reality does not reduce to individual character; despite the many dire consequences arising from Columbus's discovery of the New World, his idealism can and should be recognized and admired. Indeed, Baillie says in her preface to *Metrical Legends*, Columbus belongs "to no particular country" (xxiv), because the reach of his accomplishment and leadership span across all subsequent history and across the entire globe. Such a view embraces a realistic historical sensibility without abandoning the redemptive possibilities of idealism.

Baillie's vision, no less than Yearsley's and Barbauld's and no less than Hands's and Bannerman's, is systematically pursued across the span of her volume, and, like Yearsley and Barbauld, she celebrates and advocates on behalf of the transformative power of sympathy, virtue, and love. Moreover, like Yearsley and Barbauld, Baillie situates her vision among the complex and nuanced relations between material circumstance the human capacity to dream and work for human betterment. Baillie is neither a pure idealist nor a mechanical materialist; she recognizes the determining reality of circumstance while insisting on the transformative power of human agency and idealism. She seeks to find a way to move human experience forward toward a better world, but at the same time she acknowledges—insists—that any progressive movement must find a way to negotiate the constraining realities of material circumstance.

Other examples from the years following the first publication of Barbauld's *Poems* doubtless could be adduced to demonstrate the wide interest in visionary poetics during the long eighteenth century, as well as the visionary belief that love and sympathy were the proper means by which to change the world. In any case, the point is clear: Barbauld was not writing in a historical or literary vacuum; she was part of widespread cultural sensibility that operated across the lines of class and gender, seeking to devise a means of directing the historical changes that were already in motion by the 1760s, as evidenced by the Corsican and industrial revolutions. Barbauld's purpose, like that of her fellow visionary poets, was to find a path forward through history to a new world of human possibility. While she cast a long glance back toward the past, studying the works of Virgil, Ovid, Tibullus, and others, she did so not from a desire to move backward in time but rather from a wish to learn from the past and, equally importantly, to make visible the connecting thread of humanity through the course of its long struggle to find peace, love, and security. Only by studying the past, by reexamining its challenges and desires and drawing forward its most durable principles, she seems to suggest, does it become possible to head into the future in a meaningful way.

Over the past twenty or thirty years the scholarship on the long eighteenth century has been indispensable to recovering and explaining the works of many writers who were heretofore either little studied or not studied at all, and this scholarship has been indispensable to the present study. Scholars cited across this book—Theresa Kelley, Paula Feldman, Paula Backscheider, Susan Wolfson, Stephen Behrendt, Stuart Curran, Penny Bradshaw, Anne Mellor, Marlon Ross, among many others—have prepared a rich ground that will long be vital to research and criticism on the period, particularly the women poets of the period. But much work remains to be done. While many excellent studies have been produced that examine the character and depth of individual poems, there have not yet been comprehensive, detailed, and closely argued investigations of individual authors and their work (with the notable exceptions of McCarthy and Waldron's biographical studies of Barbauld and Yearsley, respectively).[4] The result is that very few studies exist of the sort that, more than seventy-five years ago, were produced in an effort to demonstrate (for example) the far-reaching poetic and cultural significance of such writers as Wordsworth and Coleridge.

I have tried to take one small step toward correcting this deficiency. By building on the outstanding scholarly work on the women poets of the long eighteenth century, particularly by focusing in detail on one author's most important volume of poems, I have sought to advance the understanding of the period. Not only have I tried to follow McCarthy's example (which calls for close attention to scholarly detail) by researching as comprehensively as possible the sources and associations of Barbauld's poetry; I have also tried to call attention to an area of investigation that has been little considered in the study of the women poets of the period: the importance of the poetic volume as a means of expressing the visionary. As Daniel White has shown and as Barbauld's prose writings attest, Barbauld was very much a writer who was engaged with the world around her and who sought to find ways to change that world so as to relieve it of injustice and violence. As part of the British Dissenting community, she was entirely dedicated to the principle of the liberty of conscience, and her life's work, including her poetry, was given over to examining this principle and working toward its establishment in society. And, for her, liberty of conscience was incommensurate with systems of value and forms of social life that viewed violence—political, personal, psychological—as acceptable or necessary. In her poetry, perhaps more than anyplace else, she set out to examine what it means to stand on the principle of liberty of conscience and took it on herself to consider the many implications of this principle in personal and social life. The result was a volume, *Poems*, that articulates a comprehensive and detailed understanding of the many dimensions of visionary poetry and poetics.

If my line of inquiry into Barbauld's poetry is persuasive, then it follows that much future work remains to be done on other poets of the late eighteenth century. Taking my critical point of departure from Joseph Wittreich's indispensable work on Milton and Blake, I have sought to complicate and extend Wittreich's argument by showing that visionary poetics did not die during the eighteenth century; rather, it took an odd but important detour into the imaginations of many women writers, who, writing from various class and cultural positions, believed that they saw through the constraining and dominant structures of value in Britain and had discovered a way—through principles of love, sympathy, and servitude—to break free of those structures, thereby enabling a new humanity to arise. While Barbauld may not have embraced the role of the prophet with the same degree of certainty as (say) Blake and may not have understood prophecy in the same way as Milton and Blake, she nevertheless saw that, by virtue of her gender and religious identity, she was an outsider and that her voice arose from the margins of British society. And even as she challenged the idea that prophecy is necessarily a marginalized discourse, she at the same time used her marginalized voice strategically in *Poems* to build a pacifist and loving vision of human possibility that might draw readers away from the seemingly inescapable conflicts and turmoil of their world toward a new way of imagining and constructing human experience. Moreover, Barbauld's vision, while radical, is never, unlike Blake's, articulated from a position of certainty; at every turn she questions her own presuppositions and cross-examines her conclusions to assure that she does not become entrapped by reductive and dogmatic presuppositions about truth. Her vision is flexible, shaped according to the material circumstances of human experience, and her prophecy is inviting rather than threatening, showing a path toward a better world for those who wish to follow it. And that path is marked by the liberty of individual conscience and the unifying and universal principle of love.

NOTES

Introduction

1. See especially Northrop Frye, *Fearful Symmetry*; Harold Bloom, *The Visionary Company*; Harold Bloom, *Blake's Apocalypse*; and Joseph A. Wittreich, *Angel of Apocalypse*.

2. For a brief recognition of Leapor's use of dreams as a framework in many of her poems, see Susan Goulding, "Reading 'Mira's Will,'" 78.

3. Some of the later work of Joanna Baillie also reflects an interest in visionary poetics. She explores the operations of vision in a series of narrative poems not just in *Metrical Legends of Exalted Characters* but also, two years later, in a volume that she edited entitled *A Collection of Poems*, in which she gathers poems by others, many of whom were interested in the power of vision. Note, for example, the concluding lines in the sonnet about Hannibal ("At Lake Thrasymenus"), written by Charles Johnston:

> But what was thy reward? care, labour, war
> Defeat, and exile, a self-hasten'd end—
>   Enough;—for not confin'd to life, but far
> Beyond, can minds like thine their vision send,
>   And see, tho' none beside, the ascending star
> Of glory, which their memories shall attend. (127)

4. In dating the poem, I rely on a list of poems included in Robinson's *Memoirs* that, she says, were written between December 1799 and December 1800. See Robinson, *Memoirs of the Late Mrs. Robinson*, 2:262.

5. In talking about the visionary tradition in general, Wittreich makes a point that is applicable to Blake: "If epic articulates a new stage of consciousness, prophecy is more ambitious still, attempting to bring man to the highest peak of consciousness that is possible, its objective being not to equip man to live in an advancing state of civilization but to enable man to enter the heavenly Jerusalem" ("'A Poet Amongst Poets'" 104).

6. One notable exception to this claim is Anne Bannerman, whose work I discuss in the next section of the introduction.

7. Stephen C. Behrendt's important recent study, *British Women Poets and the Romantic Writing Community*, examines books rather than individual poems, though his critical interest is not centered on the practical and theoretical significance of the poetic volume.

8. Wolfson's comment about Hemans helps to make the point that the gender dynamic of women's writing is as much a critical construct as a product of authorial agency: "Before she had been hailed (not without her bid) into the cult of the 'feminine,' the gender of Hemans's pen was less settled. She baffled the *British Review*'s reader with her unsigned *Modern Greece* (1817), its 'high polish' and 'classical' modeling seeming 'the production of an academical, and certainly not a female, pen'" (77).

9. For a discussion of these two poems, and of Barbauld's general views on gender, see Marlon Ross, *The Contours of Masculine Desire*, 215–30.

10. For a helpful and informative article on the Della Cruscans, see Edward E. Bostetter, "The Original Della Cruscans and the Florence Miscellany," 277–300.

11. The best work to date on Hands's volume is Donna Landry, *The Muses of Resistance*, 186–208. For a helpful recent study of Hands, see Cynthia Dereli, "In Search of a Poet."

12. Achitophel sees Amnon as an obstacle to the crown: "Th' ambitious Prince [Achitophel], resolv'd / At once t' avenge his sister, and remove / An obstacle betwixt him and the crown" (34).

13. For a helpful study of Hands's writing strategies, see Carolyn Steedman, "Poetical Maids and Cooks Who Wrote."

14. On matters of sexual orientation, see "An Epistle" (91–92), which is explicitly lesbian in its expressions of desire: "Let love-sick nymphs their faithful shepherds prove, / Maria's friendship's more to me than love" (91); "When I walk forth to take the morning air, / I quickly to some rising hill repair, / Then sigh to you, and languish with desire" (91); "'Tis you, Maria, and 'tis only you, / That can the wonted face of things renew: / Come to my groves" (92).

15. Very little has been written about this important poet. But see Ashley Miller, "Obscurity and Affect in Anne Bannerman's 'The Dark Ladie'"; Adriana Craciun, "Romantic Spinstrelsy"; Diane Long Hoeveler, "Gendering the Scottish Ballad"; and Andrew Elfenbein, "Lesbian and Romantic Genius."

16. My discussion here is based on a hardcopy of Bannerman's *Tales of Superstition and Chivalry*, which places the engraving of *The Prophecy of Merlin* in the front of the volume. In two online versions of the volume, the engraving appears immediately adjacent to the poem, rather than at the front of the volume. See, for instance, www.archive.org/stream/talessuperstitio00bangoog#page/n146/mode/2up and http://books.google.com/books?id=z0UgAAAAMAAJ&printsec=frontcover&dq =tales+of+superstition+and+chivalry.

17. A later translation of the play gives the lines as follows:

Do your lips ope, you lie, and if ye sigh,
Your sighs are feign'd; or if your eyes ye move,

Deceit is in your looks; in fine each act
Each semblance, all you show or hide is false. (35)

18. While the notes to Bannerman's volume suggest that she was indebted to Spenser, it should be noted as well that Geoffrey of Monmouth also published a work entitled *Prophetiae Merlini* (*The Prophecies of Merlin*). See Geoffrey of Monmouth, *The History of the Kings of Britain*. See also Caroline D. Eckhardt, ed., *The "Prophetia Merlini" of Geoffrey of Monmouth*.

19. For a helpful discussion of women's poetry in the late eighteenth century, see Stuart Curran, "Women Readers, Women Writers." For a discussion of women and education in the eighteenth century, see Backscheider, *Eighteenth-Century Women Poets and Their Poetry*, 379–80.

20. The feminist critical studies of Barbauld are too numerous to list. But I will mention three that are particularly important: William McCarthy, "'We Hoped the Woman Was Going to Appear'"; Penny Bradshaw, "Gendering the Enlightenment"; and Philip Cox, *Gender, Genre, and the Romantic Poets*, 22–37. For a more general study of women's efforts in the period to negotiate the constraints placed on them by a patriarchal society, see William Stafford, *English Feminists and Their Proponents in the 1790s*.

21. See, for example, William Keach, "A Regency Prophecy and the End of Anna Barbauld's Career"; John Guillory, "Literary Capital"; and Behrendt, *British Women Poets and the Romantic Writing Community*, 71–77.

Chapter 1 · Barbauld's Poems *in Context*

1. While the war with France ended with a British victory and the considerable expansion of British holdings in North America, it also left the nation financially strapped, a fact that led George III to impose taxes on the American colonies.

2. Catholics and Unitarians, of course, were not among those groups that enjoyed protection under the Act of Toleration.

3. In 1794 Priestley emigrated to Pennsylvania to escape the reactionary political climate of England.

4. The 1773 version of *Poems* went through several editions in the 1770s, before the new and corrected edition was published in 1792. For the story of the volume's composition, see McCarthy, *Anna Letitia Barbauld*, 107–11.

5. For an example of Barbauld's direct commentary on politics, see *Sins of Government, Sins of the Nation*.

6. For an outstanding commentary on Dissent in the age of Barbauld, see Daniel E. White, *Early Romanticism and Religious Dissent*, especially 17–33.

7. See, for instance, Milton's important essay, written during the period when the monarchy was being restored, entitled *The Ready and Easy Way to Establish a Free Commonwealth*.

8. The remainder of Priestley's statement here seems to have particular relevance for Barbauld's thought: "Let us, at least, virtually acknowledge it, by generously

cancelling all that is past, and suffering things to remain for the future as they were some years ago. (Happy years of mutual love and confidence!) This will not fail to secure the gratitude and affection of the Colonists. Nay, more, having seen our errors, and repented of them, there will be a better foundation laid for mutual confidence than ever" (144). Priestley's reference to "mutual love" directly anticipates Barbauld's poetic response, in "Rights of Woman," to Mary Wollstonecraft's *Vindication of the Rights of Woman*:

> Then, then, abandon each ambitious thought,
> Conquest or rule thy heart shall feebly move,
> In nature's school, by her soft maxims taught,
> That separate rights are lost in mutual love. (187)

The major difference between the two friends' views of "mutual love" seems to be that Priestley has reasonably little faith in it, while Barbauld invests her entire poetic vision in its possible triumph.

9. Priestley's son remarks that his father's "speculations on the subject of British politics did not go farther than a reform in Parliament, and no way tended, in his opinion, to affect the form of government, or the constitution of the kingdom, as vested in King, Lords, and Commons. He used frequently to say, and it was said to him, that though he was an Unitarian in religion, he was in that country a Trinitarian in politics" (107).

10. For an informative general discussion of Priestley's radical political views, see Robert D. Fiala, "Priestley, Joseph (1733–1804)."

11. As the title page to the 1792 edition states, Barbauld also made various small corrections, consisting mainly of changes in diction and punctuation. For instance, in the 1793 edition, she moves the date of composition for "Corsica" from the bottom of the page to just beneath the title of the poem; she also removes parentheses from a line on page 1 that had appeared in the earlier edition; on page 4, she changes the word "leav'd" to "leaved"; on page 7, she changes the word "Borne" to "Born"; and so on.

12. It is possible, however, that there is a closer connection than McCarthy asserts. An online description of the Grey family papers held at the University of Manchester notes, for instance, that among the holdings in the library are papers by "Mary, Countess of Stamford, relating to the construction of the Bridgewater Canal, 1758–1767." Barbauld's second poem in the volume, "The Invitation," discusses the canals at some length. It is possible that she drew on Lady Mary West (nee Grey) for some of her information on the topic. See Papers of Mary, Countess of Stamford (1704–72) (EGR3/7), in the Papers of the Booth Family, in Grey (Stamford) of Dunham Massey Papers, John Rylands Library, University of Manchester, Manchester, UK.

13. In her excellent discussion of Barbauld, Lucy Newlyn notes that Barbauld's poetry involves a "complicated interweaving of private with public concerns" (136). Barbauld's refusal to distinguish categorically between these concerns, Newlyn says, arose from her upbringing in Warrington: "Barbauld's objective of political interven-

tion had been fostered in early adult life by the unique atmosphere at Warrington, where no evident distinction existed between familial and civic allegiances. Warrington offered more than an educational training for Nonconformists; it was a family, a society of friends, an ideal community practicing a fraternalist ethic, a centre in which current political issues were enthusiastically debated, and a thoroughfare for the traffic of radical ideas and publications. Fifteen years of life as a young woman in this environment gave Barbauld a head start . . . in seeing how domestic life itself might be lived as a form of political praxis" (137). Newlyn's claim helps to explain how and why Barbauld might move across a disparate range of poetic modes and subjects while working toward a common visionary aim.

14. Newlyn's discussion of Barbauld's "politics of sympathy" usefully addresses the poet's search for, and investment in, the principle of a universal idea of sociability. Note especially Newlyn's comment that, for Barbauld, "stories of suffering . . . give us access to 'universally felt' emotion, teaching us 'to think, by inuring us to feel'" (164).

15. For a helpful discussion of the personal, cultural, and historical details surrounding this document, see McCarthy, *Anna Letitia Barbauld*, 332–41.

16. Barbauld's view here, in an important respect, anticipates Martin Luther King's description of nonviolent direct action in "Letter from Birmingham Jail." In this famous address to his fellow clergymen, King notes that the political activism of the sort he advocates requires four important steps: the gathering of the facts, an attempt to negotiate, self purification, and nonviolent direct action. While Barbauld's address is not quite so prescriptive as King's description, she is clear about the importance that she attaches to self-reflection, or self-purification.

17. I discuss the problem of justice in relation to nationalism a bit later in this chapter. But for now it is worth noting Barbauld's comment in *Sins of Government* that "there is a notion which has a direct tendency to make us unjust, because it tends to make us think God so; I mean the idea which most nations have entertained, that they are the peculiar favourites of Heaven."

18. For an excellent brief discussion of *Sins of Government, Sins of the Nation* and *Eighteen Hundred and Eleven*, see Stephen C. Behrendt, *British Women Poets and the Romantic Writing Community*, 70–77.

Chapter 2 · Politics, Vision, and Pastoral

1. Freedom and liberty, of course, were problematic terms in the eighteenth century, as various politically interested groups fought over their meanings. For a helpful discussion of this topic, see P. J. Marshall, ed. *The Oxford History of the British Empire*, especially Marshall's "Britain without America."

2. Note Marshall's comment that "by the middle of the eighteenth century, 'liberty' had been firmly established as 'the single most important ingredient of an Imperial identity in Britain and the British Empire.' There was, however, no agreed interpretation as to what constituted British liberty. Opposing interpretations gained acceptance on either side of the Atlantic. The revolutionary crisis made it clear

how different these interpretations were. After 1783 the British version of liberty, later reinforced by responses to the challenge of the French Revolution, became the prevailing ideology of the white populations of the British Empire" ("Britain without America" 590). For a consideration of Barbauld's handling of liberty in "Corsica" (that is different from mine), see Robert Jones, "What Then Should Britons Feel?" Jones views Barbauld's poem as "a powerful piece of patriot writing wholly committed to the cause of liberty" (285); the difficulty that Barbauld faces in presenting her views on liberty, Jones argues, revolves around the poem's uncertainty about "how far feelings can be trusted as guides when the issues are complex and the consequences severe" (299).

3. For the relations between Barbauld and Milton, see Robert W. Jones, "Barbauld, Milton, and the Idea of Resistance." See also McCarthy, "'We Hoped the Woman Was Going to Appear,'" 122–23.

4. Some years later, Wordsworth feels compelled to draw the same conclusion about political violence. See his stirring "Letter to the Bishop of Llandaff," especially the following comment: "What! have you so little knowledge of the nature of man as to be ignorant that a time of revolution is not the season of true Liberty? Alas, the obstinacy and perversion of man is such that she is too often obliged to borrow the very arms of Despotism to overthrow him, and, in order to reign in peace, must establish herself by violence" (6).

5. On Barbauld's pacifism, note Penny Mahon's comment regarding Barbauld and her brother's children's writing: "The Aikins' criticism of the militarist system of their day, with its contrast between appearance and reality, was a new element in children's literature. The original and outspoken nature of that criticism is suggested by the modern children's literature critic Gillian Avery, who noted that Barbauld's pacifism was startling" ("'Things by their Right Name'" 171). Mahon here is referring to Avery's *Nineteenth-Century Children*. See also Nicholas Birns's "'Thy World, Columbus!'" and Anne Mellor's helpful comments in *Mothers of the Nations*, 78ff.

6. For a useful commentary on Barbauld's materialist sensibilities, see William Keach's important essay on *Eighteen Hundred and Eleven*, "A Regency Prophecy and the End of Anna Barbauld's Career."

7. The eclogue from which the epigraph is taken exhibits what Judith Haber in *Pastoral and the Poetics of Self-Contradiction* refers to as "a fundamental self-contradictoriness within the genre," insofar as Virgil's poem is not a purely idyllic portrait of peace and ease but also an acknowledgment of loss and difficulty. Barbauld's use of pastoral in "The Invitation" reflects the same self-contradictoriness, as she presents pastoral as a mode that, as Haber puts it, "work[s] insistently against itself" (1). For Barbauld, as "The Invitation" shows, pastoral is not a static or prescriptive poetic form but rather a complex and multifaceted mode of expression.

8. For an important commentary on the relations between pastoral and vision, see Wittreich, *Visionary Poetics*, 117–37. While Wittreich's focus here is on Milton's "Lycidas," he provides helpful general information on the way that visionary poetry engages with pastoral poetry (among other genres).

9. On Belsham, see McCarthy, *Anna Letitia Barbauld*, especially 79–81.

10. Ann Yearsley talks frequently about the social importance of friendship as a necessary building block in society. See, for instance, her poem "Address to Friendship: A Fragment" in *The Rural Lyre* (74–81).

11. Note, for example, the similarity between Barbauld's line "drink the spirit of the mountain breeze" and Wordsworth's lines in "To My Sister": "Our minds shall drink at every pore / The spirit of the season" (64).

12. The term "enamel'd meads" refers to a form of gardening wherein the landscape is shaped by planting short flowers (pansies, for instance) in a meadow and allowing the short-cropped grass to grow up to the edge of the flowers, creating the appearance of enameling.

13. A good online history of Bridgewater's canals can be found at www.bridgewatercanal.co.uk/history.html. For a general discussion of Bridgewater, see W. H. Chaloner, *People and Industries*, ch. 3. See also Edwin A. Pratt, *A History of Inland Transport and Communication in England*, 165–86, and Hugh Malet, *Bridgewater*.

14. Bridgewater's engineer was James Brindley. For an early account of Brindley's accomplishments, see Samuel Smiles, *James Brindley and the Early Engineers*. Also, in 1801, John Aikin, Barbauld's brother, included a long entry on Brindley in *General Biography*.

15. This famous quotation, of course, appears at line 8 of Blake's epigraph poem attached to his prophetic poem *Milton* (qtd. in *The Complete Poetry and Prose of William Blake* 95).

16. For an excellent discussion of Barbauld's middle-class temperament, see John Guillory, "Literary Capital," especially 402–7. Guillory focuses only on the section of "The Invitation" that was published by William Enfield in *The Speaker* under the title of "Warrington Academy." His emphasis on "cultural property" as private property is helpful in illuminating the extent to which Barbauld was indebted to a middle-class sensibility or ideology.

17. The town of Warrington was located halfway between Manchester and Liverpool, on the Mersey River, which river is referenced further on in this passage, thereby making clear that Barbauld's reference is to Warrington Academy. Useful details about the academy can be found in Robert E. Schofield, *The Enlightenment of Joseph Priestley*, 87–158.

18. The story of the serpent and the eagle comes from book 12 of the *Iliad*, 1:223ff.

Chapter 3 · Satire, Antipastoral, and Visionary Poetics

1. According to McCarthy, Lissy was Barbauld's friend Elizabeth Rigby, who, along with her sister, Sarah, was a lighthearted free spirit whose father was associated with Warrington Academy. Elizabeth, McCarthy says, "displayed a freedom from self-consciousness and unfettered spontaneity, that worked magical effects on Anna Letitia" (*Anna Letitia Barbauld* 83).

2. McCarthy describes the erotic dimension of the poem, a claim that is supported by the reference to Venus (*Anna Letitia Barbauld* 83).

3. For a discussion of Horace along these lines, see Terry Gifford, *Pastoral*. Gifford remarks, for instance, that Horace finds the idea of pastoral retreat ironic and views Arcadia as "a myth" (22). According to Gifford, pastoral is a metaphor, and when it comes to be taken literally "it becomes dangerously open to exploitation by a culture that might prefer to hide reality in the myth of Arcadia" (23). In "Verses Written in an Alcove," Barbauld does not make this mistake, as she understands that the retreat she is describing is a myth and that the harsh realities of human experience are always close by.

4. As Barbauld observes in a note at the bottom of the poem's first page, the manuscript of "The Mouse's Petition" was placed in one of the cages in Joseph Priestley's lab: "Found in the trap where he [the mouse] had been confined all night by Dr. Priestley, for the sake of making experiment with different kinds of air" (37). According to McCarthy, "Many [of Barbauld's poems] were sent in letters to her intimate friend Elizabeth Belsham; others were deposited in places where they would be found later. The most famous of the deposited poems is 'The Mouse's Petition,' . . . left in the cage of a mouse that Joseph Priestley had captured for use in an experiment" ("'We Hoped the Woman Was Going to Appear'" 125).

5. Numerous scholars have examined Barbauld's interest in science, sympathy, politics, and conceptions of liberty as these appear in "The Mouse's Petition." See, for instance, Mary Ellen Bellanca, "Science, Animal Sympathy, and Anna Barbauld's 'The Mouse's Petition,'" and Julia Saunders, "'The Mouse's Petition': Anna Laetitia Barbauld and the Scientific Revolution."

6. McCarthy traces Barbauld's argument here to Pythagoras through James Thomson: these lines "allude less, probably, to the ancient sage Pythagoras than to James Thomson's reference to Pythagoras in his poem *Liberty*" (*Anna Letitia Barbauld* 77).

7. According to McCarthy's account, Priestley, on reading the poem, released the mouse ("'We Hoped the Woman Was Going to Appear'" 125).

Chapter 4 · *Personal Life and Visionary Poetics*

1. For a comparative analysis of Barbauld and Pope's poetry, see Kathryn Ready, "Identity, Character, and Gender." While Ready focuses on Barbauld's series of "Characters," written during her years at Warrington, in relation to several epistles by Pope rather than on "To Mrs. P——," her essay is nevertheless helpful in placing Barbauld within the context of eighteenth-century British literary history.

2. In their edition of Barbauld's poems, McCarthy and Kraft argue that "To Mrs. P——" is "technically less assured" than the other poems that Barbauld addressed to Mary Priestley (224). Even if this is true, it does not minimize the importance of the poem to Barbauld's effort in the volume to construct a meaningful visionary poetics.

3. Among the (perhaps) lesser explanations for Barbauld's interest in Pope's epistle is his reference to Elizabeth Churchill, who, after marrying Scroop Egerton, became Countess of Bridgewater. Egerton, the first Duke of Bridgewater, was the father (by

his second wife, Rachel Russell) of Francis Egerton, the third Duke of Bridgewater, and the subject of part of Barbauld's "The Invitation."

4. It perhaps goes without saying the social importance that Barbauld attaches to idleness is distinct from the virtue that Wordsworth attaches to idleness. For Wordsworth, idleness is not an opportunity to enrich one's social life and understanding but rather to enhance one's personal connection to nature. See, for example, "Expostulation and Reply," especially the lines

> Then ask not wherefore, here, *alone*,
> Conversing as I may,
> I sit upon this old grey stone,
> And dream my time away. (108, my italics)

5. I say "seems" because McCarthy implies that Barbauld may be describing drawings that she saw at the British Museum: "From Bloomsbury Square to the British Museum was a short walk, and at the museum she could see brilliant colored drawings of plants and insects of Surinam by the Dutch naturalist Maria Merian. In a poem she sent to Mary Priestley 'with Some Drawings of Birds and Insects' she alluded to them, or to Merian's great work on the subject, *Dissertatio de Generatione et Metamorphosibus Insectorum Surinamensium* (1705)" (*Anna Letitia Barbauld* 97). Even if Barbauld saw such drawings at the British Museum and perhaps has some of them in mind when she is writing her poem, her comment in "To Mrs. P——" suggests that she is writing first and foremost about drawings that she produced: "Amanda bids, at her command again / I seize the pencil, or resume the pen; / No other call my willing hand requires" (41). The reference to the pencil I take to suggest drawing, and the reference to the pen I take to suggest poetry. For a helpful general sketch of Fresnoy's ideas and his poem see David Marshall, "Literature and the Other Arts," 683ff.

6. For a discussion of the way visionary poetry engages with and transforms its antecedents, see Joseph A. Wittreich, "Opening the Seals," 26, and Wittreich, preface, xv. For a discussion of how prophecy overturns collective ideology, see Wittreich, *Visionary Poetics*, 50.

7. McCarthy briefly mentions the social implications of this poem: "In a poem devoted to describing the habits of birds and insects, she will draw from her own description a moral about human destiny" (*Anna Letitia Barbauld* 42).

8. According to Thomas B. Johnson, "The pheasant is a foreign bird, and was brought into Europe from the banks of the Phasis, a river of Colchis, whence the name, which it still retains" (*The Shooter's Guide* 133). For a history of the pheasant in England and elsewhere, see Rev. H. A. MacPherson, *Natural History of the Pheasant*, 3–23. The primary consumers of pheasants, of course, were initially the rich, and during the middle ages, the punishment for poaching pheasants *could* result in death. See William Perry Marvin, *Hunting Law and Ritual in Medieval English Literature*, 52. Subsequently, the penalty was reduced. According to James FitzJames Stephen, of the lighter penalties that eventually developed over time, "it was theoretically doubtful whether from 1604 to 1832 any one could lawfully shoot a pheasant,

partridge, or hare whatever qualification he possessed. The penalties by which this privilege was protected were not (except in the case of deer-stealers) severe, consisting principally in a moderate money fine, which might, in default of payment, be converted to imprisonment" (*A History of the Criminal Law of England* 2:281).

9. In the notes to *The Poems of Anna Letitia Barbauld*, McCarthy and Kraft observe that "in Torquato Tasso's *Gerusalemme Liberata*, 17.xxvi–vii (Fairfax translation), the hero Rinaldo, in a wood, beholds 'a marvel great and strange': first one tree, and then a hundred more, give birth to beautiful young women. ALA [Barbauld] conflates this scene with another (13.xli–iii) in which the hero Tancred stabs a tree trunk and discovers that he has stabbed Clorinda, imprisoned in it" (225). It is also worth noting Wittreich's comment on Tasso: "Behind Tasso's view of the epic poem, which emphasizes its dramatic character and predicates a movement toward new fulfillment and higher perfection, is his insistent belief that the poet, like God, is a creator, and the corollary to this belief, that the poet's universe is a replication of God's" (*Visionary Poetics* 11).

10. Keats's statement appears in his famous "vale of Soul-making letter": "I can scarcely express what I but dimly perceive—and yet I think I perceive it—that you may judge the more clearly I will put it in the most homely form possible—I will call the *world* a School instituted for the purpose of teaching little children to read—I will call the *human heart* the *horn Book* used in that School—and I will call the *Child able to read, the Soul* made from that *school* and its *hornbook*." (*The Letters of John Keats* 102).

11. In describing rather than examining this line, I realize that I am dodging the question of whether Barbauld is making an essentialist claim about the female mind. One reason for this dodge is that given the place of the poem in the larger volume, it seems reasonable to assume that Barbauld is describing (as she had done in "To Mrs. P——") her own relation to the ideas at the center of the poem.

12. Milton published a translation of the poem in 1673. His translation reads as follows:

> What slender Youth bedew'd with liquid odours
> Courts thee on Roses in some pleasant Cave,
> > *Pyrrha?* for whom bind'st thou
> > In wreaths thy golden Hair,
> Plain in thy neatness; O how oft shall he
> On Faith and chang'd Gods complain: and Seas
> > Rough with black winds and storms
> > Unwonted shall admire:
> Who now enjoyes thee credulous, all Gold,
> Who alwayes vacant alwayes amiable
> > Hopes thee; of flattering gales
> > Unmindfull. Hapless they
> To whom thou untry'd seem'st fair. Me in my vow'd
> Picture the sacred wall declares t' have hung

> My dank and dropping weeds
> To the stern God of Sea. (10)

13. At the time Barbauld was writing, there was disagreement about who wrote the poem from which she takes her epigraph. In attributing the poem to Tibullus, I am following Barbauld's own designation. But James Grainger, in his account of Tibullus and Sulpicia, attributes the poem to Sulpicia, who was a contemporary of Tibullus. In his introduction to the poems of Sulpicia, Grainger remarks, "But if the following little pieces are not the composition of Tibullus, to whom shall we impute them? Shall we, with Caspar Barthius, and Broekhusius, ascribe them to Sulpicia, the wife of Calenus, who flourished in the reign of Domitian? This opinion is by no means improbable, for we know from Martial and Sidonius Apolinarius, that Sulpicia was eminent in those days for her poetry" (225). Grainger then proceeds to offer a lengthy defense of his position against those historians and critics who attribute many of Sulpicia's poems to Tibullus (225–31).

14. For a brief account of the festival of Mars, see Leslie Adkins and Roy A. Adkins, *Handbook to Life in Ancient Rome*, 282.

15. McCarthy and Kraft state that "mild unvarying cheek/To meet the offer'd blow" are most likely taken from Matthew 5:39. They offer two possible explanations of the "Phyrgian sage": Tertullian and Epictetus (265).

16. That Barbauld doubtless had Horace's conceit in mind while writing the poem is suggested by the fact that her epigraph, also from Horace, voices a similar idea.

17. I am relying here on the information presented in the online edition of *Encyclopedia Britannica*. The Maecenas entry can be found at www.britannica.com/EBchecked/topic/356230/Gaius-Maecenas.

Chapter 5 · Reflections on Writing

1. In addition to its theoretical and literary historical interests, the work attempts to do for song writing what Bishop Thomas Percy had done for the English ballad in *Reliques of Ancient English Poetry*: provide a collection of verse that might help to establish the worth of British poetry. That Aikin knew that he was following in the footsteps of Percy is clear from his comment distinguishing his own literary efforts from those of Percy: "As it is not my design to collect pieces of this sort [i.e., poems that draw on "the marvelous" to illustrate "natural history"], which is already done in a very elegant manner by Dr. Percy, in his *Reliques of Ancient English Poetry*, I shall proceed to consider the Ballad more as an artificial than as a natural species of composition" (*Essays on Song-Writing* 23–24).

2. For further commentary on Barbauld's use of Tibullus in "Origin," see Paula Backscheider, *Eighteenth-Century Women Poets and Their Poetry*, 285. Backscheider argues that, in "Origin," Barbauld mingles "allusions to classical and British art" to make "Cupid a timeless inspiration."

3. I have listed the authors here in the order that Barbauld presents them (or their work, or characters). Her lines on these poets read as follows:

> Hence Sappho's soft infectious page;
> Monimia's woe; Othello's rage;
> Abandon'd Dido's fruitless prayer;
> And Eloisa's long despair;
> The garland blest with many a vow,
> For haughty Sacharissa's brow;
> And, wash'd with tears, the mournful verse
> That Petrarch laid on Laura's herse. (64–65)

4. I am drawing here on Poggioli's description of "the bucolic invitation," which, he says, is "to be like shepherds" (1).

5. Barbauld probably takes the name "Araminta" from William Congreve's comedy *The Old Bachelor* (1693).

6. I have been unable to trace the source of Barbauld's reference to the Persians who worshipped the sun god. It is likely that she is drawing on stories about Mithra or Hvare-khshaeta, both of whom are Persian gods associated with the sun.

7. Her most explicit political poem about the collapse of an entire culture is *Eighteen Hundred and Eleven*, though she anticipates the sentiments of that poem in *Epistle to William Wilberforce*, which concludes the 1793 edition of *Poems*.

8. The third book of elegies was published after Tibullus's death, and many scholars question whether he is their author. Barbauld seems to have had no such doubt, as she cites him by name in her epigraph. For one example of scholarly skepticism on the subject, see J. Wight Duff, *A Literary History of Rome from the Origins to the Close of the Golden Age*, 612ff.

9. I am here drawing loosely on a comment that Wittreich makes in the preface to *Milton and the Line of Vision*. In describing prophecy, Wittreich observes that the prophet is part of a tradition that "postulates a theory of influence and provides a paradigm for intrapoetic relationships" (xv). While Barbauld does not specify an author in her reference to "the storied page," it is nevertheless clear that her poem is textually engaged, even to the point of engaging in what Wittreich calls "corrective criticism" (xvi). Finally, Wittreich claims that "this corrective function is validated by the fact that, while prophets communicate with one another, they all derive their vision from Christ" (xvi). For Barbauld, the importance of Christ to her vision is found in the principle of love, which runs through the entire volume.

10. According to scholars, no definitive explanation exists of why Ovid was banished. As Charbra Adams Jestin and Phyllis B. Katz note, "We do not know the exact cause of his banishment; the poet himself speaks of a *carmen* and an *error* in one of the poems in the *Tristia*, poems he wrote during his banishment, in the hope that they would move Augustus to recall him. The *carmen* is almost certainly the *Ars Amatoria*; the *error* may be connected with the banishment of Augustus's daughter, but there is no indisputable evidence for either cause" ("Ovid's Life and Works" xx).

11. That this is exactly what happened can be seen clearly in the critical outcry against her poem *Eighteen Hundred and Eleven,* which Barbauld wrote when she

was sixty-five years old. For a brief sketch of the poem's critical reception see McCarthy and Kraft, *The Poems of Anna Letitia Barbauld*, 309–11.

12. For a discussion of the creative nature of visionary poetry, see Wittreich, *Visionary Poetics*, 31ff.

Chapter 6 · The Personal and Biblical Principles of Poetic Vision

1. The extent to which conflict is a part of the Milton line can be seen in the title of Jacki DiSalvo's wonderful book, *War of Titans: Blake's Critique of Milton and the Politics of Religion*.

2. Deirdre Coleman offers a useful account of Wollstonecraft's views on the poem and makes the helpful critical observation that Wollstonecraft does not put much stock in the idea that "the poem is an intimate poetic epistle from one woman to another" ("Firebrands, Letters and Flowers" 91). See also McCarthy's helpful account of Wollstonecraft's views on Barbauld in *Anna Letitia Barbauld*, 350ff.

3. For a general discussion of Virgil and homosexuality, see Robert Aldrich, *The Seduction of the Mediterranean*, 28–30. See also Ellen Oliensis, "Sons and Lovers"; Thomas K. Hubbard, ed., *Homosexuality in Greece and Rome*; and Craig A. Williams, *Roman Homosexuality*.

4. The reference to Amaryllis suggests that Corydon views himself as bisexual.

5. For a discussion of laws and cultural views surrounding homosexuality in eighteenth-century Britain, see Louis Crompton, *Byron and Greek Love*, 12–62.

6. McCarthy, "'We Hoped the Woman Was Going to Appear,'" esp. 131–37.

7. The image of the Doric reed is typically associated with pastoral and can be found, for example, in Virgil. It is also found in one of Barbauld's acknowledged British poetic sources, James Thomson. In the "Autumn" section of *Seasons*, for example, Thomson writes: "The Doric reed once more / Well pleased, I tune" (91). The reference to the "Lydian flute may be taken from Horace's ode 4.15, where he says,

> In the manner of our fathers, bravely,
> in verse, that's accompanied by Lydian flutes,
> we'll sing past leaders, we'll sing of Troy,
> Anchises, and the people of Venus.

The image of the Lydian flute is common in classical and neoclassical literature and can be found as well, for example, in Alexander Thomson, *Memoirs of a Pythagorean*. Thomson remarks, "I once saw the priests jig with meretricious airs to the soft music of the Lydian flute; but their levity was afterwards repaid by the votaries with a hearty flogging" (153). I should also note that McCarthy and Kraft associate the Doric reed and Lydian flute with elegiac lament rather than pastoral poetry per se, quoting from Richard Lovell Edgeworth, who met Barbauld in 1799 and subsequently wrote a commentary on "Ode to Spring," in which he states that "the Doric mood or mode was a grave species of music though sometimes mixed with the cheerful. The Lydian soft and tender so much so, as to be sometimes used at funerals" (qtd. in McCarthy and Kraft, *The Poems of Anna Letitia Barbauld* 268). In *The Lay of the Last Minstrel*, Sir Walter Scott also seems to use the image of the Doric reed to evoke an elegiac mood:

> Cliffs, which for many a later year
> The warbling Doric reed shall hear,
> When some sad swain shall teach the grove,
> Ambition is no cure for love. (35)

But "Dorian song" is a term often used to describe pastoral expression in general. See, for instance, Poggioli, *The Oaten Flute*, 69–70. See also James Sambrook's comment in *English Pastoral Poetry* associating Doric with the language of pastoral: "Theocritus writes in the Doric, that is to say a rustic dialect" (3), as well as his discussion of "Scotch Doric" (110–12).

8. For an excellent discussion of apocalyptic literature and thought, see Wittreich, *Angel of Apocalypse*.

9. For an account of Waller's plot, see Robert Wilcher, *The Writing of Royalism, 1628–1660*, 161ff.

10. For an excellent study of "Verses on Mrs. Rowe" within the context of literary history and women's writing, see Stuart Curran, "Romantic Women Poets."

11. For a brief account of Rowe's publishing history and a consideration of Theophilus's account of Elizabeth Rowe's life, see, for instance, Jennifer Richards's introduction to *Elizabeth Singer (Rowe)*.

12. For a brief discussion of Rowe and enthusiasm in relation to Barbauld, see McCarthy, *Anna Letitia Barbauld*, 109–10. See also 156–57 for McCarthy's discussion of Rowe's influence on Barbauld's poetry.

13. The best study of Barbauld and Dissent is Daniel E. White, "The 'Joineriana.'" White's notes are especially helpful in tracking the history of scholarship on the subject.

14. As Fairclough points out in a footnote here, these lines echo the opening lines of Virgil's *Eclogues*.

15. For a discussion of Pope's dramatic personae and their uses, see Maynard Mack, "The Muse of Satire."

16. For an account of Barbauld's friendship with the young Rigby sisters, see McCarthy, *Anna Letitia Barbauld*, 82–83. McCarthy says that the poem was first published in 1772 (83), perhaps because the dedication is dated December 1, 1772. But the publication date given on the title page is 1773. In the notes section of *The Poems of Anna Letitia Barbauld*, McCarthy and Kraft speculate that the poem may have been written as early as 1769, following a dustup at Warrington Academy caused by the Rigby sisters, but they are unable to establish beyond doubt a specific date of composition (231).

17. I take this information from the online version of Barbauld's *Poems*, which can be found at www.rc.umd.edu/editions/contemps/barbauld/poems1773/jennings.html.

McCarthy says that Mrs. Jennings was eighty-four at the time of her death (*Anna Letitia Barbauld* 40).

18. Even in "Hymn to Content" Barbauld draws very little upon biblical understanding or vocabulary, with the exception of referring at one point to Eve (57) and using such words as pilgrim and hermit (55). For the most part, the poem draws upon a pastoral sensibility, as Content is characterized as a nymph (54).

19. That Horace's poem is an effort to use the idea of God to make a political argument is seen in the following commentary by Sara Nolan, in "Horace Moving, Horace Rising": "Horace is caught up in this cycle of homage to the gods and the political leaders of his country, which the artist is obligated to render as praiseworthy. We can read the cultural need for Horace to fill this position of praise-giver, to place Caesar aesthetically, literally, and hierarchically beside Zeus, whose wrath strikes out at the impure. Horace's is a local muse. His poetic choice determines which of the 'neighborhood' heroes will live beyond their present life to be the remnants of the Great Roman Culture."

20. "Darkness" first appeared in Byron's *The Prisoner of Chillon and Other Poems*. While Byron's poem is perhaps more extreme than Barbauld's in its suggestion that there is not creative authority at all in the universe, the two poets share an understanding that creation—personal, historical, material—is ultimately subject to collapse.

21. For a helpful discussion of the Book of Habakkuk, see Sean P. Kealy, *An Interpretation of the Twelve Minor Prophets of the Hebrew Bible*, 136–62.

22. McCarthy argues that Rowe was "a model": "Rowe wrote several paraphrases on parts of the book of Habbakuk [sic]; Barbauld wrote a paraphrase on Habbakuk [sic] in her 'Hymn 2' . . . , which declares unmingled gratitude to God whether he blesses or blasts us, a theme congenial to Rowe" (*Anna Letitia Barbauld* 156).

23. See Samuel Willoughby Duffield, *English Hymns*, 76.

24. McCarthy and Kraft remove the quotation marks from the lines beginning "Come then" and ending "immortal shield" (*The Poems of Anna Letitia Barbauld* 257). I include them, as they appeared in the 1793 version of the poems.

25. The exact expression "pious friendship" does not appear in Cicero, but the general tenor of Barbauld's poem nevertheless echoes Cicero's sentiments. The exact phrase was fairly common in the eighteenth century and can be found, for example, in Henry Fielding's *Tom Jones*: "By which generous proceeding he very probably prevented Mr. Jones from becoming a victim to the wrath of Thwackum, and to the pious friendship which Blifil bore his old master; for, besides the disadvantage of such odds, Jones had not yet sufficiently recovered the former strength of his broken arm" (65).

26. White cites similar statements on liberty of conscience made by the Dissenters John Evans and Samuel Palmer. See *Early Romanticism and Religious Dissent*, 10–11.

27. Samuel Palmer, *The Protestant-Dissenter's Catechism*, qtd. in White, *Early Romanticism and Religious Dissent*, 11.

28. For a discussion of Barbauld's Arianism and her relation to Unitarianism, see White's helpful discussion in *Early Romanticism and Religious Dissent*, 37–41.

Chapter 7 · God, Vision, and the Political Moment

1. For a helpful discussion of "An Address to the Deity" in relation to Barbauld's Dissenting principles, see White, *Early Romanticism and Religious Dissent*, 61–65. White's argument centers on Barbauld's "nuanced arbitration between populist Puritanism, rational Dissent, and the established Anglican Church, presenting the failure of the sublime to sustain devotion for the common natures of earthly life" (61).

2. See White, *Early Romanticism and Religious Dissent*, for a discussion of the momentary nature of vision (63).

3. For discussions of Barbauld and pantheism, see Martin Priestman, *Romantic Atheism*, 128, and Jonathan Wordsworth, *The Bright Work Grows*, 21–26.

4. Variations on this expression, which describe the role of John the Baptist in preparing the way for the coming of Christ and, more generally, the isolation of the prophet from the social currents of the world, can be found in the Bible, including Isaiah 40:3, Matthew 3:3, John 1:23, and Mark 1:30. Blake, of course, also uses the expression as an epigraph to "All Religions Are One."

5. In *Anna Letitia Barbauld*, McCarthy examines the connections between Barbauld's theology and gender in the poem, commenting, for example, that "Summer Evening's Meditation" "departs from all these precursors [David Hume, Mark Akenside, John Milton], however, in presenting once again for Anna Letitia, a women's universe. In the tradition of 'A Nocturnal Reverie' (1713) by Anne Finch, and like her own 'Alcove' verses, the 'Meditation' claims the night poetically for women" (94). In "The Politics of Fancy in the Age of Sensibility," Julie Ellison also examines the gender dynamics of the poem, noting, for instance, that "the tensions among masculine authority, feminine ambition, and an interior space of aesthetic productivity are played out in the field of cosmic perspectives. The idea of the system provides an opportunity for the woman writer to expand her scope, then turns into a conceptual frame she cannot escape" (236).

6. Note especially Ellison's comment that in "A Summer Evening's Meditation," "fancy finds vistas that connect it to epic aspiration through resemblances to Milton's tours of space" (231). See also Christopher Hitt, "Ecocriticism and the Long Eighteenth Century," which draws associations between Barbauld's question addressed to God ("Where shall I seek thy presence? How unblamed / Invoke thy dread perfection") and Milton's in book 3 of *Paradise Lost* ("May I express thee unblam'd?"), claiming that "Barbauld's question is more searching, more desperate than Milton's" (141).

7. McCarthy has also noted the similarity between "A Summer Evening's Meditation" and Milton's and Blake's thought. See *Anna Letitia Barbauld*, 95.

8. Barbauld's reference to "Hesperian gardens" (138) echoes a passage in book 3 of *Paradise Lost*, wherein Milton refers to "those Hesperian gardens famed of old, Fortunate fields and groves and flowery vales, Thrice happy isles" (272).

9. Note, for instance, Barbauld's many references to silence, as she constructs a scene of meditative vision: "Nature's self is hushed" (139); "not a sound is heard / To break the midnight air" (140); "How deep the silence" (140). Coleridge uses a similar poetic strategy, for instance, in "Frost at Midnight," preparing for his speculative commentary by remarking that "'Tis calm indeed! So calm, that it disturbs / And vexes meditation with its strange / And extreme silentness" (240).

10. As McCarthy notes, *Epistle to William Wilberforce* was first published alone in 1791, by Joseph Johnson, as a quarto pamphlet and was only later incorporated into *Poems*. See *Anna Letitia Barbauld*, 294–301.

11. For a helpful account of the political circumstances surrounding Wilberforce's efforts to ban the slave trade by means of parliamentary law, see Behrendt, *British Women Poets and the Romantic Writing Community*, 154–59.

12. For an informative study of epistolary poetry in the eighteenth century, see William C. Dowling, *The Epistolary Moment*. Largely a study of the relations between poetry and philosophy, the book argues, as Dowling puts it in his introductory chapter, that "epistolary verse during that period [the eighteenth century] was an attempt to solve in literary terms the philosophical problem of solipsism as it arose between *Locke's Essay Concerning Human Understanding* and Beattie's attack on Humean skepticism" (3). Barbauld wrote another epistolary poem, entitled "Epistle to Dr. Enfield, on His Revisiting Warrington in 1789," which does not rely upon heroic couplets in presenting its largely personal subject matter. For a discussion of the poem, see McCarthy, *Anna Letitia Barbauld*, 266–68.

13. Barbauld thus rejects the idealism that is evident in Blake's poetic desire, voiced more than a decade later in "And Did Those Feet in Ancient Time" in the preface to his epic *Milton*, that the prophetic imagination might be used to recreate England as a pastoral landscape:

> I will not cease from Mental Fight,
> Nor shall my Sword sleep in my hand:
> Till we have built Jerusalem,
> In Englands green and pleasant Land. (95–96)

These famous lines are followed by the inscription, "Would to God that all the Lords people were Prophets," suggesting the relation, for Blake, between pastoral and prophecy.

14. McCarthy remarks in passing on the antipastoral dimension of *Epistle to William Wilberforce* (*Anna Letitia Barbauld* 298).

15. The reference here is to John Howard, the first British prison reformer. For a brief discussion of Howard in relation to Barbauld, see White, *Early Romanticism and Religious Dissent*, 72–73.

Conclusion

1. My vocabulary here draws on Stephen C. Behrendt's excellent essay "The Gap That is Not a Gap," 25–45.

2. See, for instance, McCarthy, *Anna Letitia Barbauld*, 60.

3. On the early reception of *Poems*, see McCarthy, *Anna Letitia Barbauld*, 117–21, and Backscheider, *Eighteenth-Century Women Poets and Their Poetry*, 3.

4. My claim here echoes Backscheider's comment that "to a considerable extent . . . the reassessment of Restoration and eighteenth-century poetry remains to be done" and attempts to contribute to the sort of reassessment for which Backscheider calls (402).

Acosta, Ana M. "Spaces of Dissent and the Public Sphere in Hackney, Stoke Newington, and Newington Green." *Eighteenth-Century Life* 27.1 (2003): 1–27.
Adkins, Leslie, and Roy A. Adkins. *Handbook to Life in Ancient Rome.* Oxford: Oxford University Press, 1998.
Aikin, John. *Essays on Song-Writing; with a Collection of Such English Songs as are Most Eminent for Poetical Merit.* London: R. H. Evans, 1810.
Aikin, John, William Enfield, and William Nicholson. "Brindley, James." In vol. 2 of *General Biography; or, Lives Critical and Historical of the Most Eminent Persons of All Ages, Countries, and Professions,* 300–306. London: Joseph Johnson, 1801.
Aldrich, Robert. *The Seduction of the Mediterranean: Writing, Art and Homosexual Fantasy.* New York: Routledge, 1993.
Avery, Gillian. *Nineteenth-Century Children.* London: Hodder and Stoughton, 1965.
Backscheider, Paula R. *Eighteenth-Century Women Poets and Their Poetry: Inventing Agency, Inventing Genre.* Baltimore, MD: Johns Hopkins University Press, 2005.
Baillie, Joanna, ed. *A Collection of Poems, Chiefly Manuscript, and from Living Authors.* London: Longman, 1823.
———. *Metrical Legends of Exalted Characters.* London: Longman, 1821.
Ball, Robert J. *Tibullus the Elegist: A Critical Survey.* Gottingen: Vandenhoeck and Ruprecht, 1983.
Bannerman, Anne. *Tales of Superstition and Chivalry.* London: Swam, 1802.
Barbauld, Anna Letitia. *An Address to the Opposers of the Repeal of the Test and Corporation Acts.* In vol. 2 of *The Works of Anna Letitia Barbauld, with a Memoir by Lucy Aikin,* 2 vols., edited by Lucy Aikin, 353–78. London: Longman, 1825.
———. *Eighteen Hundred and Eleven.* In *The Poems of Anna Letitia Barbauld,* edited by William McCarthy and Elizabeth Kraft, 152–61. Athens: University of Georgia Press, 1994.
———. *Poems.* London: Joseph Johnson, 1773.
———. *Poems.* Rev. ed. London: Joseph Johnson, 1792.
———. *Poems (1773) by Anna Laetitia Aikin: A Hypertext Edition.* Edited by Lisa Vargo and Allison Muri. www.rc.umd.edu/editions/contemps/barbauld/poems1773.

———. "The Rights of Woman." In vol. 1 of *The Works of Anna Letitia Barbauld, with a Memoir by Lucy Aikin*, 2 vols., edited by Lucy Aikin, 185–87. London: Longman, 1825.

———. *Sins of Government, Sins of the Nation*. In vol. 2 of *The Works of Anna Letitia Barbauld, with a Memoir by Lucy Aikin*, 2 vols., edited by Lucy Aikin, 379–412. London: Longman, 1825.

Behrendt, Stephen C. *British Women Poets and the Romantic Writing Community*. Baltimore, MD: Johns Hopkins University Press, 2009.

———. "The Gap That Is Not a Gap: British Poetry by Women, 1802–1812." In *Romanticism and Women Poets: Opening the Doors of Reception*, edited by Stephen C. Behrendt and Harriet Kramer Linkin, 25–45. Lexington: University of Kentucky Press, 1999.

Bellanca, Mary Ellen. "Science, Animal Sympathy, and Anna Barbauld's 'The Mouse's Petition.'" *Eighteenth-Century Studies* 37.1 (2003): 47–67.

Bentley, Elizabeth. "Ode to Fancy." In *Genuine Poetical Compositions, on Various Subjects*, 30–32. Norwich, UK: Crouse and Stevenson, 1791.

Birns, Nicholas. "'Thy World, Columbus!': Barbauld and Global Space, 1803, '1811,' 1812, 2003." *European Romantic Review* 16.5 (2005): 545–62.

Blake, William. "Auguries of Innocence." In *The Complete Poetry and Prose of William Blake*, edited by David V. Erdman, 493–96. Berkeley: University of California Press, 1982.

———. *Milton: A Poem*. In *The Complete Poetry and Prose of William Blake*, edited by David V. Erdman, 95–143. Berkeley: University of California Press, 1982.

———. "A Song of Liberty." In *The Complete Poetry and Prose of William Blake*, edited by David V. Erdman, 44–45. Berkeley: University of California Press, 1982.

Bloom, Harold. *Blake's Apocalypse: A Study in Poetic Argument*. New York: Doubleday, 1965.

———. *The Visionary Company: A Reading of English Romantic Poetry*. Rev. and exp. ed. Ithaca, NY: Cornell University Press, 1971.

Bostetter, Edward E. "The Original Della Cruscans and the Florence Miscellany." *Huntington Library Quarterly* 19.3 (1956): 277–300.

Boswell, James. *An Account of Corsica, the Journal of a Tour to That Island, and Memoirs of Pascal Paoli*. London: Robert and Andrew Foulis, 1768.

———, ed. *British Essays in Favour of the Brave Corsicans*. London: Edward and Charles Dilly, 1769.

Bradshaw, Penny. "Gendering the Enlightenment: Conflicting Images of Progress in the Poetry of Anna Laetitia Barbauld." *Women's Writing* 5.3 (1998): 353–71.

Byron, George Gordon, Lord. *Childe Harold's Pilgrimage*. Vol. 2 of *Lord Byron: The Complete Poetical Works*, edited by Jerome McGann. Oxford: Clarendon Press, 1980.

———. *The Prisoner of Chillon and Other Poems*. London: John Murray, 1816.

———. "Sonnet on Chillon." In vol. 4 of *Lord Byron: The Complete Poetical Works*, edited by Jerome McGann, 3–16. Oxford: Clarendon Press, 1986

Chaloner, W. H. *People and Industries*. London: Frank Cass, 1963.

Cicero. *De re publica.* Translated by Clinton W. Keyes. Cambridge, MA: Harvard University Press, 1928.

———. *De senectute; De amicitia; De divinatione.* Translated by William Falconer Armistead. Cambridge, MA: Harvard University Press, 1983. http://penelope.uchicago.edu/Thayer/E/Roman/Texts/Cicero/Cato_Maior_de_Senectute/text*.html.

———. "On Old Age" and "On Friendship." Translated by Frank O. Copley. Ann Arbor: University of Michigan Press, 1967.

Claudian. *Against Rufinus.* In *Claudian*, translated by Maurice Platnauer, 24–97. Cambridge, MA: Harvard University Press, 1963.

Coleman, Deirdre. "Firebrands, Letters, and Flowers: Mrs. Barbauld and the Priestleys." In *Romantic Sociability: Social Networks and Literary Culture in Britain, 1770–1840*, edited by Gillian Russell and Clara Tuite, 82–103. Cambridge: Cambridge University Press, 2002.

Coleridge, Samuel Taylor. "The Eolian Harp." In *Coleridge: Poetical Works*, edited by Ernest Hartley Coleridge, 101–2. London: Oxford University Press, 1912.

———. "Frost at Midnight." In *Coleridge: Poetical Works*, edited by Ernest Hartley Coleridge, 240–42. London: Oxford University Press, 1912.

Congreve, William. *The Old Bachelor.* In vol. 1 of *The Complete Works of William Congreve*, edited by Montague Summers, 157–225. 1924. New York: Russell and Russell, 1964.

Cox, Philip. *Gender, Genre, and the Romantic Poets: An Introduction.* Manchester, UK: Manchester University Press, 1996.

Craciun, Adriana. "Romantic Spinstrelsy: Anne Bannerman and the Sexual Politics of the Ballad." In *Scotland and the Borders of Romanticism*, edited by Leith Davis, Ian Duncan, and Janet Sorensen, 204–24. Cambridge: Cambridge University Press, 2004.

Crompton, Louis. *Byron and Greek Love: Homophobia in 19th-Century England.* Berkeley: University of California Press, 1985.

Curran, Stuart. "Romantic Women Poets: Inscribing the Self." In *Women's Poetry in the Enlightenment: The Making of a Canon, 1730–1820*, edited by Isobel Armstrong and Virginia Blain, 145–66. New York: Macmillan, 1999.

———. "Women Readers, Women Writers." In *The Cambridge Companion to British Romanticism*, edited by Stuart Curran, 177–95. Cambridge: Cambridge University Press, 1993.

Dereli, Cynthia. "In Search of a Poet: The Life and Work of Elizabeth Hands." *Women's Writing* 8.1 (2001): 169–82.

DiSalvo, Jackie. *War of Titans: Blake's Critique of Milton and the Politics of Religion.* Pittsburgh, PA: University of Pittsburgh Press, 1983.

Doody, Margaret Anne. "Sensuousness in the Poetry of Eighteenth-Century Woman Poets." In *Women's Poetry in the Enlightenment: The Making of a Canon, 1730–1820*, edited by Isobel Armstrong and Virginia Blain, 3–32. New York: Macmillan, 1999.

Dowling, William C. *The Epistolary Moment: The Poetics of the Eighteenth-Century Verse Epistle.* Princeton, NJ: Princeton University Press, 1991.

Duff, J. Wight. *A Literary History of Rome from the Origins to the Close of the Golden Age*. New York: Scribner's Sons, 1927.

Duffield, Samuel Willoughby. *English Hymns: Their Authors and History*. New York: Funk and Wagnalls, 1886.

Eckhardt, Caroline D., ed. *The "Prophetia Merlini" of Geoffrey of Monmouth: A Fifteenth-Century English Commentary*. Cambridge, MA: Medieval Academy of America, 1982.

Egerton, Sarah Fyge. *The Female Advocate; or, An Answer to A Late Satyr against the Pride, Lust and Inconstancy, &c. of Women, Written by a Lady in Vindication of Her Sex*. London: John Taylor, 1686.

Elfenbein, Andrew. "Lesbianism and Romantic Genius: The Poetry of Anne Bannerman." *ELH* 63.4 (1996): 929–57.

Ellison, Julie. "The Politics of Fancy in the Age of Sensibility." In *Re-Visioning Romanticism: British Women Writers, 1776–1837*, edited by Carol Shiner Wilson and Joel Haefner, 228–55. Philadelphia: University of Pennsylvania Press, 1994.

Fiala, Robert D. "Priestley, Joseph (1733–1804)." In vol. 1 of *Biographical Dictionary of Modern British Radicals*, edited by Joseph O. Baylen and Norbert J. Grossman, 396–401. Sussex, UK: Harvester, 1979.

Fielding, Henry. *Tom Jones*. In *The Works of Henry Fielding*, 1–275. London: Henry G. Bohn, 1845. http://etext.lib.virginia.edu/toc/modeng/public/FieTomJ.html.

Fraistat, Neil. *The Poem and the Book: Interpreting Collections of Romantic Poetry*. Chapel Hill: North Carolina University Press, 1985.

Fresnoy, Charles-Alphonse, du. *The Art of Painting*. Translated by John Dryden. London: John Heptinstall, 1695.

Frye, Northrop. *Fearful Symmetry: A Study of William Blake*. 1947. Reprint, Princeton, NJ: Princeton University Press, 1969.

Geoffrey of Monmouth. *The History of the Kings of Britain*. Translated by Lewis Thorpe. London: Penguin, 1966.

"Giaus Maecenas." *Encyclopedia Britannica*. 2010. Encyclopedia Britannica Online. www.britannica.com/EBchecked/topic/356230/Gaius-Maecenas.

Gifford, Terry. *Pastoral*. New York: Routledge, 1999.

Goulding, Susan. "Reading 'Mira's Will': The Death of Mary Leapor and the Life of the Persona." *Modern Language Studies* 32.2 (2002): 69–89.

Grainger, James. *A Poetical Translation of the Elegies of Tibullus and of the Poems of Sulpicia, with Original Text, and Notes Critical and Explanatory*. Vol. 2. London: Andrew Millar, 1759.

Guarini, Giovanni Battista. *The Faithful Shepherd: A Pastoral Tragi-comedy, Written in Italian by the Celebrated Signor Baptista Guarini*. London: Richard Montagu, 1736.

———. *Il Pastor Fido; or, The Faithful Shepherd, A Pastoral Tragi-comedy*. Edinburgh: Charles Stewart, 1809.

Guillory, John. "Literary Capital: Gray's 'Elegy,' Anna Laetitia Barbauld, and the Vernacular Canon." In *Early Modern Conceptions of Property*, edited by John Brewer and Susan Staves, 389–412. London: Routledge, 1995.

Haber, Judith. *Pastoral and the Poetics of Self-Contradiction: Theocritus to Marvell.* Cambridge: Cambridge University Press, 1994.

Hands, Elizabeth. *The Death of Amnon: A Poem, with an Appendix Containing Pastorals, and other Poetical Pieces.* Coventry: Noah Rollason, 1789.

"History." Bridgewater Canal Company Limited. www.bridgewatercanal.co.uk/history.html.

Hitt, Christopher. "Ecocriticism and the Long Eighteenth Century." *College Literature* 31.3 (2004): 123–47.

Hoeveler, Diane Long. "Gendering the Scottish Ballad: The Case of Anne Bannerman's *Tales of Superstition and Chivalry.*" *Wordsworth Circle* 31.2 (2000): 97–101.

Horace. Ode 1.4. In *The Odes and Carmen Saeculare of Horace*, translated by John Conington. 3rd ed. 1865. http://ancienthistory.about.com/od/horace/ig/The-Odes-of-Horace-/Horace-Ode-I-4.htm.

———. Ode 1.5. In *The Odes and Carmen Saeculare of Horace*, translated by John Conington. 3rd ed. 1865. http://ancienthistory.about.com/od/horace/ig/The-Odes-of-Horace-/Horace-Ode-I-5.htm.

———. Ode 1.12. In *The Odes and Carmen Saeculare of Horace*, translated by John Conington. 3rd ed. 1865. http://ancienthistory.about.com/od/horace/ig/The-Odes-of-Horace-/Horace-Ode-I-12.htm.

———. Ode 3.8. In *The Complete Odes and Satires of Horace*, translated by Sidney Alexander, 113–14. Princeton, NJ: Princeton University Press, 1999.

———. Ode 4.15. In *Odes of Horace*, translated by Anthony S. Kline. 2003. www.poetryintranslation.com/PITBR/Latin/HoraceOdesBkIV.htm.

———. Ode 10.13. In *Odes of Horace*, translated by Anthony S. Kline. 2003. www.poetryintranslation.com/PITBR/Latin/HoraceOdesBkIII.htm#_Toc40263858.

Hubbard, Thomas K., ed. *Homosexuality in Greece and Rome: A Sourcebook of Basic Documents.* Berkeley: University of California Press, 2003.

Jestin, Charbra Adams, and Phyllis B. Katz. "Ovid's Life and Works." In *Ovid: Amores, Metamorphoses: Selections*, edited by Charbra Adams Jestin and Phyllis B. Katz, xvii–xx. 2nd ed. Mundelein, IL: Blochazy-Carducci, 2000.

Johnson, Samuel. *Rambler* no. 107. In vol. 4 of *The Rambler*, edited by W. J. Bate and Albrecht B. Strauss, 208. New Haven, CT: Yale University Press, 1969.

Johnson, Thomas B. *The Shooter's Guide; or, Complete Sportsman's Companion.* 5th ed. London: Gale and Fenner, 1816.

Jones, Robert W. "Barbauld, Milton, and the Idea of Resistance." *Romanticism* 9.2 (2003): 119–40.

———. "What Then Should Britons Feel? Anna Laetitia Barbauld and the Plight of the Corsicans." *Women's Writing* 9.2 (2002): 285–303.

Keach, William. "A Regency Prophecy and the End of Anna Barbauld's Career." *Studies in Romanticism* 33.4 (1994): 569–77.

Kealy, Sean. P. *An Interpretation of the Twelve Minor Prophets of the Hebrew Bible: The Emergence of Eschatology as a Theological Theme.* Lewiston, NY: Edwin Mellen, 2009.

Keats, John. *The Letters of John Keats, 1814–1821*. Vol. 2. Edited by Hyder Edward Rollins. Cambridge, MA: Harvard University Press, 1972.

———. "Sleep and Poetry. In *Keats: Poetical Works*, edited by H. W. Garrod, 51–61. London: Oxford University Press, 1956.

Landry, Donna. *The Muses of Resistance: Laboring-Class Women's Poetry in Britain, 1739–1796*. Cambridge: Cambridge University Press, 1990.

Leapor, Mary. *Poems upon Several Occasions*. London: James Roberts, 1748.

"Life of the Late James Boswell." In *The Annual Register; or, A View of the History, Politics, and Literature, for the Year 1795*, 32–33. London: W. Otridge and Son, 1800.

Lucan. *Lucan's "Civil War."* Translated by P. F. Widdows. Bloomington: Indiana University Press, 1988.

Mack, Maynard. "The Muse of Satire." *Yale Review* 41.1 (1951): 80–92.

MacPherson, H. A. *Natural History of the Pheasant*. In *The Pheasant, Fur and Feather Series*, edited by Alfred E. T. Watson, 3–104. New York: Longman, Green, 1895.

Mahon, Penny. "'Things by Their Right Name': Peace Education in *Evenings at Home*." *Children's Literature* 28 (2000): 164–74.

Malet, Hugh. *Bridgewater: The Canal Duke, 1736–1803*. Manchester, UK: Manchester University Press, 1977.

Marshall, David. "Literature and the Other Arts." In *The Cambridge History of Literary Criticism*. Vol. 4 of *The Eighteenth Century*, edited by H. B. Nisbet and Claude Rawson, 681–718. Cambridge: Cambridge University Press, 1997.

Marshall, P. J. "Britain without America—A Second Empire?" In *The Oxford History of the British Empire: The Eighteenth Century*, edited by P. J. Marshall, 576–96. Oxford: Oxford University Press, 2001.

Marvin, William Perry. *Hunting Law and Ritual in Medieval English Literature*. Cambridge, UK: D. S. Brewer, 2006.

McCarthy, William. *Anna Letitia Barbauld: Voice of the Enlightenment*. Baltimore, MD: Johns Hopkins University Press, 2008.

———. "'We Hoped the Woman Was Going to Appear': Repression, Desire, and Gender in Anna Letitia Barbauld's Early Poems." In *Romantic Women Writers: Voices and Countervoices*, edited by Paula R. Feldman and Theresa M. Kelley, 113–37. Hanover, NH: University Press of New England, 1995.

Mellor, Anne K. *Mothers of the Nations: Women's Political Writing in England 1780–1830*. Bloomington: Indiana University Press, 2002.

———, ed. *Romanticism and Feminism*. Bloomington: Indiana University Press, 1988.

———. *Romanticism and Gender*. New York: Routledge, 1993.

Mill, John Stuart. *Autobiography*. 2nd ed. London: Longmans, 1873.

Miller, Ashley. "Obscurity and Affect in Anne Bannerman's 'The Dark Ladie.'" *Nineteenth-Century Gender Studies* 3.2 (2007). www.ncgsjournal.com/issue32/miller.htm.

Milton, John. "Areopagitica." In *John Milton: Complete Poems and Major Prose*, edited by Merritt Y. Hughes, 717–49. Indianapolis, IN: Hackett, 2003.

———. Ode 1.5, by Horace. In *John Milton: Complete Poems and Major Prose*, edited by Merritt Y. Hughes, 10. Indianapolis, IN: Hackett, 2003.

———. *Paradise Lost*. In *John Milton: Complete Poems and Major Prose*, edited by Merritt Y. Hughes, 173–470. Indianapolis, IN: Hackett, 2003.

———. *The Ready and Easy Way to Establish a Free Commonwealth*. In *John Milton: Complete Poems and Major Prose*, edited by Merritt Y. Hughes, 880–99. Indianapolis, IN: Hackett, 2003.

———. Sonnet 19. www.dartmouth.edu/~milton/reading_room/sonnets/sonnet_19/index.shtml.

More, Hannah. "The Black Slave Trade." In vol 2. of *The Works of Hannah More: A New Edition with Additions and Corrections in Eleven Volumes*, 107–21. London: Thomas Cadell, 1830.

Newlyn, Lucy. *Reading, Writing, and Romanticism: The Anxiety of Reception*. Oxford: Oxford University Press, 2000.

Nolan, Sara. "Horace Moving, Horace Rising." www.brown.edu/Departments/Classics/bcj/13-07.html.

Oliensis, Ellen. "Sons and Lovers: Sexuality and Gender in Virgil's Poetry." In *The Cambridge Companion to Virgil*, edited by Charles Martindale, 294–311. Cambridge: Cambridge University Press, 1997.

Ovid. "The Onset of Age." In *Tristia*, translated by Anthony S. Kline. 2003. www.poetryintranslation.com/PITBR/Latin/OvidExPontoBkFour.htm#_Toc34217193.

Poggioli, Renato. *The Oaten Flute: Essays on Pastoral Poetry and the Pastoral Ideal*. Cambridge, MA: Harvard University Press, 1975.

Pope, Alexander. "Epistle to Dr. Arbuthnot." In *The Poems of Alexander Pope: A One-Volume Edition of the Twickenham Text, with Selected Annotations*, edited by John Butt, 597–612. New Haven, CT: Yale University Press, 1963.

———. "Epistle to Mr. Jervas." In *The Poems of Alexander Pope: A One-Volume Edition of the Twickenham Text, with Selected Annotations*, edited by John Butt, 249–51. New Haven, CT: Yale University Press, 1963.

Pratt, Edwin A. *A History of Inland Transport and Communication in England*. New York: E. P. Dutton, 1912.

Price, Richard. *A Discourse on the Love of Our Country, Delivered on Nov. 4, 1789, at the Meeting-House in the Old Jewry, to the Society for Commemorating the Revolution in Great Britain*. 3rd ed. London: Thomas Cadell, 1790.

Priestley, Joseph. *A Political Dialogue on the General Principles of Government*. In *The Theological and Miscellaneous Works of Joseph Priestley*, vol. 25, edited by John Towill Rutt, 81–108. London: George Smallfield, 1831.

———. *Present State of Liberty in Great Britain and Her Colonies*. In *Joseph Priestley: Political Writings*, edited by Peter N. Miller, 129–44. Cambridge: Cambridge University Press, 1993.

Priestman, Martin. *Romantic Atheism: Poetry and Free Thought, 1780–1830*. Cambridge: Cambridge University Press, 1999.

Ready, Kathryn. "Identity, Character, and Gender: Anna Barbauld and Pope's Characters of Men and Women." *Women's Writing* 11.3 (2004): 377–98.

Richards, Jennifer. Introduction. In *Elizabeth Singer (Rowe)*, vol. 7, pt. 2, of *The Early Modern Englishwoman: A Facsimile Library of Essential Works, Series II, Printed Writings, 1641–1700*, edited by Jennifer Richards, ix–xvi. Burlington, VT: Ashgate, 2003.

Robinson, Mary. *Memoirs of the Late Mrs. Robinson, Written by Herself.* 2 vols. London: Richard Phillips, 1803.

———. "To the Poet Coleridge." In vol. 1 of *The Poetical Works of the Late Mary Robinson, Including Many Pieces Never before Published*, 226–29. London: Richard Phillips, 1806.

Ross, Marlon B. *The Contours of Masculine Desire: Romanticism and the Rise of Women's Poetry.* New York: Oxford University Press, 1989.

Rowe, Elizabeth Singer. *The Miscellaneous Works, in Prose and Verse, of Mrs. Elizabeth Rowe.* 2 vols. 4th ed. London: Henry Lintot, 1756.

Sambrook, James. *English Pastoral Poetry.* Boston: Twayne, 1983.

Saunders, Julia. "'The Mouse's Petition': Anna Laetitia Barbauld and the Scientific Revolution." *Review of English Studies* 53.212 (2002): 500–516.

Schofield, Robert E. *The Enlightenment of Joseph Priestley: A Study of His Life and Works from 1733 to 1773.* University Park: Penn State University Press, 1997.

Scott, Walter. *Lay of the Last Minstrel.* Vol. 4 of *The Works of Walter Scott.* Edinburgh: Longman, 1813.

Smiles, Samuel. *James Brindley and the Early Engineers.* London: John Murray, 1864.

Stafford, William. *English Feminists and Their Proponents in the 1790s: Unsex'd and Proper Females.* Manchester, UK: Manchester University Press, 2002.

Steedman, Carolyn. "Poetical Maids and Cooks Who Wrote." *Eighteenth-Century Studies* 39.1 (2005): 1–27.

Stephen, James FitzJames. *A History of the Criminal Law of England.* 3 vols. 1883. Reprint, London: Routledge, 1996.

Thomson, Alexander. *Memoirs of a Pythagorean, in which are Delineated the Manners, Customs, Genius, and Polity of Ancient Nations; Interspersed with Various Anecdotes.* London: George G. J. and John Robinson, 1785.

Thomson, James. *The Seasons: Containing Spring, Summer, Autumn, Winter.* Philadelphia: Jacob Johnson, 1808.

Tibullus. Elegy 2.1. In *Tibullus and Sulpicia: The Poems*, translated by Anthony S. Kline. 2001. http://tkline.pgcc.net/PITBR/Latin/Tibullus.htm.

———. Elegy 3.3. In *The Elegies of Tibullus: Being the Consolations of a Roman Lover Done in English*, translated by Theodore C. Williams, 98–99. Boston: Houghton Mifflin, 1908.

———. "Sulpicia's Garland." In *Tibullus and Sulpicia: The Poems*, translated by Anthony S. Kline. 2001. http://tkline.pgcc.net/PITBR/Latin/Tibullus.htm.

Virgil. *Aeneid.* Translated by Anthony S. Kline. 2002. www.poetryintranslation.com/PITBR/Latin/VirgilAeneidVI.htm#_Toc2242942.

———. *The Bucolics and Georgics of Virgil.* Translated by A. Hamilton Bryce. Philadelphia: David McKay, 1797.

———. *The Eclogues of Virgil*. Edited and translated by A. J. Boyle. Melbourne, AU: Hawthorne Press, 1976.

———. Eclogue 2. Internet Classics Archive, edited by Daniel C. Stevenson. http://classics.mit.edu/Virgil/eclogue.2.ii.html.

———. *Georgics* 4. In vol. 1 of *Virgil*, translated by H. Rushton Fairclough, 196–236. London: William Heinemann, 1916.

Waller, Edmund. *The Poems of Edmund Waller*. Edited by G. Thorn Drury. 2 vols. London: George Routledge and Sons, 1900.

White, Daniel E. *Early Romanticism and Religious Dissent*. Cambridge: Cambridge University Press, 2006.

———. "The 'Joineriana': Anna Barbauld, the Aikin Family Circle, and the Dissenting Public Sphere." *Eighteenth-Century Studies* 32 (1999): 511–33.

Wilcher, Robert. *The Writing of Royalism, 1628–1660*. Cambridge: Cambridge University Press, 2001.

Williams, Craig A. *Roman Homosexuality: Ideologies of Masculinity in Classical Antiquity*. Oxford: Oxford University Press, 1999.

Wittreich, Joseph A., Jr. *Angel of Apocalypse: Blake's Idea of Milton*. Madison: University of Wisconsin, 1975.

———, ed. *Milton and the Line of Vision*. Madison: University of Wisconsin Press, 1975.

———. "Opening the Seals: Blake's Epics and the Milton Tradition." In *Blake's Sublime Allegory: Essays on* The Four Zoas, Milton, Jerusalem, edited by Stuart Curran and Joseph A. Wittreich Jr., 23–58. Madison: University of Wisconsin Press, 1973.

———. "'A Poet Amongst Poets': Milton and the Tradition of Prophecy." In *Milton and the Line of Vision*, edited by Joseph A. Wittreich, 97–142. Madison: University of Wisconsin Press, 1975.

———. Preface. In *Milton and the Line of Vision*, edited by Joseph A. Wittreich, xiii–xx. Madison: University of Wisconsin Press, 1975.

———. *Visionary Poetics: Milton's Tradition and His Legacy*. San Marino, CA: Huntington Library, 1979.

Wolfson, Susan J. *Borderlines: Shiftings of Gender in British Romanticism*. Stanford, CA: Stanford University Press, 2006.

Wordsworth, Jonathan. *The Bright Work Grows: Women Writers of the Romantic Age*. Poole, UK: Woodstock, 1997.

Wordsworth, William. *The Excursion*. London: Thomas Davison, 1814.

———. "Expostulation and Reply." In *Lyrical Ballads and Other Poems, 1797–1800*, edited by James Butler and Karen Green, 108. Ithaca, NY: Cornell University Press, 1992.

———. "Letter to the Bishop of Llandaff." In vol. 1 *The Prose Works of William Wordsworth. For the First Time Collected, with Additions from Unpublished Manuscripts*, edited by Alexander B. Grosart, 1–23. London: Edward Moxon, 1876.

———. "To My Sister." In *Lyrical Ballads and Other Poems, 1797–1800*, edited by James Butler and Karen Green, 63–64. Ithaca, NY: Cornell University Press, 1992.

Yearsley, Ann. *The Rural Lyre: A Volume of Poems Dedicated to the Right Honourable the Earl of Bristol, Lord Bishop of Derry.* London: G. G. and J. Robinson, 1796.

Young, Edward. *Night Thoughts by Edward Young, D. D., with the Life of the Author, and Notes Critical and Explanatory.* London: Thomas Heptinstall, 1789.

INDEX

abolitionism, 191, 194
Account of Corsica (Boswell), 56–58, 60
Act of Toleration of 1689, 34, 207n2
"Address to Friendship: A Fragment" (Yearsley), 211n10
"Address to the Deity" (ALB), 173–79, 180, 193
Address to the Opposers of the Repeal of the Test and Corporation Acts (ALB), 40–41
Aeneid (Virgil), 36, 92, 93, 154
Against Rufinus (Claudian), 109–12, 114
Aikin, John, 117–19, 122, 124, 126, 215n1
Alexander, Sidney, 115–16
"All Religions Are One" (Blake), 220n4
American Revolution, 1, 34, 36, 37–38, 186
anapestic tetrameter, 13
animism, 162, 175
apocalypse, 149, 151, 161
Apollo, 101, 130–31
Arcadia, 20, 21, 87, 121, 123, 212n3
"Areopagitica" (Milton), 62–63
art, 94, 95, 96, 97, 98, 99, 104, 147
Arthur, King, 18, 23, 24–25, 26, 27
Art of Painting (Fresnoy), 97–98
"At Lake Thrasymenus" (Johnston), 205n3
"Auguries of Innocence" (Blake), 174
Augustus, 115, 139, 160, 216n10
Autobiography (Mill), 94

Baillie, Joanna, ix–x, 3, 18, 44, 199–201, 205n3
Ball, Robert J., 119
Bannerman, Anne, xii, 3, 8–9, 28, 205n6, 207n18; "Basil," 23, 25; commentary/notes of, 25–26; epigraph, 20, 21, 24; "Fisherman of Lapland," 23–24, 26; "Murcian Cavalier," 25; "Prophecy of Merlin," 19–20, 23, 24–25, 26; "Prophetess of the Oracle of Seam," 23, 25–26; *Tales of Superstition and Chivalry*, 18–28, 206n16
Barbauld, Anna Letitia, 3; as British poet, 67; grandmother of, xiii; marriage of, 34; poetic statements of, x; sources and influences on, xiii; and visionary poetics, ix–x; writing under name Aikin, 34
"Basil" (Bannerman), 23, 25
beauty: and "Address to the Deity," 174; and Bannerman, 25; and "Characters" poems, 106; and "Corsica," 59; and "Delia," 136; and *Epistle to William Wilberforce*, 189, 190; and Horace, 81; and "Invitation," 65, 70, 71; and "Ode to Spring," 148, 149; and "On the Backwardness of Spring 1771," 83; and Pope, 96–97; and "Summer Evening's Meditation," 179; and "To Mrs. P——," 98, 100; and "Verses Written in an Alcove," 87; and Virgil, 146
Belsham, Elizabeth, 66
benevolence, ix, xiv, 44; and "Address to the Deity," 176, 178; and ALB, 40; and "Ode to Spring," 149–50; and self-reflection, 46; and "Summer Evening's Meditation," 180, 183; and "To a Lady," 147; and "To Miss R——," 156; and "Verses on Mrs. Rowe," 154. *See also* friendship; goodness; love; sympathy/compassion
Bentley, Elizabeth, 3
Bible, xi, xii, xiii, 144, 220n4; and "Address to the Deity," 175, 178; and Bannerman, 9, 18, 22; and Blake, 1, 2, 3; and Dissenters, 168; garden in, 145; Genesis, 10; Habakkuk, 163–64; and Hands, 3, 9, 10, 12, 13, 17; and "Hymn 2," 163; and "Hymn 5," 165–66; and "Hymn 6," 167, 168;

Bible (cont.)
    and "Hymn 8," 169, 171; and "Hymns," 159, 160, 166; and "Hymn to Content," 219n18; Matthew, 168; Old Testament, 9, 159, 163, 164, 166, 183, 187; and "On the Death of Mrs. Jennings," 158, 159; Psalm 41, 164; Revelation, xii; Samuel, 9, 10; as source, 196; and "Summer Evening's Meditation," 180, 181, 183, 184, 185; and "To a Lady," 145, 146; and women writers, 3
"Black Slave Trade" (More), 191
Blake, William, xi, xii, xiii, 203, 205n5; "All Religions Are One," 220n4; "Auguries of Innocence," 174; and Bannerman, 18; and ALB's "Hymn 4," 166; and Bible, 1–2, 3, 160; and Cato, 177; and England, 34; and God, 161, 179; and industrialism, 71; *Marriage of Heaven and Hell*, 84; *Milton*, 221n13; and Milton, 1, 2, 9, 195; and prophecy, 183, 194, 202; "Song of Liberty," 175; and subservience, 176; Urizen in, 189; and verbal and visual texts, 48; and wilderness isolation, 178
blank verse, 18, 55, 59, 186
Bonnivard, François, 54
Boswell, James, xiii, 56–58, 60
Brindley, James, 71, 72, 211n14
"Bristol Elegy" (Yearsley), 198
"Brutus" (Yearsley), x, 92
Butler, Samuel, 3, 18
Byron, Lord, 54, 161, 199, 219n20

Cato the Younger, 176–78, 179
"Characters" (ALB), 94, 105–8
"Characters" no. 1 (ALB), 105, 106, 107
"Characters" no. 2 (ALB), 106, 107, 133
Charles I, 150
Charles II, 150
Childe Harold's Pilgrimage (Byron), 199
Christianity, 24, 89, 91, 102, 162, 164, 169, 180. *See also* faith; Jesus Christ; religion
"Christopher Columbus" (Baillie), x
Church and King riots, 35, 42
Cicero, 156, 157, 167–69, 219n25
classical thought, 180, 182, 183, 184, 185, 196
Claudian, 109–12, 114
Coleman, Deirdre, 217n2
Coleridge, Samuel Taylor, 1, 181, 201, 221n9; "Eolian Harp," 90; "Kubla Khan," 3, 27, 58;

Lyrical Ballads, with a Few Other Poems, x, 4; "Rime of the Ancient Mariner," 24, 128
Collection of Poems (Baillie), 205n3
Columbus, Christopher, 200
commerce, 75, 187–88
community, 44; and ALB, 41; and epigraph from Virgil, 48, 49; and "Invitation," 75; nonhierarchical vision of, 90; and "Ovid to His Wife," 139, 140, 141; and service to others, 4, 146, 199; and "To Mrs. P——," 104. *See also* society/social relations
"Complaint" (Young), 153
conscience, 44; and "Corsica," 64; and "Hymn 5," 165; and "Invitation," 73, 74; liberty of, 36, 44, 47, 64, 197, 202; and Price, 168; and "Summer Evening's Meditation," 179
"Consolation" (Young), 184–85
"Contentment" (Hands), 16–17
Corporation Act, 34
corruption, 46, 145, 196; and Britain, 46; and Claudian, 111, 112; and "Delia," 137, 138, 139; and *Epistle to William Wilberforce*, 187, 189, 192; and Hands, 15; and industrial revolution, 186; opposition to, 44; and "Ovid to His Wife," 141; and power, 11; and self-interest, 14; and "Summer Evening's Meditation," 183, 185; and "To a Lady," 145; understanding of, 43
Corsica, 201; and Boswell, 56–58; constitution of, 53; and "Corsica," 53–54, 57–60; and Scotland, 53
"Corsica" (ALB), x, 50–65, 79, 196, 208n11, 209–10n2; composition date of, 50–51; epigraph to, 31–32, 50, 51–53, 54, 55, 56; and *Epistle to William Wilberforce*, 193; and "Groans of the Tankard," 80, 83; and Horace, 81; and "Hymn to Content," 114; and "Invitation," 65, 66, 67, 68, 71, 73, 77; and "Mouse's Petition," 88; nationalist revolution of independence in, xi; and "On the Death of Mrs. Jennings," 158; and the pastoral, 50, 54–55, 56, 59, 63, 64, 67; in *Poems*, 1773 edition, 50; in *Poems*, 1792 edition, 50; and politics, 40, 43, 44, 47, 50, 51, 53, 55, 56, 61, 62, 63, 64, 65, 88, 196; and "Summer Evening's Meditation," 182; and "To Mrs. P——," 98, 101; and worldly engagement, 29
"Country Festival" (elegy 3.3) (Tibullus), 119–20, 133–35, 136
Cristall, Ann Batten, xii

"Critical Fragments on Some of the English Poets" (Hands), 9, 17–18, 27
Cupid, 119–20, 121–23, 126, 127, 129, 130, 140

"Darkness" (Byron), 161, 219n20
death, 44; and "Address to the Deity," 177, 178; and Apollo, 131; and Bannerman, 23, 24, 25, 26; and ALB, 29; of civilization, 132; and "Delia," 136; and *Epistle to William Wilberforce*, 189; existential reality of, 196; and "Hymn 3," 164; and "Hymn 6," 167; and "Hymn 8," 170, 171; and "Hymns," 172; and love, 135; and "Mouse's Petition," 89; and "Ode to Spring," 150, 151; and "On the Death of Mrs. Jennings," 156–57; and the pastoral, 128, 129; and "Song V," 130, 132; and "Song VI," 132; and "Summer Evening's Meditation," 179–80, 184; and Tibullus, 134; and "To Miss R——," 155; and "To Mrs. P——," 102; and transformation, 132; and "Verses Written in an Alcove," 86; and Young, 153
Death of Amnon (Hands), 2–3, 9–18, 28
"Delia: An Elegy" (ALB), 117, 132–39, 142
democracy, 38–39, 42, 77, 124, 182
De re publica (Cicero), 156
Discourse on the Love of Our Country (Price), 168
Dissenters, ix, 29–30, 34, 37, 41, 44, 85, 202–3; and "Corsica," 64; and "Hymn 6," 168; and "Hymns," 160; and "Invitation," 72, 73–74; and Rowe, 151–52; and Warrington Academy, 34
Doody, Margaret Anne, 88
Dowling, William C., 221n12
Drayton, Michael, 23, 25
Dryden, John, 13, 97

eagle, 100, 101
Eclogues (Virgil), 36, 48–49, 65–66, 92, 145–46, 210n7
Eden, 145
Edgeworth, Richard Lovell, 217–18n7
Egerton, Francis, Duke of Bridgewater, 69–71, 72, 84, 208n12, 212–13n3
Egerton, Sarah Fyge, 6
Eighteen Hundred and Eleven (ALB), 46, 182, 189, 192, 196, 216n7, 216–17n11
ekphrasis, 94
elegiac couplet, 139
elegy, 43, 117, 132, 138–39, 142
Elizabeth I, 23

"Eolian Harp" (Coleridge), 90
epic, ix, xi, 2, 17, 53, 63, 159, 196
"Epistle" (Hands), 206n14
epistles, 2, 3, 18, 28, 48, 186
"Epistle to Dr. Arbuthnot" (Pope), 155–56, 157
"Epistle to Mr. Jervas" (Pope), 95–98
Epistle to William Wilberforce (ALB), 42, 43, 159, 173, 186–94, 196, 216n7; and Britain, 186–88, 189, 190, 191, 192, 193, 194; and corruption, 187, 189, 192; and morality, 187, 189, 191, 192, 194
Epistolary Moment (Dowling), 221n12
"Essay on Song-Writing in General" (Aikin), 118–19, 122, 124
Essays on Song-Writing (Aikin), 117–18
eternity, 2, 161; and "Address to the Deity," 175; and Blake, 1, 3; and consciousness, 29; and *Epistle to William Wilberforce*, 194; and Hands, 12; and "Hymn 8," 171; and lived experience, 175; as principles, 29; and "Summer Evening's Meditation," 180; and visionary poetics, ix, 2
Europe, 51, 60
Evans, Evan, 23
Excursion (Wordsworth), x
"Expostulation and Reply" (Wordsworth), 213n4

Fable of the Bees (Mandeville), 99
Fabliaux; or, Tales (Way), 23
Faerie Queene (Spenser), 23
faith, 115, 173, 197; and "Address to the Deity," 173, 174, 178; and "Hymn 2," 163; and "Hymn 3," 164; and "Hymn 4," 165; and "Hymn 6," 167, 168; and "Hymns," 172; and "On the Death of Mrs. Jennings," 158; and "Summer Evening's Meditation," 173, 179, 180, 181, 182–83, 184; and "Verses on Mrs. Rowe," 153, 154. *See also* Christianity
family, 155, 156, 157, 158
Female Advocate (Egerton), 6
feminism, 4, 5, 7, 29, 30
Fielding, Henry, 219n25
Finch, Anne, 220n5
"Fisherman of Lapland" (Bannerman), 23–24, 26
flowers, 145, 146, 147, 148, 151
force, 46; and freedom, 78; and "Groans of the Tankard," 82; and "Mouse's Petition," 89, 90, 92; and the pastoral, 129; and "Summer Evening's Meditation," 185; and "To Mrs. P——," 100; and transformative sensibility, 145;

force (cont.)
    and Virgil, 92; and Yearsley, 198, 199. See also military/militarism; power; violence
France, 34, 44, 53, 60, 193
French Reign of Terror, 34
French Revolution, 1, 34, 35, 36, 39, 186, 209–10n2
Fresnoy, Charles-Alphonse du, 97–98
friendship, 44, 48, 197; and ALB, 29, 31; and "Characters" poems, 105; as foundational principle, 68; and "Hymn 3," 164; and "Hymn 6," 167, 168; and "Hymn 7," 168–69; and "Hymn 8," 169; and "Invitation," 66–67, 68, 69; and Pope, 96, 97; role of, 196; and "To a Lady," 147; and "To Mrs. P——," 95, 96, 98, 99, 104; and Yearsley, 211n10. See also benevolence; sympathy/compassion
"Frost at Midnight" (Coleridge), 221n9

gender, 4–5, 43, 201, 202–3, 206n8; and Backscheider, 30; and Baillie, 199; and Bannerman, 21; and ALB, 29, 31, 32; bias concerning, 8; debates over, 7; and Hands, 9, 13, 17; and "Ode to Spring," 147; and vision, 2–8; and Wolfson, 7. See also sexuality
Genoa, 50, 53, 60, 193
Genuine Poetical Compositions (Bentley), 3
Geoffrey of Monmouth, 207n18
George III, 16, 44, 182, 207n1
Georgics (Virgil), 83–85, 154
Gerusalemme Liberata (Tasso), 102, 214n9
God, 197; and "Address to the Deity," 174, 175, 176, 177–78; belief in, 173; and "Corsica," 60, 62; and Hands, 11, 12; and "Hymn 1," 160–63; and "Hymn 2," 163; and "Hymn 6," 167; and "Hymns," 159, 160, 173, 180; metaphysical questions about, 177; and More, 191; relations with man, 9; and self-reflection, 46; and "Summer Evening's Meditation," 179, 181, 183, 185
goodness: and "Characters" poems, 105; and Claudian, 111; and Hands, 11; and "Hymn 6," 168. See also benevolence; morality; virtue
gothic, the, 18, 21, 22, 24, 25, 26, 87
Great Britain, 34, 51, 196; constitution of, 39, 53; and "Corsica," 53, 54, 60, 61; and *Epistle to William Wilberforce*, 186–88, 189, 190, 191, 192, 193, 194; and France, 34, 44; and "Groans of the Tankard," 82; and "Hymn 1," 160; and

"Invitation," 66, 74–76, 77; and liberty, 209–10n2; and "On the Backwardness of Spring 1771," 84–85; and Priestley, 37–40; and "Summer Evening's Meditation," 182; transformation of, 85; urban industrial, 72; and "Verses Written in an Alcove," 87
Greatheed, Bertie, 9
Greece, 59
"Groans of the Tankard" (ALB), 79–83, 88
Guarini, Giovanni Battista, 18–19, 20–22

Hands, Elizabeth, xii, 3, 8–18, 28; and Bannerman, 23; "Contentment," 16–17; "Critical Fragments on Some of the English Poets," 9, 17–18, 27; *Death of Amnon*, 2–3, 9–18, 28; "Lob's Courtship," 14–16; "On Contemplative Ease," 16–17; "On the Supposition of an Advertisement in a Morning Paper," 3, 9, 13, 14, 15, 17; "On the Supposition of the Book Having Been Published and Read," 3, 9, 13–15, 17; "Pastoral," 15; "Pastoral Song," 15; "Rural Maid," 14–16; "Written on Their Majesties Coming to Kew," 16–17
happiness, 197; and "Characters" poems, 105; and Claudian, 109–10; and "Delia," 134; and Horace, 116; and "Hymn to Content," 109, 112, 114; and "Invitation," 66, 67, 69, 70; and "Ode to Spring," 148, 151; recreational, 48; and "To Mrs. P——," 96, 102; and "To Wisdom," 114, 115; and "Verses Written in an Alcove," 88
heaven: and "Corsica," 60; and "Hymn 6," 167, 168; and "Hymn 7," 169; and "Hymn 8," 169, 170; and "Hymns," 172; and "Invitation," 77; and "To Mrs. P——," 98
Hemans, Felicia, 206n8
heroic couplet, 13, 18, 97, 155, 186
history, ix, xiii–xiv, 44, 45, 196; and Baillie, 199, 200; and Bannerman, 18, 22, 23, 25; and ALB, 29, 57; and Boswell, 57; and "Corsica," 54, 56, 57, 61–62, 63, 64, 65; and Cupid and pastoral retreat, 124; and "Delia," 137–38, 139; and *Epistle to William Wilberforce*, 190, 191–92, 193, 194; and "Groans of the Tankard," 80, 82; and "Hymns," 166, 167, 173; and "Hymn to Content," 113, 114; and "Invitation," 71, 73, 74, 75, 76, 77; and love, 134; and militarism, 78; and "On a Lady's Writing," 109; and "On the Backwardness of Spring 1771," 85; and "Origin

of Song-Writing," 123, 124, 125; and the pastoral, 128–29; and pastoral imagination, 71; and "Summer Evening's Meditation," 183; and "To Mrs. P——," 98–99. *See also* past, the

History of Joseph (Rowe), 151

Homer, 175, 178

homosexuality, 146–47, 206n15. *See also* sexuality

Horace, 80–81, 86, 87, 106–7, 114, 115–16, 159–61, 212n3, 219n19

Howard, John, 221n15

hudibrastic verse, 18

human/lived experience, 47, 144; and "Address to the Deity," 175; and Bannerman, 24, 25, 27; and ALB, 33, 42–43; and *Epistle to William Wilberforce*, 190, 193; and Hands, 16; and "Hymn 1," 161; and "Hymn 2," 164; and "Hymn 4," 165; and "Hymn 8," 169; and "Hymn to Content," 112; of individual people, 94; and "Mouse's Petition," 88; and "Origin of Song-Writing," 121; and "Ovid to His Wife," 140; and spirituality, 160; and Tibullus, 120; and "To Mrs. P——," 95, 98, 99, 104. *See also* material reality

"Hymn 1" (ALB), 160–63, 164, 178

"Hymn 2" (ALB), 163–64

"Hymn 3" ("For Easter Sunday") (ALB), 164, 165, 166

"Hymn 4" (ALB), 164–66, 178

"Hymn 5" (ALB), 165–66

"Hymn 6" (ALB), 159, 166–69

"Hymn 7" (ALB), 159, 166–67, 168–69

"Hymn 8" (ALB), 159, 166–67, 169–71

hymns, xi, 32, 42, 43, 48, 144, 196; and ALB, 28; and "Corsica," 64

"Hymns" (ALB), 29, 62, 145, 159–72, 173; epigraphs to, 159–61, 166–67; and "Mouse's Petition," 91; and "On the Death of Mrs. Jennings," 158; and "Summer Evening's Meditation," 180

Hymns of the Protestant Episcopal Church, 165

"Hymn to Content" (ALB), 94, 109–14, 159, 219n18

idealism, 144; and Baillie, 200, 201; and ALB, 32, 41; and "Characters" poems, 106; and "Corsica," 55, 59, 79; dedication to, 144; and "Delia," 134; and "Groans of the Tankard," 82; and Guarini, 21; and Hands, 15, 16; and history, xiii; and "Hymn 1," 161; and "Hymn 2," 163, 164; and "Hymn 8," 171; and "Hymn to Content," 112, 113, 114; and "Invitation," 71, 72, 75, 79, 80; and lived experience, ix; and militarism, 78; and "Mouse's Petition," 88, 90, 91; and "Origin of Song-Writing," 124; and "Ovid to His Wife," 140; and the pastoral, 81, 117, 124, 129, 148; and pastoral idealism, 150, 151; and politics, 44, 47; and "Song V," 129, 130; and "Summer Evening's Meditation," 179; and Thomson, 53; and Tibullus, 120; and "To a Lady," 145–46, 147; and "To Mrs. P——," 98, 101, 102, 103, 104–5; and "To Wisdom," 116; and "Verses on Mrs. Rowe," 154; and "Verses Written in an Alcove," 85, 87

imagination, 3, 144; and "Address to the Deity," 174, 175; and Bannerman, 22, 26; and ALB, 29; and "Corsica," 53, 61, 62; and "Delia," 138; and *Epistle to William Wilberforce*, 189–90; and "Groans of the Tankard," 80; and Hands, 17, 18; and "Hymn 1," 162; individual, 94; and "Invitation," 69, 77; and Pope, 97; and "Summer Evening's Meditation," 179, 181; and "To a Lady," 147; and "To Mrs. P——," 95, 97, 99, 103, 104; and "Verses Written in an Alcove," 87

imperialism: and "Corsica," 53; and "Delia," 136; and *Epistle to William Wilberforce*, 187, 188, 191; and "Groans of the Tankard," 82–83; and "Invitation," 74; and "To Mrs. P——," 99, 100, 103, 104. *See also* military/militarism

"Indifferent Shepherdess to Colin" (Yearsley), 198

industry/industrial revolution, 34, 44, 69–71, 79, 124, 186, 201

insects, 94, 96, 97, 98, 99, 101–3, 104

"Intimations Ode" (Wordsworth), 90

"Invitation: To Miss B——" (ALB), 50, 65–78, 79, 208n12, 210n7, 211n16; epigraph of, 65–66; and "Groans of the Tankard," 80; and history, 71, 73, 74, 75, 76, 77; and liberty, 65, 66–67, 73, 74, 75, 77; and "On the Backwardness of Spring 1771," 83, 85; and "Origin of Song-Writing," 124; and the pastoral, xi, 65, 66, 67, 68, 70, 71, 72–73, 74, 75, 76, 77, 83, 210n7; and society, 66, 67, 74, 75, 76, 77; and "To Mrs. P——," 95, 98; and "Verses Written in an Alcove," 87

Jennings, Anna, 156–57

Jesus Christ, xi, 220n4; and "Address to the Deity," 174–75; and Baillie, 199; and Bannerman, 24; and Dissenters, 168; and "Hymn 3,"

Jesus Christ *(cont.)*
    164, 166; and "Hymn 4," 164, 165, 166, 178;
    and "Hymn 5," 166; and "Hymn 7," 168, 169;
    and "Hymn 8," 170–71; and "Hymns," 62, 172,
    173, 180; and love, 197, 216n9; and "Mouse's
    Petition," 89; pacifism of, 183; and "Summer
    Evening's Meditation," 183, 184; and "To Mrs.
    P——," 103
Johnson, Joseph, 34, 44
Johnson, Samuel, 57, 169–70
Johnson, Thomas B., 213–14n8
Johnston, Charles, 205n3
John the Baptist, 220n4
joy. *See* happiness
justice, 2, 44–45, 47, 79, 196, 197; and ALB, 29, 43;
    and "Corsica," 55; and "Delia," 132, 138; and
    Epistle to William Wilberforce, 187, 189, 190,
    191, 192; and Hands, 12; and "Hymn 6," 168;
    and "Hymn 8," 170; and "Hymn to Content,"
    113, 114; and "Invitation," 77; and "Mouse's
    Petition," 88, 89; and self-reflection, 46; and
    "Verses Written in an Alcove," 88

Keats, John, x, 4, 48, 102, 214n10
King, Martin Luther, Jr., 209n16
"Kubla Khan" (Coleridge), 3, 27, 58

labor/laborers, 136; and Bridgewater, 84; and
    Hands, 15, 16; and "Invitation," 70–71; and
    Priestley, 39; and Virgil, 84; and Yearsley, ix.
    See also social class
"Lady Griseld Baillie" (Baillie), 199
*Lamia, Isabella, The Eve of St. Agnes, and Other
    Poems* (Keats), x, 4
Lay of the Last Minstrel (Scott), 217–18n7
Leapor, Mary, 2
lesbianism, 147, 206n15
"Letter from Birmingham Jail" (King), 209n16
Letters of John Keats (Keats), 214n10
"Letter to the Bishop of Llandaff" (Wordsworth),
    210n4
liberty, 79, 93, 197; and Boswell, 56–57; British,
    209–10n2; building of, 43; and Byron, 54; and
    "Characters" poems, 105; of conscience, 36, 44,
    47, 64, 197, 202; and "Corsica," 50, 51, 53, 54,
    55–56, 58, 59, 60, 61, 62, 63, 64, 65, 66, 71, 193,
    209–10n2; and "Delia," 132, 138, 139; of enquiry,
    173; and *Epistle to William Wilberforce*, 189,
    192, 193; of expression, 173, 179; and Hands, 17;
    and "Hymn to Content," 114; of imagination,
    18; and "Invitation," 65, 66–67, 73, 74, 75, 77;
    and militarism, 78; and Milton and ALB, 195;
    of mind, 44, 54, 55–56, 64, 66, 68, 77, 193, 196;
    need to struggle for, 47; and "Ode to Spring,"
    149; and politics, 41, 42; and Price, 168; and
    Priestley, 37–38; private path to, 56; and
    self-reflection, 45; and "Song IV," 128; struggle
    for, 124; and "Summer Evening's Meditation,"
    179, 180, 185; of thought, ix, 18, 44, 73, 74; and
    "To Mrs. P——," 101; and "Verses Written in an
    Alcove," 87; and visionary reflection, 42; and
    world transformation, 2; of worship and
    assembly, 34; and Yearsley, 198–99
"Lob's Courtship" (Hands), 14–16
love, ix, xiv, 44, 117, 201, 203; and "Address
    to the Deity," 176, 178; and Baillie, 200; and
    Bannerman, 26; and ALB, 28, 29, 40; and
    "Characters" poems, 105, 106, 107; and death,
    135; and "Delia," 132, 134, 136–38, 139; and fear
    and dread, 135; and Hands, 14; higher form of,
    121–22; and historical reality, 134; and Horace,
    106–7; and human tribulation, 134–35; and
    "Hymn 1," 162, 163; and "Hymn 2," 163; and
    "Hymn 3," 164, 166; and "Hymn 4," 164, 165,
    166, 178; and "Hymn 5," 165, 166; and "Hymn
    6," 167; and "Hymn 7," 168–69; and "Hymn 8,"
    170, 171; and "Hymns," 166, 173; and individual
    passion, 127; and Jesus Christ, 197, 216n9; and
    larger visionary ideals, 127; and materialism,
    134; and meaning, 134, 135; and "Mouse's
    Petition," 91; and "Ode to Spring," 149–50; and
    "On the Death of Mrs. Jennings," 157, 158; and
    "Origin of Song-Writing," 121, 122–23, 124, 125;
    and "Ovid to His Wife," 139, 140; and the
    pastoral, 125, 127, 134; and pastoral sentiment,
    119; and politics, 133–34; and power, 137–38;
    and power and wealth, 133–34, 135; and
    prophecy, 122; and purpose in life, 134, 135;
    and redemption, 138; restorative power of,
    134; and society, 197; and "Song I," 125–26;
    and "Song II," 126; and "Song III," 126–27; and
    "Song IV," 127–28; and "Song V," 129–30; and
    "Summer Evening's Meditation," 179, 180, 183;
    and Tibullus, 107–8, 120, 133–35, 136; and "To a
    Lady," 147; and "To Miss R——," 156; and
    "Verses on Mrs. Rowe," 153, 154; and Virgil, 48,

49, 146; and Waller, 150; and Yearsley, 198. *See also* benevolence; sympathy/compassion

Lucan, 176–78, 179

Lydian flute, 148, 149, 217–18n7

lyric, ix, 18, 28, 48, 159, 196

Lyrical Ballads, with a Few Other Poems (Wordsworth and Coleridge), x, 4

Macaulay, Catherine, 6

Manchester, 69

Mandeville, Bernard, 99

Marriage of Heaven and Hell (Blake), 84

material reality, 9; and "Address to the Deity," 175, 176; and Baillie, 200–201; and "Corsica," 61, 62; and *Epistle to William Wilberforce*, 187, 191; and "Hymn 1," 161, 162; and "Hymn 8," 171; and love, 134; and "Mouse's Petition," 88, 90, 91; and "Ode to Spring," 149; and the pastoral, 129; and "Song II," 126; and "Summer Evening's Meditation," 180; and "To Mrs. P——," 97–98, 102; and "To Wisdom," 114. *See also* human/lived experience

meaning, 105, 197; and "Characters" poems, 105; and "Hymn 6," 168; and "Invitation," 66; and love, 134, 135; and "Ode to Spring," 149–50, 151; and "On the Death of Mrs. Jennings," 158; and "Ovid to His Wife," 140; and self-reflection, 46; and "Song V," 130; and "To a Lady," 145, 147; and "To Wisdom," 114; and "Verses on Mrs. Rowe," 153

Memoirs of a Pythagorean (Thomson), 217n7

meter, 79, 85, 155

Metrical Legends (Baillie), ix–x, 18, 44, 199–201, 205n3

middle class, 72; and Baillie, ix; and ALB, ix; and "Invitation," 76, 77–78; and "On the Backwardness of Spring 1771," 83. *See also* social class

military/militarism, 68, 79; and "Corsica," 53, 62, 64, 65, 78; and "Invitation," 74, 75–76, 78; and "Ovid to His Wife," 142; and Thomson, 53; and "To Mrs. P——," 103. *See also* force; imperialism; violence; war

Mill, John Stuart, 94

millennialism, 42

Milton (Blake), 221n13

Milton, John, xii, xiii, xiv, 214n12; age of, 1, 2; "Areopagitica," 62–63; and Bannerman, 18, 22;

ALB as distinct from, 28–29; ALB's appropriation of, 196; ALB's movement away from, 49, 79, 117, 178, 179, 180, 183; and Blake, 1, 2, 9; and "Corsica," 54, 59, 62–63, 68; and Hands, 9, 10, 11, 12, 13, 17, 18; and "Invitation," 66; *Paradise Lost*, 10, 11, 12, 55, 65, 71, 179, 220n6, 220n8; and Priestley, 38; and prophecy, 202; and Romantics, 9, 195; *Samson Agonistes*, 12; "Sonnet 19: On His Blindness," 158; and tradition, 145; and women writers, 3

mind/mental life: and Bannerman, 25; and ALB, 29; and "Characters" poems, 106; and "Corsica," 55–56, 64; and *Epistle to William Wilberforce*, 193; and faith and love, 173; freedom of, 44, 54, 55–56, 64, 65, 66, 68, 77, 193, 196; and "Groans of the Tankard," 82; and Hands, 11–12; and "Invitation," 75; and "Mouse's Petition," 90; and negative and oppositional modes of thought, 44; and "On a Lady's Writing," 109; retreat into, 56

Miscellaneous Works, in Prose and Verse, of Mrs. Elizabeth Rowe (Rowe), 151–52

mock heroic poetry, 43, 79–83

monarchy, 17, 42, 182

morality, 47; and Claudian, 112; and *Epistle to William Wilberforce*, 187, 189, 191, 192, 194; and "Mouse's Petition," 89, 90. *See also* goodness; virtue

"Moral Vision" (Leapor), 2

More, Hannah, 191

"Mouse's Petition" (ALB), 32, 79, 88–93, 175, 212n4; epigraph of, 92, 93; and "Origin of Song-Writing," 124; and political reality, 47; power in, 89, 90, 91–93; and "To Mrs. P——," 100

"Murcian Cavalier" (Bannerman), 25

Muses, 122

Napoleon I, 199

nation: and Bannerman, 26; and Behrendt, 8; and *Epistle to William Wilberforce*, 192; and "Invitation," 74; and "To Mrs. P——," 99

nationalism: and ALB, 31; and "Corsica," 56, 77, 193; and *Epistle to William Wilberforce*, 193; and "Hymn 1," 160; limiting forms of, 197; and self-reflection, 46; and Thomson, 52

natural rights, 88

nature, 43; and "Address to the Deity," 176; and ALB, 58–59; and Bridgewater, 84; as

nature *(cont.)*
　foundational principle, 68; and "Invitation," 68, 69, 71, 75, 84; and "Mouse's Petition," 89; and "Ode to Spring," 148, and "On the Backwardness of Spring 1771," 83, 84–85; and "To a Lady," 147; and "To Mrs. P——," 99, 102–3; and "Verses Written in an Alcove," 87; and Virgil, 84, 146
"Nature's self is hushed" (ALB), 221n9
Newlyn, Lucy, 208–9n13, 209n14
New World, indigenous peoples of, 200
Night Thoughts (Young), 153–55, 184–85
"Nocturnal Reverie" (Finch), 220n5

Odes (Horace), 80–81, 86, 87, 106–7, 115–16, 159–61
"Ode to Fancy" (Bentley), 3
"Ode to Spring" (ALB), 144, 147–51, 217–18n7; epigraph to, 150–51
Ode to the West Wind (Shelley), 89
"On a Lady's Writing" (ALB), 94, 105, 108–9, 186
"On Contemplative Ease" (Hands), 16–17
"On Discontent" (Leapor), 2
On Friendship (Cicero), 167–69
On Old Age (Cicero), 157
"On the Backwardness of the Spring 1771" (ALB), 79, 83–85, 86
"On the Death of Mrs. Jennings" (ALB), 144, 156–59
"On the Supposition of an Advertisement in a Morning Paper" (Hands), 3, 9, 13, 14, 15, 17
"On the Supposition of the Book Having Been Published and Read" (Hands), 3, 9, 13–15, 17
"Origin of Song-Writing" (ALB), 117–25, 133, 144; epigraph of, 119–21; and "Ovid to His Wife," 140
Orpheus and Eurydice, 154
Othello (Shakespeare), 10
Ovid, 139–43, 178, 186, 201, 216n10
"Ovid to His Wife" (ALB), 117, 139–43, 144, 149, 174

pacifism, 145, 196–97, 203, 210n5; of ALB's fellow visionaries, 4; and "Corsica," 62, 63, 64; and Jesus Christ, 183; and *Sins of Government, Sins of the Nation*, 44, 45; and "Summer Evening's Meditation," 183; and Yearsley, 199

paganism, 3, 160
Paine, Thomas, 43
painting, 43, 147
"Panegyric to My Lord Protector" (Waller), 150
pantheism, 175–76, 181
Paoli, Pasquale, xiii, 31, 50, 53, 55, 60–61, 62–64, 67, 193
Paradise Lost (Milton), 10, 11, 12, 55, 65, 71, 179, 220n6, 220n8
Parliament, 186, 187, 194
past, the, 196; and Bannerman, 19, 22; and "Corsica," 54; and "Delia," 132, 138, 139; study of, 201. *See also* history
Pastoral (Gifford), 212n3
"Pastoral" (Hands), 15
pastoral, the, ix, xi, 2, 159, 196; and "Address to the Deity," 174–75; and Aikin, 118–19, 124; and Bannerman, 18, 21; and Blake, 202; and Boswell, 57; and "Corsica," 50, 54–55, 56, 59, 63, 64, 67; and death, 129; as deceptive and reviving, 124; and "Delia," 132, 137, 138, 139; and Doric reed, 217n7; and education, 73; and *Epistle to William Wilberforce*, 189–90; and geography, 85; and Guarini, 20–21; and Hands, 3, 9, 14–16, 17, 18; and hardship, 117; and history, 71, 85, 124, 128–29; and hope, 131; and human experience, 94; and "Hymn 8," 171; and idealism, 81, 117, 124, 129; as idle pastime, 124; and individual, 129; as insufficient, 128; and "Invitation," xi, 65, 66, 67, 68, 70, 71, 72–73, 74, 75, 76, 77, 83, 210n7; and life's complexities, 65; and love, 119, 125, 127, 134; and material circumstance, 129; and "Mouse's Petition," 32, 88, 89, 91, 92; and "Ode to Spring," 147, 148, 149, 151; and "On a Lady's Writing," 108; and "On the Backwardness of Spring 1771," 83, 85; and "Origin of Song-Writing," 119, 121, 124; and "Ovid to His Wife," 140, 141, 143, 190; problematic character of, 32, 55, 56, 144; and prophecy, 74, 121, 131; and reflection, 67, 68; rejection of, 48; and retreat, xi, 32, 47, 50, 54–55, 59, 63, 67, 69, 72–73, 74, 76, 77, 87, 89, 121, 124, 127, 129, 130, 131, 134, 139, 140–41, 149, 171, 174, 175, 212n3; and society, 128–29; and "Song II," 126; and "Song III," 126–27; and "Song IV," 128; and "Song V," 129, 130; and "Song VI," 130, 132; and "Summer Evening's Meditation," 181; and Thomson, 53; and Tibullus, 120; and "To a

Lady," 145; and "Verses on Mrs. Rowe," 153–54;
and "Verses Written in an Alcove," 85, 86–88;
and Virgil, 36, 49, 145; and visionary aims, 28;
and visionary idealism, 148, 150, 151; and
visionary poetics, 138; and Warrington
Academy, 72–73, 74
"Pastoral Song" (Hands), 15
Pastor fido, Il (Guarini), 18–19, 20–22
patriarchy, 4, 6, 28
peace, ix, xiv, 79; and "Characters" poems, 105;
and Claudian, 110–11, 112; and "Corsica," 55,
64; and "Delia," 138; and *Epistle to William
Wilberforce*, 190; and "Hymn to Content,"
109; and "Invitation," 65, 66, 70, 75, 76; and
"Mouse's Petition," 92, 93; and "Ode to Spring,"
148; and "Summer Evening's Meditation," 185;
and Tibullus, 119, 120; and "To a Lady," 145; and
"To Wisdom," 115, 116; and "Verses Written in
an Alcove," 86, 87; and Virgil, 66
Percy, Thomas, 215n1
personal life, 94, 196; and ALB, 29; and "Delia,"
137; and *Epistle to William Wilberforce*, 186,
192; and hymns, 159; and "Origin of Song-
Writing," 123; and "Ovid to His Wife," 140;
and "Song IV," 128; and "To Mrs. P——," 95,
104. *See also* private sphere; society / social
relations
Petrarch, Francis, 123
Pharsalia (Lucan), 176–78, 179
pheasants, 100, 101, 213–14n8
Poems (ALB), ix, xi, 43, 199, 202, 203; dream vs.
reality in, xi; early reception of, 196; epigraph
to, 36–37; idealism of, xi
Poems (ALB), 1773 edition, 41, 179, 182, 185–86,
207n4; "Corsica" in, 50; dedication of, 41; front
matter of, 41, 43; and historical context, 34, 35;
publication of, 34
Poems (ALB), 1792 edition, 38, 41, 42, 208n11;
"Corsica" in, 50; front matter of, 41, 43; and
historical context, 34–35; hymns in, 159, 166;
publication of, 34–35
Poems on Several Occasions (Rowe), 151
Poems upon Several Occasions (Leapor), 2
poetry: coherent statement in, 43; and painting,
97, 98; and poems in conversation, 4, 16; and
relations between poems, 31, 32; and "To Mrs.
P——," 95, 97, 98, 101
Poggioli, Renato, 120

Political Dialogue (Priestley), 36, 38–39
politics, xi, 29, 48, 173; and ALB, 29, 31, 36, 37,
40–41, 42, 43, 44–45; and "Characters" poems,
105; conservative, 34; conventional structures
of, 47; and "Corsica," 40, 43, 44, 47, 50, 51, 53, 55,
56, 61, 62, 63, 64, 65, 88, 196; debilitating forms
of, 197; and "Delia," 132; and *Epistle to William
Wilberforce*, 186, 189, 193; and "Hymn 1," 160,
163; and "Hymn 8," 171; and idealism, 44, 47;
identity, 30; and "Invitation," 72, 74; and
liberty, 41, 42; and love, 133–34; and Mande-
ville, 99; and "Mouse's Petition," 88, 90, 93; and
"Origin of Song-Writing," 123; and power, 84;
and Priestley, 36, 42; rejection of, 56; retreat
from, 65, 67; struggles in, ix; and "Summer
Evening's Meditation," 182; and Thomson, 52;
and "To Mrs. P——," 94, 95, 96, 99; and "Verses
Written in an Alcove," 85, 87; and Virgil, 146;
and Yearsley, 198
Poly-Olbion (Drayton), 23, 25
poor people, 14, 15. *See also* social class
Pope, Alexander, 3, 13, 18, 95–98, 123, 155–56, 157,
186, 212–13n3
power: abuses of, 73, 89; arbitrary, 90, 100; and
ALB, 40; and Claudian, 110; and *Epistle to
William Wilberforce*, 188, 189; and Hands, 11,
17; and "Invitation," 73, 74, 75; lack of, 89; and
love, 137–38; and "Mouse's Petition," 89, 90,
91–93; and "Summer Evening's Meditation,"
182, 185; and Tibullus, 133, 135; and "To Mrs.
P——," 99, 100–101; and transformative
sensibility, 145; and Virgil, 92, 146. *See also*
force; violence
prayer: and "Address to the Deity," 173, 175, 178;
and *Epistle to William Wilberforce*, 191; and
"Hymn 8," 171; and "Hymns," 171; and "Hymn
to Content," 112, 113, 114; and More, 191; and
"Summer Evening's Meditation," 180, 183–84;
and Tibullus, 108, 135
Prelude (Wordsworth), x
Presbyterians, 81, 82–83, 180
*Present State of Liberty in Great Britain and Her
Colonies* (Priestley), 36–38, 61
Price, Richard, 168
Priestley, Joseph, xiii, 43, 207n3, 207–8n8, 208n9,
212n4, 212n7; influence on ALB, 35–36, 41, 182;
and "Invitation," 72; and "Mouse's Petition,"
88, 89, 90, 91, 92–93; *Political Dialogue*, 36,

Priestley, Joseph *(cont.)*
  38–39; *Present State of Liberty in Great Britain and Her Colonies*, 36–38, 61; and riots, 35, 42
Priestley, Mary, 94, 95, 97
Prisoner of Chillon and Other Poems (Byron), 219n20
private sphere, 208–9n13. *See also* personal life
progress, 71–72, 83
progressives, 34, 72, 73–74
Prometheus Unbound, with Other Poems (Shelley), x, 4
prophecy, 28, 144, 173; and "Address to the Deity," 177, 178; and Bannerman, 21, 22–23, 25, 26, 27; as call to others, 48; and Claudian, 111; and "Corsica," 50, 54–56, 57, 59, 60, 61, 63, 64, 65, 68, 194; dangers associated with, 131; and "Delia," 137, 138; and *Epistle to William Wilberforce*, 187, 189, 194; failure of, 65, 68; and "Groans of the Tankard," 82; and Guarini, 21–22; and historical and political context, 42; and hope, 131; and human experience, 94; and "Hymn 1," 162; and "Hymn 5," 165–66; and "Hymn 8," 171; and "Invitation," 66–67, 69, 77; and love, 122; and Milton, 202; and "Mouse's Petition," 88, 92, 93; and "On the Death of Mrs. Jennings," 159; and "Origin of Song-Writing," 122, 123, 125; and "Ovid to His Wife," 140; and the pastoral, 47, 74, 108, 121, 131; problematic character of, 56; retreat from, 65; satire on conventional, 79–80; and "Song VI," 130–32; and "Summer Evening's Meditation," 183, 185, 187; and sun, 101; and "To Mrs. P——," 95, 101, 102, 104; and "Verses Written in an Alcove," 85, 87, 88
"Prophecy of Merlin" (Bannerman), 19–20, 23, 24–25, 26
Prophecy of Merlin (engraving in Bannerman's *Tales*), 18–20, 21, 206n16
"Prophetess of the Oracle of Seam" (Bannerman), 23, 25–26
Prophetiae Merlini (Geoffrey of Monmouth), 207n18
Proserpine, 154
prostitution, 170
Protestantism, ix
public sphere, 68, 197, 208–9n13; and ALB, 29, 30, 40; and *Epistle to William Wilberforce*, 187, 193,

194; transformation of, 196. *See also* society/social relations
Pythagoras, 212n6

quietism, 55, 61

Rambler (Johnson), 169–70
rape, 9, 11
Recluse (Wordsworth), x
redemption, 123; and "Address to the Deity," 175; and Baillie, 200; and "Delia," 135–36, 138; and *Epistle to William Wilberforce*, 187, 190; and Hands, 13; and "Hymn 4," 165; and "Hymn 7," 169; and "Invitation," 74; and love, 138; and "Song I," 126; and "Song III," 127; and "Summer Evening's Meditation," 179
religion, 42, 175, 196; and ALB, 29, 41, 44, 45–46; and clusters of poems, 32; conventional structures of, 47; and Hands, 13; and "Invitation," 76–77; and "On the Death of Mrs. Jennings," 158; and self-reflection, 46. *See also* Christianity; faith
Reliques of Ancient English Poetry (Percy), 215n1
"Remonstrance in the Platonic Shade" (Yearsley), 198
Rigby, Elizabeth, 211n1
Rigby, Sarah, 155, 156
Rigby, Sarah Taylor, 155
"Rights of Woman" (ALB), 7, 207–8n8
"Rime of the Ancient Mariner" (Coleridge), 24, 128
Robinson, Mary, 3
Romanticism, 1, 6, 9, 195
Rome, 92
Romeo and Juliet (Shakespeare), 169
Rousseau, Jean-Jacques, 56
Rowe, Elizabeth Singer, 151–55, 163–64, 219n22
Rowe, Theophilus, 151–52
Rowe, Thomas, 152
Rural Lyre (Yearsley), ix, 44, 197–99, 211n10
"Rural Maid" (Hands), 14–16

Samson Agonistes (Milton), 12
Sappho, 122
Satan, 11, 12, 14, 55, 65, 71, 103
satire, 2, 48, 79, 94, 159, 196; and ALB, 28; and "Groans of the Tankard," 80, 81, 82; and

Hands, 3, 9, 13, 15, 17, 18; and "Mouse's Petition," 88, 89, 93; and "To Miss R——," 155, 156
science, 31, 75, 88, 123, 183, 184, 196
Scotland, 52–53, 56, 59–60
Scott, Sir Walter, 217–18n7
seasons, 68, 86, 148–49, 151
Seasons (Thomson), 31–32, 50, 51–55, 217–18n7
Selden, John, 23, 25
self-absorption, 129, 140
self-awareness, 165
self-criticism, 4; and "Corsica," 50, 64, 65; and "Groans of the Tankard," 83
self-interest: and Baillie, 199; and ALB, 40; and "Corsica," 65; and Hands, 11, 14; and "Mouse's Petition," 92, 93; resistance to, 135; and self-reflection, 46; and "Song V," 129, 130; and "Verses Written in an Alcove," 88
selfishness, 167, 168
selflessness, 62
self-reflection, 45–46; and ALB, 40; and "Corsica," 65; and "Delia," 138; and "Groans of the Tankard," 83; and "Invitation," 73, 74, 77; and "Song III," 127; and "Song VI," 130; and "To Mrs. P——," 94–95; and visionary poetry, 117
self-sacrifice, 62
Seneca, 57–58
sentimentality, xiv, 106, 133, 137
Seven Years' War, 34, 182, 207n1
Seward, Anna, xii
sexuality, 11, 20, 206n14. *See also* gender; homosexuality
Shakespeare, William, 9, 10, 122, 123, 169
Shelley, Percy Bysshe, 9; *Ode to the West Wind*, 89; *Prometheus Unbound, with Other Poems*, x, 4
Shooter's Guide (Johnson), 213–14n8
sin, 169, 172. *See also* corruption
Singer, Walter, 152
Sins of Government, Sins of the Nation (ALB), 34, 40, 44–46, 209n17
slavery, 41, 44, 186–87, 194
slave trade, 42, 187, 188–89, 190–91
"Sleep and Poetry" (Keats), 48
sociability, 209n14
social class, 201; and Hands, 9, 13, 17; and "Invitation," 72; and "Mouse's Petition," 90. *See also* labor/laborers; middle class; poor people

society / social relations, 29, 44, 197; and "Address to the Deity," 176; and Baillie, 199; and ALB, 40, 43; and "Corsica," 55–56; engagement in, 144; and *Epistle to William Wilberforce*, 186–87, 188, 189, 191; and "Groans of the Tankard," 81; and Hands, 14, 15, 16, 18; and "Hymn 4," 165; and "Hymn 6," 167; and "Hymns," 159, 167; and "Invitation," 66, 67, 74, 75, 76, 77; and love, 197; and "Mouse's Petition," 88, 89; and "On the Backwardness of Spring 1771," 83, 85; and "Origin of Song-Writing," 123; and the pastoral, 128–29; and pleasure, 67; and Pope, 96, 97; rejection of, 56; and "To Mrs. P——," 97, 99, 100; and Virgil, 83–84; vision of, 45. *See also* community; public sphere
solitude: and *Epistle to William Wilberforce*, 193; and God, 175; and "Invitation," 67; and love, 134; mental, 55, 57, 67; and "Ovid to His Wife," 140; pastoral, 75; and redemption, 127; retreat into, 47, 126
"Song I" (ALB), 125–26, 129
"Song II" (ALB), 126, 129
"Song III" (ALB), 126–27, 129
"Song IV" (ALB), 127–28
"Song V" (ALB), 129–30, 132
"Song VI" (ALB), 130–32, 136, 144
"Song of Liberty" (Blake), 175
songs, 28, 32, 196; writing of, 43, 118, 119, 124
"Songs" (ALB), 117, 125–32
"Sonnet 19: On His Blindness" (Milton), 158
"Sonnet on Chillon" (Byron), 54
Specimens of Welsh Poetry (Evans), 23
Spenser, Edmund, 1, 18, 23, 26, 27, 117, 207n18
spirit, 42; and "Corsica," 60, 62; and "Origin of Song-Writing," 123; and "To Mrs. P——," 98; unsubmitting, 52, 53–54, 55, 56
spirituality, 42, 45–46, 48, 196, 197; and "Address to the Deity," 175; and "Hymn 1," 163; and "Hymn 8," 171; and "Hymns," 172; and lived experience, 160
spring, 144, 148–50
Stoicism, 176, 177
subservience, 145, 197; and "Address to the Deity," 176; and Baillie, 199; and Jesus Christ, 197; and "Mouse's Petition," 93; and "To Mrs. P——," 101; and Yearsley, 198
"Sulpicia's Garland" (Tibullus), 107–8

"Summer Evening's Meditation" (ALB), 29, 161, 173, 179–86, 187, 193, 220n5, 220n6; epigraph to, 184–85; and faith, 173, 179, 180, 181, 182–83, 184
sun, 101, 130, 132, 136
superstition, 24, 25, 27, 75
sympathy/compassion, ix, 44, 201; and "Address to the Deity," 178; and Baillie, 200; and ALB, 28, 40; and "Hymn 6," 167, 168; and "Mouse's Petition," 88, 90, 91, 93; and "To Miss R——," 156. *See also* benevolence; friendship; love

"Tables Turned" (Wordsworth), 67
Tales of Superstition and Chivalry (Bannerman), 18–28, 206n16
Tasso, Torquato, 102, 214n9
"Ten-Penny Nail" (Leapor), 2
Test Acts, 34
Thomson, Alexander, 217n7
Thomson, James, 2, 31–32, 50, 51–55, 212n6, 217–18n7
Tibullus, xiii, 2, 107–8, 119–20, 201, 215n13, 216n8
"To a Lady" (ALB), 144, 145–47, 153
"To a Very Young Lady" (Waller), 150–51
"To Miss R——, on Her Attendance upon Her Mother at Buxton" (ALB), 144, 155–56, 157
Tom Jones (Fielding), 219n25
"To Mrs. P——" (ALB), 94–104, 105; and art, 94, 95, 96, 97, 98, 99; and friendship, 95, 96, 98, 99, 104; and idealism, 98, 101, 102, 103, 104–5; and imagination, 95, 97, 99, 103, 104; and politics, 94, 95, 96, 99; and power, 99, 100–101; and society/social relations, 97, 99, 100
"To My Sister" (Wordsworth), 211n11
"To the King, upon his Majesty's Happy Return" (Waller), 150
"To the Poet Coleridge" (Robinson), 3
"To Wisdom" (ALB), 94, 114–16, 117, 129
transformation, 144–45; and "Address to the Deity," 176; and Baillie, 199, 200; and "Characters" poems, 105; and "Corsica," 55–56; and death, 132; and "Delia," 132; and *Epistle to William Wilberforce*, 186, 190, 193–94; and "Hymn 4," 165; and "On the Death of Mrs. Jennings," 158; and "Ovid to His Wife," 142; personal and cultural, 123; of public world, 196; and "Song III," 127; and "Summer Evening's Meditation," 183; and "To a Lady," 145, 146, 147;

and "To Mrs. P——," 98; of world, 2, 56, 69, 79, 91, 98, 164, 196; and Yearsley, 198
Tristia (Ovid), 139, 140–43

Ulysses, 175, 178
Unitarianism, 180
utopianism, ix, 44, 77–78

"Verses on Mrs. Rowe" (ALB), 144, 151–55, 157
"Verses Written in an Alcove" (ALB), 32, 47, 79, 85–88, 89, 91, 212n3
Vindication of the Rights of Woman (Wollstonecraft), 207–8n8
violence, 197; and Claudian, 110, 112; and "Corsica," 61, 62, 64, 65, 66, 71; and "Delia," 137; and *Epistle to William Wilberforce*, 190; and "Groans of the Tankard," 82; and Horace, 116; and "Hymn to Content," 112–13; and "Invitation," 67; and "Ovid to His Wife," 142; and "To Mrs. P——," 99, 100, 103. *See also* force; military/militarism; power; war
Virgil, xiii, 2, 115, 117, 122, 123, 201; *Aeneid*, 36, 92, 93, 154; *Eclogues*, 36, 48–49, 65–66, 92, 145–46, 210n7; epigraph from, 41; *Georgics*, 83–85, 154
virtue: and "Address to the Deity," 176, 177, 178; and Baillie, 199, 200; and ALB, 28, 29, 41; and Claudian, 111; and "Corsica," 62–63, 64; and *Epistle to William Wilberforce*, 189, 194; and "Hymn 3," 164; and "Hymn 6," 167, 168; and "Hymn 7," 169; and "Invitation," 65; and "On the Death of Mrs. Jennings," 157, 158; and "Summer Evening's Meditation," 179, 180, 183, 185; and "To Miss R——," 156; and "To Wisdom," 114. *See also* goodness; morality

Waldron, Mary, 201
Wallace, William, 31–32, 52, 53, 55, 56, 60, 199
Waller, Edmund, 123, 150–51
war: and ALB, 41; and Behrendt, 8; and "Invitation," 76, 77; and "To Mrs. P——," 103; and Virgil, 92. *See also* military/militarism; violence
Warrington Academy, 34, 41, 71–74, 85, 121, 182, 208–9n13, 211n17
"Washing Day" (ALB), 7
Way, Gregory L., 23
West, Lady Mary, 41

Wilberforce, William, xiii, 186, 187, 191, 192–93, 194

Wollstonecraft, Mary, 6, 7, 145, 147, 207–8n8, 217n2

women, 2, 4–5, 105, 195, 201; address to, 43, 144; and Baillie, 199; and Bannerman, 21; and education, 28; marginalization of, 5, 6; poems about, 32; and "To a Lady," 145

Wordsworth, Jonathan, 181

Wordsworth, William, xi, 1, 117, 201; *Excursion*, x; "Expostulation and Reply," 213n4; "Intimations Ode," 90; "Letter to the Bishop of Llandaff," 210n4; *Lyrical Ballads, with a Few Other Poems*, x, 4; and Milton, 9; *Prelude*, x; *Recluse*, x; "Tables Turned," 67; "To My Sister," 211n11

"Written on Their Majesties Coming to Kew" (Hands), 16–17

Yearsley, Ann, ix–x, xi, xii, 3, 94, 200; "Address to Friendship: A Fragment," 211n10; "Bristol Elegy," 198; "Brutus," x, 92; "Indifferent Shepherdess to Colin," 198; and "Invitation," 66; "Platonic Shade," 68; "Remonstrance in the Platonic Shade," 198; *Rural Lyre*, ix, 44, 197–99, 211n10

Young, Edward, 2, 9, 153–55, 184–85